Soul Pc

CW00815883

Paul Williamson

www.capallbann.co.uk

Soul Pathways

ISBN 186163 1812

Cover design by Paul Mason

Published by:

Capall Bann Publishing
Auton Farm
Milverton
somerset
TA4 1NE

Dedication

I would like to dedicate this book to my two sons, Julian and Johannes. With love and in the hope of understanding

By the same author, also published by Capall Bann:

Atlantis - The Dark Continent
Healing Journeys

Contents

Chapter 1 - Beginnings

People with enquiring minds, naturally want to discover meaning for their lives. I believe that it is a compelling quest for all of us to seek to a lesser or greater extent to do this. However, in the living of our lives, it can be very difficult to extract a sense of reason and purpose, especially when we suffer and experience pain. This book represents an attempt to try to understand our lives from an inner perspective, and how we may use these insights to navigate through life's trials.

I wish to introduce some tools, and thoughts for helping people to live in harmony with their soul and thoughts, tools that may not necessarily make life feel more comfortable, but which may help people to feel how their lives can be a richer and deeper experience.

Many of the topics in this book are very close to my heart. I intend to write both from a general and very personal stand point. There are life stories from people with whom I have been acquainted, people who have crossed my path. Also, I have given details of some of my own challenges and inner crises. These life stories are intended to be illustrations and to convey images of universal problems faced by our humanity.

There are challenges that we all have to meet such as our struggle to assert our individuality, and learning how we can be open to feel loved and able to give love under many different circumstances. Because of the complexities of our human nature, we also need to come to terms with difficult inner conditions such as relating to feelings of rejection, guilt, obsession and issues of control, amongst others. In this book, I want to describe some of the dynamics connected to these inner states of being and their possible impact upon our lives. I wish to show how this then links with our faith and our relationship with 'Spirit' or 'God' as we may term it.

If we have openness to Spirit, then when we feel close to that, we will feel peace and contented with our lot. Very often though, especially when we are confronted with problems, we may become separated from Spirit. Consequently, we may then feel lost and dissatisfied with our lives. In these times we may be more likely to make mistakes that create suffering and confusion in our lives. These are issues, which I will explore extensively, in the forthcoming chapters.

It is my belief that we each have Spiritual guides helping to protect us and love us during our time in physical incarnation. These Spiritual beings are near to us and we can learn to make contact with them.

The main theme of this book though, is the proposition that we each have a soul pathway, a map that our soul has made in Spirit, of the necessary learning experiences and interactions that we need to make in order to fulfil our lives on Earth. In as much as we can connect with this map and be true to it, then we may be at peace.

If we ignore our soul pathway or disregard it, then we will be essentially in conflict with our inner self and this may cause us many problems and possibly even destructive behaviour.

However, the soul pathway that we have chosen for ourselves may not be particularly easy and there may be many lessons contained within it for us to learn. There may be temptations for us to back off and refuse lessons that seem too much for us, and this can create times of crisis in our lives. For us to become familiar with our soul pathway is one thing, but for us to be prepared to live that pathway is another. There may not be many of us who are able to be completely successful at the task our souls have set for us. However, even in the midst of despair, I want to suggest that life can be worthwhile and, with courage, we can still make necessary and important inner steps.

It is my intention for this book to contain notions and teachings that may inspire and help readers to connect more with their own pathway. No matter how difficult life may feel to be sometimes, I believe that there is hope and that we are never totally alone.

Chapter 2 -
The Life Stories

Many of the dynamics of challenges that we need to confront as human beings are common to us all. Yet, at the same time we are all unique and we have our own specific patterns that we create by the way we choose to unfold our lives. We all need to learn to cope with experiences that may provoke feelings of guilt, fear, isolation, rejection and many other difficult emotions. As well as developing our mental intelligence, which is what our education systems seem to concentrate upon, we also need to learn about using our Will appropriately, managing our emotions, and making choices in our lives that are wise and will reflect our deeper inner needs. Often we make mistakes, so we also need to come to terms with that. This may mean that we need to learn forgiveness to be able to accept others and ourselves when things do not work out quite as we would wish.

As human beings, most of us enjoy and crave for companionship. We can become tangled up with each other and lost in each other's feelings and desires. At the other extreme, when we do not have some substantial contact with other human beings we can become withdrawn and sad. We may be afraid of what would happen if we did have contact with others. By interacting with love though, I feel that we can learn much by sharing our journeys with each other. When we open our hearts to others we can feel how much of what other people have experienced is what we have experienced too. This enables us to develop compassion and we may then feel more connected to others and less isolated.

I want to suggest that we cannot learn everything in one lifetime. There is too much for us to absorb and integrate within one limited life span (unless we are very dedicated!). Hence, what tends to happen is that there may be particular themes that we concentrate upon, themes that repeatedly challenge us throughout our lifetime, in various forms, until we are able to cope and perhaps master those themes as experiences. This kind of learning is the learning of the soul.

Our soul can arrange for us to meet up with certain people and situations that will test our ability to act with integrity. On a personality level we may be quite unaware of such challenges being prepared for us. However, I do believe that with all that we experience, there is purpose and meaning, if only we can discern it, and therefore, nothing is random. These are my beliefs and I know that there are many contrary opinions about this. But, from my own experiences, looking back over my life and gaining much knowledge of other people's lives through the therapy work that I do, I have experienced enough miracles to convince me that there is purpose and a Spiritual plan for all of us.

Whenever I have had the privilege to listen to someone else's life story, when it has been told openly and honestly, it has filled me with awe and respect for that person. I feel there is something of great beauty in every person's life. It does not matter how many mistakes that person may have made or how `bad' he or she may have been. We all have our shadows, which connect with the themes that we may be working out. The challenge though with any life story is the person's willingness to be honest.

When we have been through an experience in our life where we know that we have not been at our best, then in our memory of that event, we will tend to diminish any thoughts of negativity in our own actions and perhaps exaggerate the faults of others. If we have low self-esteem, we may tend to remember our own actions in a worse light than was the case. 'We do this as an inner act of self-protection. So I know that it takes a lot of inner strength for people to acknowledge their life and its experiences in a true light. Inside, I believe that we all know the truth of our actions, but very often many of us do not want to know or accept this truth. Our deeper emotional responses to some of our actions can be quite disturbing to us, especially where we may feel shame or guilt and when we know that we have brought suffering to others. We all have had experiences of this nature. Basically, we would rather not be disturbed.

5

In the world we live in, I find it hard to conceive that any of us could act without bringing suffering of one sort or another to other people. With all our various interests and unique needs, we cannot help but be in conflict with each other, and even with two people who are very close, there will and not be complete harmony. Therefore, we bring suffering to others, and we naturally suffer ourselves by virtue of the law of cause and effect. To find peace in the midst of suffering is what I believe then to be our main human challenge.

When people tell their own life story, they will find this to be a very emotional and engrossing experience. For people to admit the suffering they have felt and the suffering they feel that they may have brought to others can bring many troubling feelings to the surface. It is not an easy thing to do, but it can also have its rewards. As people can acknowledge the deeper feelings and thoughts that they have held about their life, this can help them gain understanding of the overall patterns in their life and how various aspects of their life links together. Being truthful can act like a torch to illuminate a lifetime's overall meaning.

In this book, I have included the life stories of seven people. Mostly, they have composed these stories themselves, but with input from me, more with some than others. They are all people with whom I feel that I have been quite well acquainted, although all of them have included information, telling about aspects of their lives in their writing that surprised me. The reason that I chose people whom I know was because I wanted to check with my own perception whether there were any important distortions or significant omissions from their accounts. Where I found this to be so, I would confront them about this. I wanted their stories to be as truthful a representation of how they perceived their own lives to be as possible.

When I proposed to each of them to do this as a project, I asked that they be as honest and frank as they could. I believe that this presented each of them with a difficult challenge. Most of them needed several drafts and considerable time before they could finish. With all of these people, I interviewed them at various stages to clarify details of what they wrote, and tried to help them with any areas of their accounts where they felt stuck. I edited what they wrote. Through the interview process and mutual feedback, it was sometimes possible to become aware of inner themes running through their lives. These needed to be highlighted. In some cases, I substantially wrote or rewrote the story for them. My aim though was that each of the stories would reflect accurately, the prevailing thoughts, both said and unsaid, that they all held about the various stages and significant events of their lives. It needed to be a co-operative effort, where for each contributor, ultimately we could both feel satisfied by what was expressed. It was quite a searching and demanding process for them all. Some of them needed considerable space to reflect and meditate after the writing was completed just to be sure that it felt `right', so they could be committed to it.

For each of them, I believe, as they wrote their story, it brought up strong emotions. They were confronted with places in their lives where they did not want to visit. To go into the places of darkness in their lives and write about those meant that they had to experience those energies again to some extent. Where in their lives they had reacted with fear and lost their way, they needed to acknowledge that. Consequently, they all needed emotional support to cope with this. A few of them asked more for help from me, whereas others turned to their friends. Sometimes a balance needed to be reached in terms of the need for personal privacy so that not everything was included in the writing.

In several of the stories there were relationship problems and issues that were integral parts of the stories being told. I tried to encourage my contributors to write of their own experience, to take responsibility for that, and as much as possible, not to project too much judgement about other people's behaviour. But I also wanted them to be honest and not to diminish other people's roles and influence in their lives. Obviously, if these other people had written their own story, they may have cast quite a different light upon those events where they shared experiences with those who wrote the stories in this book. Hence, I have tried not to cause offence, and some names have been slightly altered or omitted to protect the identity of people concerned. However, all the people who have written their stories have used their own name for this. Most of them have wanted to share their stories with other loved ones as a testimony to the lives that they have lived.

In gathering feedback from my contributors, they all felt positive about the experience of writing their stories. Many of them termed it as a therapeutic exercise. It must have been, on the one hand, humbling, for them to admit their shortcomings, and on the other hand, strengthening to affirm their aspirations and achievements. Each of them has gained, I feel, a fuller and deeper perspective of their lives through the writing. Because of the memories and thoughts that arose for them, some of the contributors needed therapy to help come to terms with aspects of their experience, especially those thoughts and feelings that they normally tried to suppress.

There were several other people whom I asked to make contributions that did not complete it. Some of these obviously found the prospect of such writing rather too daunting and refused. Others made attempts and found the process too emotionally demanding to continue. In one case, a man was prevented from writing his story by his wife. She did not wish to be confronted with the difficulties of her past through his writing.

I was disappointed not to have more contributions from men. I did ask nearly as many men as women, but the men tended to be the ones who backed down rather than the women. Because of the small sample size though, I could not draw any definitive conclusions about this.

The people who have made contributions have either been friends and loved ones (as in the case of Eleyna, my partner) or people who have been associated with me through my work. All of them have undergone therapeutic work with me at some point in their lives. In this way, I have had prior knowledge of their histories. Not all of them have shared a consistently positive relationship with me. In fact, one of the contributors, Helga, has written about some of the problematic aspects of her relationship with me.

8

Because I know that I have had a strong impact upon the lives of many of the contributors, I cannot expect that my own personality would appear glowing for all of these stories where I am mentioned. I know that I have got myself into my fair share of difficulties in life. Therefore, I have tried to present an honest account of my own shortcomings and weaknesses where I have written about myself, and allowed others to do the same.

All of the contributors have undergone some form of Spiritual awakening at some point in their lives. Some of them have also had phases in their lives where they have turned away from Spirit too. I have wanted to bring out accounts of the impact, which the act of turning towards and away from Spirit has had upon these people's lives.

As I have already suggested, in reading the stories of my contributors, it was possible to delineate themes that ran through their lives, problems that kept recurring for them. So, I have tried to interweave the stories with chapters about the strong themes running through each of their lives, presenting thoughts about how these themes may have a common element for everyone.

I cannot claim to have covered all the underlying themes of human existence in this book. However, I hope that I have been able to touch upon some of the main ones, and show how, as souls, we try to learn to tread our way through these dilemmas in our physical lives, until we can find peace.

Chapter 3 -

The Spiritual Dimension

Over the years, I have come to believe that there is a Spiritual dimension of being beyond the physical reality in which we live our lives. I believe that our soul descends from this Spiritual dimension into our material world for our physical incarnation and that essentially part of us remains in Spirit for this duration. Then, once we have passed through the transition that is death, we can be united more fully and consciously with the aspect of us that has remained in Spirit.

My perception of the Spiritual dimension is that it is very loving compared with our physical world, and very alive with creations of thought and feeling. These can have real power and energy. I cannot pretend to know all about it but I do feel an awe and wonder in its presence.

Before we are born, I feel we make a plan of how we want our life to be, the lessons we want to learn, the people we want to meet, our parents, the challenges and opportunities that we want to give ourselves. I believe that this plan is imprinted upon the aspect of us that remains in Spirit once we are born. Therefore, knowledge of this plan can be available to us in as much as we are in contact with the Spiritual dimension of ourselves.

I believe that it is possible for each one of us to consciously connect with our Spiritual self, and with this next dimension of life. There are a number of advantages for us to attempt to do this. If we can gain access to Spirit, then we can become more aware of our life plan and what we need to be doing here on Earth. This can help us to feel more whole and united with ourselves. Because the Spiritual dimension is a realm of incredible love, by contacting this aspect of ourselves, we can bring this love into our physical reality and this can help us greatly to feel more happy and able to cope.

One of the best methods of contacting the Spiritual realms of our being, I feel, is by regular meditation. By stilling our minds and reaching within for help, I feel that Sprit draws closer to us and we can feel the peace and the love that is there. With this beginning, thoughts and feelings may come to us to help us on our way.

From within the Spiritual dimension, I feel that we are not left on our own. I believe that we each have a personal Guardian Angel or Spiritual Guide who stays with us throughout our lifetime, to protect our space and to help us where that is possible. Over the years I have helped many people to make contact with their Spiritual guides, to the extent where I believe firstly that these beings do exist, and secondly, that people can learn to reach out to them.

I have found that Spiritual guides can provide wonderful insights, energetic help and love, especially to the one to whom they are guiding. To have contact with our guides, I believe, can be a blessing.

When we are living our lives on Earth, we need to make our own choices about the ways in which we proceed. One of the gifts we are given is the use of a free will. Therefore, to a large extent, we can do what we want. However, if we are not careful, we can also get ourselves into a big mess and trouble.

It is possible in our life that we can make choices to go against the plans and wishes of our Spiritual self. If we are caught up in some turmoil, then we may not even realise that we are doing it. However, once we are acting contrary to the plans of our Spiritual self, then we feel inner conflict, and are separated from our essential self and from the love and peace, which Spirit can bring. Then, in all probability, we will not be very happy and the further we go along this path of separation the more unhappy we may become. This state of being could be likened to what I have referred in this book as `living in the darkness'.

Once in this state of being, it can be difficult to get out of it. If a person becomes determined to follow a course of action, even though from deep inside he or she knows that it is not right or is afraid of facing up to what is right, then after a while that person may become confused and not even realise what is right or wrong or for the best anymore. The path of being cut off from our Spiritual self can feel very lonely and isolated. This can lead a person to behaviour of self-destructiveness and despair.

I believe that from our life plans, we give ourselves tests about how well we can remain true to ourselves when we are facing challenges. When we manage to succeed with this, then it can make our soul stronger. When we are facing one of these tests, our Spiritual guide cannot help us, our friends cannot help us - we have to make essential decisions ourselves. From our guides we may find peace and clarity about what we need to do, and with friends we may gain love and support. But in the end, each decision is our own making and we are responsible for the life we create.

If we are in a state of `living in the darkness', it is possible through fear, for people to create all kinds of limiting beliefs and prejudices that may interfere with the capacity for them to perceive their own inner truth and love. People can easily delude themselves when they do not want to know the truth that is there. However, I feel that it only needs a sincere asking for help from within and perhaps a willingness to seek help from other people and things can start to turn around.

It may be very difficult for any of us to live our life plan out fully, to be in harmony with this through every moment. However, I feel that each thread of our plan that we can live and be in loving connection with our Spiritual self can give us joy so we know that we have made some accomplishment.

No one can tell another what to do. We each have to live out our own life path ourselves. However, as we dare to reach inwards, asking for help to embrace the truth of our origins and essential Spiritual nature, then we won't feel alone and our life may feel much more filled with love.

The Teachings of Sojah

In my first book, *Healing Journeys*, I wrote of my meeting with Marjorie Wilson and becoming familiar with her Spiritual guide, `Sojah'. There I included a channelled transcript of his teachings.

Through the time I have known Marjorie, I have come to respect Sojah very much. His presence inspired me to believe that Spiritual Guides are an authentic reality. When I listen to him, I feel a lot of love, kindness and simplicity. He does not create an impression of being grandiose, but is much more, a humble Spirit. However, his knowledge has always impressed me with awe, and his teachings have instilled in me a thirst to want to learn more about Spirit and Spiritual life.

To access Sojah, I am able to guide Marjorie into a hypnotic trance. Marjorie then, is able to let her consciousness move to one side, so that Sojah is able to come forward, connect through Marjorie's mind and speak using her voice. At the end of the session, when Sojah withdraws and Marjorie returns to her normal consciousness, she has no recollection of what has been said.

I felt that it would be useful to include another transcript of Sojah's teachings in this book. *Soul Pathways* is very much about the difficulties and trials which people need to confront in their lives and how they may face up to these and overcome them. One of the main remedies that I am suggesting is for people to discover how to connect with Spirit, to live a more Spiritual path and be true to their essence. I do not want to suggest that doing this will be the answer to all people's problems, but more, that it can be a support in the background, and as a means to feel peace. What follows is a channelled session of questions and answers, where I have asked Sojah about Spiritual love, connecting with Spirit and how people can better cope with life on Earth. When I write about people's Spiritual self, Sojah refers to this as the 'psychic ego'. I am hopeful that this transcript may provide some help from a Spiritual source for readers to better feel able to understand the dynamics of how Spirit can help us in our lives on Earth.

Channelling

Paul: Can you tell about the importance of Spiritual love and how Spiritual love can help human beings?

Sojah: *We on this side are here to help you on Earth. It is very important that we reach you if possible, because life is very difficult. By reaching Spirit you can obtain help and be given strength to live the life that you have chosen to live. Also, if you have disease or illnesses, we on this side try to help you with this and give you healing. These things are most definitely here and therefore being able to tune in and use Spirit is a most marvellous thing. The more you tune in, the stronger you become, and the easier it is for you to cope with life. I know that it is not always easy, and also many do not believe that we are here to help. So we cannot make ourselves known unless people ask for help. And this is where in many cases we fail, because we cannot interfere with the life that our one has chosen. But we are always here and ready and willing to help when we can.*

Paul: How can people begin to make contact with Spirit if they feel they do need help?

Sojah: *The first thing I would say is trust - trust that there is someone there. Do not listen to the ones that ridicule this or tell you that it isn't so. But do work it out in your mind and think - `Well this is possible and therefore, I'm going to believe this'. And that is the first thing - trust.*

The second thing is to be calm and to listen. There are so many noises and interruptions and babble going on around you. Your head becomes so full of conversation, the noise of instruments, music being played loudly, cars making their noise on the roads, and many other things. All these noises are hammering onto your subconscious and it is very difficult to just sit down and clear them out. But the only way that you can do this is through meditation. Many have their own ideas of how they meditate and it is appropriate for people to explore and find the way that they feel is right, so that they find the thing that helps them the most. I always think a candle is very helpful or the image of a candle if you do not actually wish to light one. But then it is the calmness that you must first feel within you - the peace and the quiet and the calm. You need to close doors on all the noise, all the activities that are going on around you and go inwards instead of outwards. To help you, you could say the words over and over 'peaceful and calm..peaceful and calm...' These words will go into your subconscious and gradually you will feel yourself relaxing. . This is the first step.

The second thing is then to ask in your mind the things that you want to know. And as I have said many times - then listen. You will not hear a loud voice or anything outstanding. At first you may think you are not receiving any sort of information. But just go on listening. Go on asking questions and listen. You could also do this with a tape recorder if you wish. You will find that gradually, you are reaching a light or beginning to feel a presence or energy. Once you begin to feel this, you realise you are being drawn towards love and Spirit. You already are beginning on your road to success in reaching us.

Paul: Once people have made contact in this way, how can they develop this contact?

Sojah: *Well once they have made contact, they may question - 'Is this really someone in Spirit speaking to me in my mind, or is it my subconscious that is sorting out all the information that I'm asking about?' But what we try to help you understand is that everyone has a psychic ego. This is in Spirit, and by quieting yourself and reaching out, you are rising up to this particular psychic part of you which is already with us.*

You have attached to your body a silver cord and the messages are transferred from Spirit and through the psychic ego almost like a telegraph wire, coming down the silver cord and into your mind. If you do not wish to think you have a guide, if you feel happier with saying that it is your own psychic ego that is talking to you, if it helps you, then do it this way. But do believe that you belong in Spirit and therefore you are attached to Spirit. All the knowledge and help you need is there for you.

You will most certainly have doubts. You may believe for a while and then something unfortunate may happen to you because your life will not be perfect. You could begin to say `Well if this can happen to me, then of course there is no one there that cares, and it's all a load of rubbish'. But it is not. This particular disaster that happens to you may have been meant and come as a challenge. And that is the time really when you must be stronger in your beliefs instead of less. Don't let yourself doubt. Come even closer to Spirit, ask for help and overcome these trials. This way I think you will find that you are receiving help.

Some people in a sense of shock may have an experience where they don't know how they got from one place to another or how they survived something. Well think about this. Something somewhere was helping them even if they were not aware of it. How many times have people suddenly come to their senses and not really remembered what they did half an hour before because they were suffering from shock? But something was cushioning the shock and helping them. When you receive something very, very traumatic, a bad accident, or hear some news for instance, people often pass out with shock. They do this because the Spirit body leaves the physical body for just a short time. This is when the help is being received. Then the Spirit body will go back into the physical body again, and when you awaken, you will realise that you have received help from somewhere even if you are not quite sure from whence it came. But learn from these experiences. This is why sometimes disasters happen, because it is the only way you will learn. How can we prove that we are here if we can't prove to you in a time of trial that we are helping you? So these things are usually planned, and we are most certainly here to help. But it is entirely up to you to trust and believe.

We cannot force it on you, if you become angry and close doors. And you are quite entitled to do this. For once you have linked up with Spirit and your guide, you know deep down that we are here. There may be times where you are sulking or refusing to speak to us. But after you have got over whatever disaster has befallen you, the shock, or the thing that hurt you most, and begun to calm down, you find yourself turning back to Spirit again. You may realise that it was not Spirit causing you the trouble, but either someone else, or even yourself for taking the wrong path or doing the wrong thing. And we always want to pick up the pieces, dry the tears and help you to begin again.

Paul: How important is it for people to make contact with Spirit?

Sojah: *It is important if you wish to have help. A lot of people will struggle through life, fighting, getting themselves in a mess and take the wrong path, getting in with the wrong people and loosing all sense of what is good. We say that they have no conscience. This is because they have closed all doors. They have not listened to their inner self, their Spirit or whatever you want to call it, and they have just gone haywire. Until they find some way of help, they will not get better, they will get worse.*

So, of course, believing in Spirit is very important indeed. But what it boils down to in the end is love. That is what everyone needs and what every one should strive for. Not love for themselves, but love for their fellow beings, and for people around them - even some that they find difficult to love. Love is energy, but it is also God. God is love and therefore this is important, very important indeed. You will only find this if you turn in the direction of Spirit, or through prayer if you prefer this.

Many people have their religions and their various denominations and they find their peace and love there. Well that is perfectly all right. As long as they find it, it doesn't matter what road or way they choose. It is a case of learning to live with others, learning to cope with things, not letting life make you bitter and helping you to understand.

Paul: Can you say a little more about what love is in terms of souls and people's path through life?

Sojah: *Well, I can only ask people 'What is your idea of love? What kind of love do you feel?' There are many kinds. There is a love between partners- husband and wife. There is a love of your children and children loving their parents. But there is also a love of human beings and generally humankind as a whole.*

You can look at people and even if you don't know them, if they are looking happy and contented then you can feel happy and contented for them. If someone is smiling, you wish to smile back. This person is happy and you are glad they are happy. Now if you see someone looking wretched and unhappy, your first thought is to reach out and try to help them. They may not want your help. But if you feel at all compassionate towards this person, then there you are, you have all the right ingredients about what love is all about. It's not just caring for yourself and the ones very close to you. It is caring on the whole for everyone with whom you come into contact.

Now, of course, you cannot love everyone, and it is very difficult to love someone who has treated you very badly and made you very unhappy. But if you can't love, please forgive, because while there is hatred against someone in your heart, then that blocks off other channelling and you cannot develop with hatred in your heart. So although it may be difficult, if you cannot love that person again, you can at least try to forgive them.

The whole thing is embracing, embracing whatever you do, from getting up in the morning to going to bed at night - even the jobs you do, the walk down the road, going around the shops, whatever you are doing, embrace it with warmth. Set out with the intention of doing this - even though it may be very harassing. You are putting before you love and knocking down barriers by doing this.

Paul: So you feel it is important for people on their Soul pathway to remove barriers from inside themselves?

Sojah: *Yes, this is very difficult, for depression and suffering block the channels. They will not open up if they are very unhappy and bitter. They do need trust and some sort of counselling although not necessarily thrown at them immediately. It is better to just talk to them and let them sort themselves out first. Then as they begin to listen to you, speak to them in a way as if you are learning also. Don't throw it at them. Give the information you have learned gently and they will begin to listen to you and think about it. Once they do this they will become interested.*

18

This approach will give people room for thought. Anyone very depressed and ill will grasp at this, because really they don't want to feel like that. They want to be brave; they want to face the challenges that come their way. They just need a helping hand and it is up to the strong to help the weak. That is really what it is all about.

Paul: So if someone is feeling depressed or suffering a lot - as I would say `living in the darkness', what can they do to help themselves? What is the best thing they can do?

Sojah: *Well, someone must speak to them first, because they can't just find the answer from nowhere, if they have never believed. Therefore, someone must give them some help and explain. Then, the all-important thing is looking inwards and trying to be calm - sorting out your mind and all the things you know should not be there - the hatred and the confusion. Toss out all the things that you know don't feel right in your mind. Start replacing them with things you know make you feel better. You can use visualisation in many ways to get rid of anger or bitterness. Each can find their own way. But I do say that they possibly need help to do this in the beginning.*

For someone who is learning to help, it is better to find out just how someone would like to work. Then once you help them on to the right road, they are able to do it alone. This is as I say by meditating, asking questions, listening and trying to unblock the channels that are preventing you from receiving the energy that we are trying to send and give to you.

Paul: What are your main wishes for us human beings from the Spirit side?

Sojah: *Well for you to be able to contact us and find something that will help you. For you to try and live your life as best you can, and naturally in many cases you will fail. But anything that comes your way is a challenge, and you can either do two things. You can lie down and let this thing take over, or you can say this is a challenge and stand up and face it. It won't always be easy, but with guidance you will get there. What we wish is that our love* and wisdom in Spirit will reach you and help you in this way. It is not possible to live perfectly in your world because you are born physically with too many emotions. No matter how hard you try jealousy, envy, greed and many things will step in. Even if you feel you are most saintly, you may find yourself one day wishing wicked thoughts against someone, or not feeling happy, because that is the way that you have been created. You have been created like that to face this particular life. So never worry about it, just accept, and try to do your best. There is no more than that. Just try to live. Then at the end of a lifetime, if you can say `well I did all I could and I did try my best', then that's the answer and there is no more to it than that.

Paul: When people come into a time of struggle in their lives, where things are not going easily, how can they best get through this time?

Sojah: *Well, it depends on how much they believe, and how many friends they have to help them. People do need others to help them, they cannot struggle alone. If, as they go through life, they have made helpful friends that care about them then, when this time of struggle comes, they will turn around to find these people, with love, waiting to help them. So that is why it is good to start as soon as possible caring about people, because as you care about them, then they will care about you. Someone who sits down and complains that no one cares whether they live or die or loves them, is someone who has never bothered to care about anyone else. The first thing you do is caring for them. The struggle through life is not easy; it depends on how many people you've helped along the way, so that they can later help you when your time of difficulty comes. We are all put upon the Earth to help one another. One cannot live alone in life and expect to survive. It is good to remember that life is like a circle. It is a link and everyone is helping everyone else.*

Chapter 4 -

Living in the Darkness

In this book, I want to refer many times to a state of being, which I will term `living in the darkness'. This is an inner state of being and may not reflect how people express their personality outwardly to others and to the world. Basically, it is a condition of separateness, feeling lonely, isolated, confused, depressed, devoid of inspiration - feeling blocked from being able to envision a way ahead. To a large extent, I believe that this is a state of being which is common to nearly all people, that may affect us to a lesser or greater extent at various stages of our lives.

It is a kind of condition that people often tend to try and keep secret, so that even those closest may not know that we feel like that. From studying this condition, I am interested in helping people to identify some of the problems that may befall us when we suffer like this, and how we may be able to work our way out of this state of being to be able to feel more happy and fulfilled. My own belief is that it is necessary for all of us at some stage of our lives to learn about what it is to be living in the darkness, that this is a primary experience that we have to confront as human beings.

I expect that it must feel frightening for many souls to come and live physical lives upon the Earth. To be separated from the love, peace and familiarity of the Spirit realm is very difficult. Yet, it is an ordeal that we all go through. I imagine that deep within each one of us, is that yearning to be united with our Spiritual self, to return to that home from where we have come. However, our Spiritual self wants us to find our way home by our own actions and decisions, by being true to our deepest inner desires and living the life that we have chosen. There is no reward for opting out early. Basically, we are here because, in essence, we want to be here.

I believe that sometimes our souls set hard tasks for us to live in the physical realm, testing how well we can cope and manage these tasks. This may involve going into some very dark places within our lives. For instance, we may be born into a family where there is a cruel and abusive parent, or we may face situations where we are rejected in love, or where there is no warmth or affection for us. How are we going to respond to these situations? Are we going to be able to search within for guidance and peace, perhaps finding a friend to support and help us? Alternatively, are we going to tend to react more negatively, blame the world and shut ourselves off from others?

We may decide very firmly that we really don't want to be here, and this decision may be fundamentally at odds with what our soul wants from us. As we decide things within, that are at variance with the essential truth of who we are as souls, then this will begin to cause splits inside of us, with different parts of us pulling in different directions. Thus we will become less at peace with ourselves and less able to act in the manner that we wish.

Our thoughts about ourselves, our inner beliefs and decisions about what is possible, can have a very powerful impact upon what we can achieve. As our lives go on, some of these inner beliefs and decisions can get buried in such a way that they may operate without us even knowing consciously that they are there. Inner thoughts and feelings that have very little resemblance to our essential being can determine our actions. Therefore we can either get more and more lost or begin a search for our true nature.

When people feel connected with their inner self, knowing that they are living in accordance with what they really want, then they will feel happier and lighter. If people are living a life where they sense somehow that they are not being true to themselves, then they will feel less at ease, generally unhappy and their lives will feel darker.

Sometimes, the dark places where people enter may seem so bleak that people may perceive that there is only the faintest line of possible help, and even that may appear very fragile. Suffering may be almost inevitable then, and it is a severe test for our inner resources to be true and kind to ourselves. Under such circumstances, many people become damaged. We may feel that we lack access to people who are living their lives better, people who as models for us could help to move us out of self-destructive patterns of hurt and isolation. We may feel desperate and that all is hopeless. There may seem to be no way out that would work for us.

From the viewpoint of reincarnation, it may happen that a soul continues to make similar mistakes in life after life. Hence, when placed in a certain type of darker situation, this soul tends to react negatively, by either withdrawing or causing hurt to others, so that the task of working through that situation and finding unity once more with their essential self, does not happen. Therefore, that soul keeps choosing a similar kind of path in life after life until the lesson is learnt.

It seems that in any life we live, there may be opportunities given to us, times when we may be able to reach out of a place of darkness if only we dare. There may be a person that we meet or the chance for us to move away from some circumstance or destructive relationship that we are in. It may take a lot of courage to move on from a situation where we are stuck, because it has become so familiar to us. Usually, in these places of darkness, there is a lot of fear and consequently a lack of trust that any other situation could be better. The choice between the devil you know and the unknown can make it very daunting to make a life changing decision.

It is the pattern of thoughts and beliefs from within people's consciousness that needs to change first before any external change will be possible. As people continue to believe that life can get no better for them, or whatever it is that limits people via their inner beliefs, then this will keep them stuck. Sometimes a meeting, a dream, a release of tears or some realisation that comes suddenly, will make a difference, and bring a shaft of light into that person's life. Whether people then make steps to nourish the light and allow it to shine brighter, or slowly withdraw again into a very dark reality, is up to them.

People may enter into a place of darkness knowing and feeling that they have made mistakes, perhaps caused hurt to others or acted foolishly. They may become lost inwardly as a way of punishing themselves. Then it may appear to those people that they deserve to be in such a place of darkness, that they are worthy of no better.

When people are living in darkness, they will tend to project that darkness onto others. Their view of life will affect how they see others. Some people will not want others to be happy if they are not. It is a natural herd-like instinct in us to wish for others to feel like we do. Therefore it must be very courageous to step beyond that, to take a different path, to dare to be an individual making our own choices.

There may be periods in our lives that are difficult, where for example, through illness, adverse circumstances or concerns we may have for our loved ones, we may be tested upon our faith in life and our ability to trust that a way forward can be found. These testing times may have nothing to do with the conditions of our early upbringing. Instead they may be a character test, in which we either feel compelled to continue to be true and determined to do what we feel is right, or else yield to the huge temptations to give up and hide away.

Of course, what we feel is right may be an illusion in our minds, so to be really true to ourselves, we need to challenge our own behaviour. My belief is that somewhere inside ourselves, we will know the truth that is right for us, if we are willing and ready to face it.

When we feel afraid, the tendency in us will be to want to work things out on our own. We may not consider other people's thoughts and feelings. Fear can bring with it a panic that we don't know what to do. Then we may perceive other people's behaviour, as more threatening than we otherwise would feel it. Inside ourselves we may erect barriers and cut ourselves off from others and the help that we need. Our hearts can close down and once the love is not flowing, then we are lost. The only result can be suffering, both to others and ourselves.

Sometimes we need to be on our own. Solitude can be a great healer. As much as we can really use these times to still our minds, to seek help from within, then clarity may be able to shine a light upon our circumstances and we can gain a fuller perspective about what is happening for us. However, being alone can also be a means of escape, a place that feels safer because within that place, no one can hurt us or intrude upon our thoughts and feelings. By this means, solitude becomes isolation and will feel very empty. Some people will also try to hide away from being on their own because they will feel terrified of loneliness. So it is a challenge for all of us to learn how being on our own can be a positive experience.

As children we may expect to feel supported and helped to be. But that confidence can be quickly shaken, and once it is shaken we may struggle to either feel able to ask for help from other people or from Spirit. We may feel that we have to do everything on our own. Once we cut ourselves off like this, we can easily make mistakes and take on a more negative attitude about our lives. This will influence how we relate to others, the kind of life experiences we manifest for ourselves, and how we cope with them.

Once we make mistakes, it can be hard to forgive ourselves. We know what we have done and how it has affected the others concerned. It is easy to engage in self-pity and wish to punish ourselves. However, we cannot live as human beings without sometimes hurting another, whatever we do to try to prevent it. The challenge may be for us to accept that this is so. Until we are able to acknowledge and let go of the past, it will haunt us and dwell in us as darkness. Then we will not be open to manifest a more constructive future.

But the biggest obstacle to our finding peace to live fully in the present is fear. Many people will stray from their path through fear, and so this needs to be understood, and fears need to be released as fully as possible.

Chapter 5 -

Fear

With our minds, we like to be able to control others and the world around us, so that everything fits in with our personal needs. When we cannot do that and our expectations are not being met, then we can become afraid. If we feel hurt, physically, mentally or emotionally, then this can also generate fear. Feeling afraid, we either want to stand and fight or else we want to run away. Fear is an instinctive response and it is something that is very difficult for us to control.

When we are afraid, we construct energy barriers to separate ourselves from others, to try to keep ourselves safe and protected. It can be like a shell that contracts our energy field and makes us smaller, so that we turn more within and have less contact with other people and the external world.

Fear is a cold energy. If we let our bodies express fear that has been trapped within us, then it is likely that our bodies will want to shiver. Even if we are in a very warm room, while fear is expressing or releasing itself, we will tend to feel very cold. The main antidote to overcome the experience of fear, I feel, is the warmth of love. Once a person understands that there is no need to be afraid, that a fear is groundless, then this fear may be released.

Fear is governed to a large extent by our inner beliefs and imagination. If we imagine that a certain type of situation is likely to be dangerous for us, or difficult, then this will tend to breed fear. If we lose trust in a situation so that we imagine that what might happen would be an outcome outside our control and something that does not suit us, then we will tend to freeze and not go any further along that way.

Fear does not necessarily have anything to do with what is real or true. It is also a reaction that can be engendered by others. I remember as a child, many times being told that I must not go into a certain situation because something bad may happen to me if I did. Then I would be afraid of entering those situations even though I had no experience of them. This was because I relied on my mother's guidance to protect me. Her thoughts about what was safe for me and what wasn't, influenced me tremendously. It was only much later, when as an adult and away from my mother's influence, that I felt that I could test situations for myself and gradually work through inner fear barriers that I had established for myself. I needed to learn that I could decide about these things for myself.

Fear is very much linked to our inner beliefs about a situation. Therefore, if we believe that a particular circumstance is threatening, then we will feel afraid of it. If our inner attitude towards the same circumstance is that it is non-threatening, then we may feel quite relaxed about it.

However, telling ourselves mentally that there is nothing for us to fear is unlikely to make any difference to the feelings that bubble up from within us. What we need to do is to make an energetic link in our body with the actual feeling of fear. While that is pulsing through us, if we then realise that what we believe to be threatening is not, or that there are other possibilities of action that would reduce the threat, then the energy of the fear may release itself quite quickly from us. Hypnotherapy is a useful tool that can help in these types of processes.

In other words, if we try to impose on our minds positive beliefs, when underlying these are grave doubts and fears about how we will cope with a particular situation, then it will not matter how determined we are to meet that situation positively, the fears from within will still express themselves. Our personal Will and thought/mind processes cannot shift fears fundamentally. This is because our minds want to control our fears, but the fears inside us say that we are impotent to be able to control what is happening. Therefore, these two forces cannot meet each other effectively.

To help a fear, we need to get to know this fear in us, to accept it, and not to try and struggle against it. Our fears need very delicate, caring and loving handling to be helped. We may want to speak with our fears, but even more important, I feel is for us to listen. If we close our eyes and journey into the feelings of our body, where we feel the fear, we may be able to go right inside and learn about our fear. As we travel within, we may find ourselves experiencing an event from our past, a memory. It could be that this is the root of our fear. Otherwise, we may also experience thoughts and feelings with associations of many previous times. If we keep breathing with what we experience, gradually, we may be able to sift out what is true.

The fear will not go to the core of our being. It will only go so far inside us. Then, beyond that, closer to our essential being and soul, will be peace. If we can reach that place of peace, then we will be in a much better position to be able to know the truth of our fear, to speak with it and communicate, so that the decisions created by the fear may be healed. Sometimes, even if we do not comprehend our fear fully, by letting the energy of it express itself, once we have made energetic contact with it, then this will help take our awareness deeper towards peace.

Fears can be generated when we feel that we have made mistakes, and also when we feel we are being attacked. We may meet with a situation that does not conform to what we expect and this may startle us. As we feel not in control, unless we can accept this, then we will feel fear. The sensation of fear can be quite overwhelming and this may blind us to various options of behaviour that we would have otherwise seen. Thus we begin a pattern of restrictive behaviour based on fear, because we failed to gain a fuller perspective of what was happening to us.

I believe that the most common source of fear is connected with feelings of not being loved and accepted, in other words, of feeling rejected. Ultimately, we all want love more than anything. So, when it feels that love is withheld form a source where we feel we want and need it, then this can be quite terrifying to us. We need to learn about love, where we can find it, and how we can sustain ourselves with it. In the course of our learning, we may realise that the sources we had set up in our minds of where we expected most to receive the love that we need, are not so reliable, and waiting on these sources may bring more pain than happiness. If we can be helped or realise through self-exploration, that we do not need to be so fixed on these sources to feel loved, then this can be very worthwhile. On the other hand, if someone with whom we share a close bond, can be a reliable source of love to us, then this can be very nourishing indeed.

Very often, people will grow up feeling dependant upon their parents or family to feel loved. As they get older, other people may fill the roles of parents or family substitutes, and so the pattern goes on. If the parents concerned have not been such good providers of love, then people suffering from this may feel a big lack in their lives, and this can generate fear.

If people can experience that deep within them that there is love, there is, say, Spiritual help, there is the strength to know what their life is all about, then they do not need to cling anymore to less reliable sources of support. They can still be linked to their family or family substitute, but from a position of strength rather than weakness, and without the attachment or dependency. It can be a great gift when a person is able to attain an experience like this.

Mostly, fears need a lot of patience and gentle handling to be overcome. We need human love as well as the love of Spirit. People need to be open to this before it can be given.

Love tends to shine a light on fears. That is why many people are afraid of love, because it will show up the fears that are there. Very often, it will feel easier to run away from love, than to face it with all the reflections it will show of what is feared inside.

My belief is that love can overcome fear, and this is the only pathway for people to find greater peace and happiness. For people to emerge from inner places of darkness and fear, they have to embrace love, no matter how painful the process may feel along the way.

Chapter 6 -
Life in Crisis

My Marriage Breakdown

Some little time ago, my life seemed to be quite stable and secure. My marriage appeared safe and was proceeding smoothly, I was enjoying my children and my work was giving me considerable satisfaction. There was little sign of any pending upheaval or disruption.

Glancing back in retrospect, I feel that my marriage had been stagnating. My wife and I had been living lives more independently of each other, rather than doing things together. I had been sharing more of my inner life with other people rather than with her. Yet, we shared a warmth and cosiness which made us stay together. Our bond was most strong around our family with our two boys and this felt a very nurturing place for all of us to be.

I feel that at that time, I was living my life more upon the surface, not as involved emotionally with people as I could have been. However, as I projected ahead and tried to imagine how my life could be in the future, I saw no reason to suppose that it would be different to any significant degree. But then it all changed.

My friend Eleyna told me that she loved me. Immediately, I blocked her with my heart and kept up that block for some time.

From my past, there had been other women who had been attracted to me, women also to whom I fleetingly was wanting to be close as well. However, with Eleyna, it was different. I knew that it was more serious. My bond with Eleyna had first established itself when she typed my book *Healing journeys*. I felt with her then, a mutual common Spiritual interest, and a heart connection that wanted to grow and deepen. We had become close and practised Spiritual healing together. I had tried to help her with problems she had around her home life. At the time she first shared her love for me, I was in daily contact with her, in many ways sharing more of myself with her than with my wife.

I felt to be facing a very difficult dilemma and needed time to think. Already, for my wife, the amount of close contact I had with Eleyna was difficult for her. She could not easily tolerate that to increase. However, my friendship with Eleyna felt very precious and important to me and I did not wish to damage it in any way. What could I do?

After a month or so, I began to remove my inner barriers and open my heart to Eleyna, deciding that I wanted to explore what was there. Gradually, even though I had initially tried to resist it, I felt a growing sense of love for her as well. I felt that soul bond which I knew existed between us.

As part of our Spiritual and emotional work together, we had done much past life exploration. For both of us, through numerous regressions, we found the other one to be there in one form or another, for most of these past lives. Some of the contacts were very intense. It felt as if we were never really apart, that we were close companions, testing and trying to help each other. I could not help myself from getting closer to Eleyna. Because of this, my problems became more severe.

My marriage was under threat. Circumstances made it increasingly clear to me that I could have my marriage and family life preserved or I could have a relationship with Eleyna, but I could not have both. I had to make a choice.

When I considered my love for my family, for my wife and children, and also the feelings they had concerning the importance of keeping our family unit together, there seemed only one choice possible. Yet my love for Eleyna felt even deeper, and I could not give her up.

My usual self-control collapsed, and for days on end, I was in floods of tears. Feeling that my best approach would be openness, I shared with my wife, my children and also Eleyna, my emotions and the problems, doubts and questions that I had.

No one could tell me what to do. Somehow, if I could, I needed to find the answers within myself. There was so much pulling, soul searching and suffering during this period. At various stages, I felt a depth of love towards everyone concerned, greater in intensity than I had ever felt before. My emotions were opening up and in an unexpected way, this felt very freeing.

My Spiritual work had taught me that at times of crisis like this, I needed to ask for help from within, to let the strength and love of Spirit support me. However, I could not get the answers from this source either. The main prompting I appeared to receive was for me to be true to my heart, to let the decisions come from there. In this case though, my heart was split in two, and I could not bear what I might lose if I went either one way or the other. And so it continued like this for more months of agony.

The decision, when it eventually came, was made for me by my wife. After I spent a week with Eleyna, she asked me to leave. Returning from that trip away with Eleyna, neither of us had been certain how we could take things forward. Yet, I can understand my wife's reaction. And the effect was devastating. Even though I had moved a long way in the direction of Eleyna, I had not decided fully to be with her. I still needed to make that decision in order to find peace. In the upheaval of these days though, the shock waves were so enormous, I needed a lot of support just to keep going. It was very challenging for me to be aware of the suffering of others, especially my children. Yet there was nothing I could do. The marriage was now broken.

To make my own decision, I arranged a ritual for myself, about two months later, for this purpose. Having a few of my closest friends in attendance, I invited the Spirit of my wife to be present, and I spoke to her. I shared with her all that I wanted to say, both positive and more difficult. But then I needed to know how I could proceed.

The question entered my mind 'How can you leave someone that you love?' I was stuck there and could not move. I thought of all the people condemning me for breaking up my family. I thought of the pain felt by my wife and children. I wondered how selfish I would be to do anything except stay with them.

But then I heard a quiet voice within me, and I spoke this voice aloud. It said, `I am leaving you because it is my path to do so.' As I uttered these words, I felt a strength beginning to fill me and at last I could move. Hesitantly, I got to my feet and walked thorough a symbolic gateway that had been constructed for me to represent the path into my new life. No one could help me. I had to do this myself. Once through this gateway, I felt peace and it felt right. Much of the guilt that had been entangling me was gone. I had made my decision and released the marriage. There was no turning back now, no other way possible. My path lay in front of me to tread. Eleyna was waiting for me, but she had her own challenges and trials to face. The process of separation from my marriage and coming together with Eleyna had shaken me to my core. It was the hardest decision I had made in my life.

Chapter 7 -

Eleyna

Background

I first met Eleyna in 1990, when she came to work with me as a client. She was then pregnant with her fourth child and experiencing fear and anxiety surrounding what may happen during the birth. I enjoyed my work with her and she has described from her own perspective, her contact with me from this time, in her story.

During this initial contact, although she had not told me, I sensed that she was troubled by quite a number of problems. Therefore, during her final session, I offered to lead her in a guided meditation to discover what other inner work she may need to do. Agreeing to this with her inner consciousness Eleyna found herself entering a house. Within this house, there were numerous rooms that she could sense behind closed doors. She knew that it was not the time for her to open those doors and felt that she was not ready.

I did not see Eleyna again for six years. Then she phoned me to arrange an appointment, and I remember feeling delighted that she had made contact with me again. However, when I saw her, I was quite shocked at how she had changed. The level of distress and inner confusion in her was obvious. Without telling her, I struggled to know how I could help her. In the weeks and months that followed, I admired greatly her courage and determination in persisting with our sessions. Some of them were very difficult, dealing with despair and depression. It was hard for me to believe at times that we were really making progress.

Gradually, though, things seemed to clear for her. The sessions were very important for her. Coyly, she has confessed to me how she used to sit in her car outside my home, trembling and not knowing what may happen once she entered my therapy room.

However, I know that she also used to concentrate upon every detail of what transpired in these sessions. Afterwards, she would reflect about some of her experiences for many hours, struggling to understand her inner feelings and thought patterns, gradually untangling the knots that were there.

I believe that by doing this work with me she was beginning to open the doors of that inner house which she had visited all those years before. There were some horrible things in these rooms. They were the rooms of her soul. Within her, there were memories, thoughts and feelings that were very dark, and preventing her from being happy. She knew that she needed to confront these places in her, but at times, she was also very afraid and resistant of doing so. On occasions, Eleyna has remarked to me that her sessions with me were a matter of life and death for her, that coming to work with me saved her life.

Eleyna is a woman of great heart and sensitivity. As a mother, I feel she has enormous love and nurturing ability with her children. She also has a fine analytical mind. However, undermining these qualities, she has tended to have a very low opinion of herself, doubting her worth and often looking upon her life as a failure. Over the years, from her childhood onwards, the significant people in her life have reflected those negative beliefs back to her in various forms, reinforcing them in her own mind.

Since connecting with Spirit, she has been able to challenge those beliefs and begin a process to acquire a more realistic assessment of her own qualities. But it is a long process to peel back all that conditioning. Fundamentally, she has questioned if it is worthwhile even for her to be alive, and so she has been challenged with the task of whether she can say `yes' to life, especially when circumstances have been tough.

Since becoming her partner, I have needed to confront my own level of self-acceptance and self-worth. She has helped me to appreciate life more deeply and to feel in my heart how much life does matter. What follows is her story.

Eleyna's story

As with most children, I did not really question or consider my childhood to be different to anyone else. My physical needs were well cared for and my parents always had my comforts central to their lives. It was only as I grew older that I became more and more out of step with my parents way of being and felt isolated and confused within myself. It is difficult for me to judge where the turning point came, there were many events in my childhood where my emotional needs were not met, and these just seemed to accumulate as a great huge barrier of hurt and despair that over time caused me to close my heart.

My parents have good intentions and wanted me very much. I was adopted at the age of three months. My parents were thirty-six years old when they adopted me. Their attitudes and approach to life, however, always made them seem a great deal older. I did not learn of my adoption until I was eight years old. My mother decided to tell me, and needing some moral support, she requested the presence of her favourite uncle. He was however a stranger to me, and when my mother began to tell me about my adoption, I felt acutely embarrassed for her to be discussing these things in front of this unknown man. Very firmly, I told her that I did not want to ever talk about such things again. This moment was very significant in that I placed a total block on the knowledge of my adoption and to all intents and purposes the conversation had never taken place.

Some years later, when I was expecting my first child at the age of nineteen, I had discovered I was adopted because of my birth certificate. I felt betrayed. Talking to my best friend of many years about my discovery, she said she had known for years and could never understand my apparent lack of knowledge. It began to seem to me that everyone knew this secret apart from me. In the middle of a furious row about something I have now forgotten, I yelled at my mother "And why did you never tell me I was adopted?" In response to this question she said she had, and quoted back to me the words I had used eleven years before.

It was as though a floodgate had opened, the barrier I had created in my mind disappeared and the memory of that day long ago was there in my mind. It was just like an old black and white melodrama. I would not have believed the mind to be so powerful if I had not experienced this for myself. Even so, apart from going into some kind of shock, I did not even then feel capable of dealing with the situation.

It was only in 1984 when I was making my marriage arrangements, and my life felt as stable as at any point so far, that I decided to pursue tracing my natural parents. It felt very important to me that I could do this without having too much emotional attachment to the outcome. I had already received considerable psychiatric help to deal with depression resulting from my difficult childhood and relationship problems and as a result felt stronger internally and better able to cope with whatever challenges might come. I went to the local university and using the microfilm records and my original birth certificate, managed to find the telephone number and address of the midwife who had delivered me and also registered the birth. I wrote her a very simple letter, which was first passed onto my aunt and finally to my natural mother who was living in Derby. My natural mother wrote me a long letter in reply. She had thought I was dead because I had not traced her as soon as I had turned eighteen. Shortly after followed an emotional reunion. I was excited and wondered how I would feel about this mother I had never met.

It was very odd for me; I felt no immediate rush of love or even a wish to develop a close relationship. This probably reflected my difficult relationship with my adopted mother and my inability to trust. It was startling to meet someone who looked exactly like me, and also wished to mother me like a baby even though I was twenty-three years old. She spent most of the day holding me very close and even when we went out for a walk she held my hand. I felt uncomfortable, but accepted that this was a very difficult time for her and tried to be sensitive to her needs.

I was open to my mother initially, but difficulties soon began. She would often speak very frankly about things or bring issues to my

37

attention from her work as a minister, that placed me in considerable distress and caused me to close down to her more and more. During this period, she was working as a hospital minister and through her work, frequently had to counsel mothers who had had a stillbirth or miscarriage. At the time, I was expecting my second child and found her sharing of these events very difficult to deal with. Also she became very angry with me because she felt I had encouraged my half sister to not pursue her college place, but leave to be with her fiancée. I did not feel that this was true. Much as I wished it to be different, I found her to be an intrusive presence in my life. Once again, in my second pregnancy, I was experiencing a horrendous emotional upheaval. My response was to stop answering the phone so that my husband could shield me from the worst of her stories and reactions.

Later in our relationship she disclosed other distressing details. In particular, she told me that I had been conceived because she had been raped. I did not know whether I could believe her. It was a shocking idea that I could have come into the world in that way. Anyway, this conversation marked the point at which my barriers to a close relationship with my natural mother were finally put into place.

Events my natural mother had shared with me, did not in any way help towards healing my relationship with my adoptive mother either. My natural mother gave birth to me shortly before her seventeenth birthday. She was the youngest of a very large family and her father was very harsh and dictatorial. He had decided that I must be adopted. She gave birth to me in the family home and then was sent to a home for unmarried mothers where she cared for me. I had been breast-fed for the first three months of my life, and she had embroidered baby clothes for me with butterflies. She had loved me very much. We must have begun to build a very close bond.

Once I was taken, my adoptive mother had disposed of the baby clothes not wishing for there to be any reminders of my previous existence. She even felt that the day in July when I was taken away by them was more significant than my birth.

My adoptive mother had very high expectations. She made sure that I was always very tidy, that my manners were perfect, and that I was well fed. Her attention was wholly with me. However, she did not deal with difficult emotional situations well. Frequently, I had nightmares and wet the bed until teenage years. I was afraid of the dark and felt there to be danger every - where. I would lie in bed too scared to move and would call out into the night for my mother to come to me. She never did.

My father is a man who finds it difficult to deal with his emotions and would easily become stressed and angry. Although he was rarely violent to me, there was always this threat present and my mother would keep me separate from him to protect me. Yet in a way I needed him to protect me from the worst excesses of my mother's emotional abuse.

For even the tiniest wrongs my mother would completely withdraw her love from me and would not even begin to show me any compassion until I had begun to cry and show uncontrollable distress. This pattern repeated itself so many times that gradually over time my immediate response to any difficult situation was to cry desperately. Even now I am not completely free from that pattern although it is much better that it was.

As I entered my teenage years I became very interested in having a permanent relationship. Looking back I feel I was trying to compensate for a lack of love in my life. I was sexually active from a young age and was lucky to not become pregnant whilst still at school.

At the age of sixteen I met someone who seemed sensitive and understanding, and I leapt at the chance of building a relationship with him. He seemed to be everything that I wished for in a man. He appeared to be kind, fun and outgoing. We began a relationship. However, things began to be difficult very early on.

I talked to him briefly about my earlier sexual experiences, because I wished to have a physical relationship with him also. This was a disaster. He had imagined me to be a virgin, and the news that I was not was devastating to him. He said he did not want a physical relationship with me, but wanted to wait. This remained the case for about a year. In the meantime I had come to see that he had some very difficult sides to his nature and that his apparent sensitivity was entirely superficial.

Really he found close relationships very difficult because he was unable to communicate about his own feelings. However, I felt that I loved him so deeply, that these difficulties could only be transient things and that we could work through them. And so after one year, we did begin a physical relationship.

Already my feelings for him had changed. The early passion had evaporated and I no longer really wished for intimate contact with him. The sexual relationship between us lacked spontaneity, but most of all it lacked love. Once again within myself I was determined to fix this.

Running through all of these earlier experiences in childhood and early adult life was a drive to have a connection with God. It had begun very early. One of my earliest memories is at about three years of age gazing up at a statue on my aunt's sideboard, thinking it was like the Madonna.

Later around the age of eight or nine, I had the impulse to wish to attend church. My mother arranged for me to go with another woman from the estate. She did not want to take me, as she really had no time for such things. Waiting for over an hour, which felt like an eternity to a young child, no one came to collect me from the corner where I was waiting. I felt totally devastated. It felt as though even God had deserted me. I still don't know to this day whether the woman forgot or my mother told me a deliberate lie. When I returned home my mother was totally indifferent to my upset. I did not pursue this any further until secondary school where I tried to follow a Christian path, again with no support from home. I led the Christian union and regularly read my Bible.

Elements of the Christian faith disturbed me. I felt especially that the wrathful and vengeful God of the Old Testament was not as it is. Also, I felt more of a sense of personal responsibility for my actions, and the Bible and church seemed to want people to somehow give this responsibility to Jesus.

Despite the obvious difficulties, the relationship I began at sixteen became permanent. My partner came from a Spiritualist background. As I learnt more about their beliefs and approach, I felt much more at home. Here was a faith that recognised our own responsibilities for our actions and also recognised the divine part in each of us. I began to regularly attend meetings. There were still aspects that made me feel uneasy, the concentration on using medium-ship for seemingly trivial matters and for people to have life after death proved, appeared to me to be pointless. I know that for people who have lost a loved one it can give comfort, but for it to be a substantial part of each meeting seemed odd, when almost everyone present presumably believed.

At some of these meetings I began to sense a Spiritual presence. Most commonly this occurred as a sensation of a heavy book or box being placed in my hands. I did not recognise it at the time, but I believe now that this was my guide, Jonah, trying to contact me. Although I felt at home in many respects in the Spiritualist church, I also found some of the experiences frightening. I was still afraid of the dark and frequently sensed beings in my room. Consequently, I spent many nights in terror.

When I was eighteen I made a crucial decision that changed my life, although I did not recognise its significance at the time. One day I entered my bedroom and told all beings to leave me alone and very consciously built a shield of light around myself. When I returned that night to sleep, the room felt cleansed and empty.

My initial response was one of great relief. I had begun to feel almost tormented and now I felt I could rest. Once again, looking back, I see that this also was a first step towards the very dark depression that followed. I cannot be certain that all of the influences around me at that time were good, but my request to be left alone and the shielding I created were so effective, that I entered a period of nearly twenty years without feeling any Spiritual connection. I still attended the church but my own personal relationship with Spirit was severed and the experiences felt empty.

I made many of the decisions and choices in my relationship. Although there were many warning signs of potential difficulties I was determined that the relationship would work. I was afraid of being alone.

One day when I was cleaning the house, I stopped and thought about my life. Apparently I had everything: two children, our first little home, a hardworking and seemingly loving husband. Yet my life felt empty and meaningless. I had received considerable psychiatric help for the frigidity I experienced following the birth of my first child, and had overcome these problems. However I still did not enjoy sex with my husband and was glad of any excuse to avoid it. The weekends were difficult because he expected sex then and although he would never admit it, his anger and violence became more common if he went without sex for any considerable length of time. So the scene was set for a pattern which remained for the next fourteen years.

I retreated into a world of fear and fantasy. I feared the consequences if I did not fulfil his needs and used ever increasing dark fantasies to help me to orgasm. He would never stop intercourse until I had climaxed and so it was essential for me to learn to do this no matter what the inner cost. He was rough and inconsiderate during sex and so it was also important for me to learn to do this as quickly as possible. I do not think he once said he loved me during intercourse. He just needed to satisfy his own physical needs and also carried out the act in his own particular black fantasy world. He expected me to act out roles to help support his fantasies, which also added to my abhorrence of the sexual act.

It did not help my circumstances that, in order to satisfy my own needs, I occasionally looked to other men. I had a few brief sexual encounters, but mostly I tended to feed my own need for love by fixing my attention on someone I worked with and imagining what it would be like to be in a relationship with them. This of course did not help the situation with my husband at all. He reacted violently to discovering my infidelity, but worse than that he expected me to tell him of my sexual encounters during intercourse so he could imagine me having sex with other men.

Perversely, he even offered to pay men to have sex with me so that he could watch, something that I always refused. But it further served to me as an indication of his own confusion.

During this time I trained to be a teacher and started working in a school in the south of the Lake District. It was while I was at teacher training college that I had the most serious of my brief liaisons, leaving my husband and two children for a brief period of time. This caused so much distress to my children that I resolved to never do such a thing again. My personal happiness was secondary to theirs. Something inside of me died.

Following the reconciliation with my husband I became pregnant again. I was unaware at the time, but I was slipping deeper and deeper into despair. I was trying to fill my life with work, children, houses, anything to try to escape my reality. Very soon after my third child was born, I conceived again. My husband did not want any more children. Although he loved them, he also felt them to be a burden both financially and as an emotional responsibility. He soon had a vasectomy.

Once again I cannot be certain when I began drinking to excess. We had always made our own wine, and although I did not drink whilst pregnant, following the birth of our fourth child I began to drink more and more. So at the worst point I was drinking between one and two bottles of wine a night. I felt better when my connection to the world was weakened. My husband often said he hated me and I spent some months on tranquillisers to help me cope. Leaving more and more of the family responsibilities to my husband, I felt useless and worthless. I could fulfil some of the worst of his sexual demands when very drunk. Dimly, I remember wishing to be completely unconscious during the act. I had learnt over time of my husband's homosexual tendencies and he had also begun to have other relationships with women. He was unable to achieve intercourse with these women and this only intensified his obsession with me. My weight had increased by another two stone in addition to what I had gained during the pregnancies. I was preoccupied with thoughts of suicide, trying to imagine how I could kill myself in a way that would protect the children financially.

Something had to change. I felt that there was a different person somewhere inside. I had a sense of this person from earlier in my life. Desperately, I wanted to rediscover myself and begin to free myself from the dark fears I carried.

The birth of my third child had been particularly difficult and there had not been enough time for the fear associated with this to subside when I became pregnant with my fourth child. With each visit to the maternity unit, my sense of dread increased. I sought the help of a Hypnotherapist - Paul Williamson.

Going for just a few sessions, there was a considerable improvement in my mental health. Even though I was aware that I had many difficulties, I insisted that we deal with just this one issue. Now six years later, I wondered if he could help me again. I lost count of the number of times I looked at his ad in the local paper and still did nothing. Finally I plucked up the courage to ring; I really did have nothing to loose.

On the first visit of an hour and a half I poured out this tale of woe, amidst tears and general distress. When this monumental period of release was over, Paul said very little, except that he would endeavour to help me find a place of peace within myself. Immediately, I felt the whole exercise to be a complete waste of time. My mind was in such a constant state of turmoil and filled with blackness that I felt it was impossible for me to ever be at peace. But I am extremely stubborn and having made it this far I was prepared to try anything even if I was highly sceptical.

I am not sure I knew what I was beginning. Week after week we dealt with layers and layers of problems and difficulties, removing barriers and confronting fears, until one session I came to a startling conclusion - I did not love my husband. This came to me as a shock for I had convinced myself that this element of my life was an essential foundation to my being, despite all the problems. My mother and others around me regularly all confirmed how lucky I was and I felt that it must be true. To look at my life and all the choices and plans I had made and to reflect that I might have made some unwise decisions was very challenging for me.

Once this realisation had impacted itself upon me, nothing could stay the same. To begin with, even with this startling new knowledge, I decided that my happiness was secondary to the children's. I would have to stay with my husband and continue to please him for the children's sake if for no other reason. However my inner conflict began to increase.

Alongside this realisation, my connection with Spirit had been renewed. At the end of one session, Paul had invoked a healing experience to help me release the session and begin my transition back to normal consciousness; something that he frequently did. On this particular occasion I was filled with an overwhelming feeling of love, peace and well being. This clearly was something external to me and I immediately recognised it as a connection with God. This experience had a reality to it and a depth that it is really impossible to describe. All that I know is that it now forms part of the unshakeable foundation in my belief in God and any doubts or questions in my mind were and are no longer relevant.

Prior to this profound experience, my faith had been beginning to grow, but there seemed to be a barrier to my progress in the form of an intense pain on the top of my head. This corresponded to the position of the crown chakra. It took many months for this barrier to weaken and finally crumble. I had to work through my feelings of anger towards God. I felt a victim and wanted to be able to blame God for all the things I felt had gone wrong with my life. When I finally accepted my own role in the choices I had made for this life, only then, could this barrier be removed and my progress continue.

During some of the sessions, I had also experienced the familiar sensations of weight being placed in my hands. This time with support, I was able to make contact with my guide Jonah and he was there alongside me as my Spiritual development began. It became clear that Jonah had been present throughout all the trials of my earlier life but now it seemed his work was coming to an end.

One night in a dream like state, I heard a name called very clearly to me. It was "Echmael". This was the name of my new guide and marked another important step. Echmael had only come forward in my life because of the changes and choices I had made. His arrival marked really the beginning of Spiritual service in my life. He wished to help others who were lost as well as guiding me through my life.

Alterations were occurring in my family life. My relationship with my daughters began to improve. Because I had withdrawn from family life, the process of reclaiming my role within the family seemed daunting. The first steps inside myself came following therapy work in accessing a particularly harrowing past life set in Victorian times. As a man I had sexually abused women and this had left a prejudice towards girls and women in my present life. The image of the Madonna and some of my earlier memories of strange experiences all were connected to this life. Particularly interesting to me was the fact that I had sexually abused and killed my present life husband, who was a woman in that life. I began to gain an understanding of karma and its role in our present existence.

Following on from my Spiritual experience, I soon made some important personal decisions. In the matter of a few short months I gave up drinking, became a vegetarian and learnt about healing. After just nine months, many of my destructive patterns had been removed. I was still determined to stay in the family home and serve my children. However, I was beginning to reduce my sexual contact with my husband, but my fear of his reaction still dominated and I was unable to make very large steps with this. There were still many more changes to come.

A friend of mine from the healing group had visited Findhorn and I had listened with fascination to her stories and experiences. I have always had a part of me wishing to be independent and strong and felt that some elements of my journey needed to be completed on my own without the support of the healing group and Paul. I had a real sense of the important parts of the jigsaw coming together. Experience week in the community gave me the opportunity to really explore my own needs and to feel my connection with Spirit in a way that was difficult in my everyday life. Enjoying the feeling of community, the idea of work being love in action and the whole rhythm of the day suited me completely.

On returning home I began to try to live a life more and more true to my heart. Unfortunately this had drastic consequences for my family life. Soon, I informed my husband about my feelings towards him and we began a very difficult and painful road towards separation. I did not know this at the time, because I still had the intention of staying at home to be with my children, but I wished to no longer share a bed with my husband or engage in any kind of sexual activity with him. I faltered on this decision many times but gradually my resolve increased. This had major consequences in terms of any kind of normal family life. My husband's own sense of loneliness and inner turmoil increased and day to day living was a constant trial. With every drama and angry incident I moved further away from him.

Alongside this I had been battling with my feelings for Paul. Initially I thought the growing feelings I had were the same feelings of infatuation I had experienced many times before. I determinedly set about to ignore them and remained focussed upon my own healing and growth. One day Paul was telling me about his first book. That day, he had received disappointing news. His intended typist had returned the manuscript, because she felt uneasy with its content and he did not know where he could turn. Suddenly I had the impulse to ask if I could type the manuscript. Paul refused. I thought no more of it until, when going out of the door to the therapy room, a voice clearly said "ask again". This I did and Paul accepted my offer. I did not know it at the time but this marked a real turning point in our relationship. Up to that time we had clearly been client and therapist, but from that point forward we began to develop a closer friendship.

My guide, Echmael, who had made contact with me following my major transformation, continually encouraged me to share about my feelings with Paul, but I refused to do so. I valued our friendship too much and did not want to jeopardise it in any way. It was still not clear to me how much of my feelings were fantasy. However, my struggles to suppress my feelings were in vain.

Every day almost, I could feel my love for Paul growing and Echmael constantly urging me to share. As Christmas approached a phone call with Paul finally confirmed for me within myself that my feelings were genuine and I needed to listen to the words of my guide. When Paul returned from his annual Christmas holiday, and we next met, I told him that I loved him. He listened with interest to what I had to say, was polite and seemed to appreciate my honesty. I knew that I was not the first woman to feel this way about him and was also aware that this had sometimes resulted in the ending of contact. I had a lot to loose.

Initially, Paul did not wish to become involved with me. Although he too felt very close to me and valued my friendship, he had a wife and two children to consider. He very delicately rejected my interest but still wished to keep me as a close and trusted friend and member of the healing group. I felt devastated. Spirit had urged me to speak and there seemed to have been no point. At least all was not lost - I had not been thrown out of the group in disgrace.

Then began another inner battle. I still felt the same unconditional love for Paul as before. How could I reconcile these feelings and use the energy constructively for others? Over the weeks and months that followed I gradually regained my sense of inner peace and finally reached a point where it did seem possible to love Paul and carry on working through the challenges in my life. Almost at the same instance as I reached these conclusions, something shifted in Paul. His feelings had also been growing and had now reached the point where he too had to speak.

One evening at healing we sat close together during the meditation and the feeling that passed between us was electric. Given the sensitivities of the others present, it was almost embarrassing in its intensity. Gradually over time we found more and more reasons to contact each other and our growing friendship began to cause disquiet in others, particularly our partners. We were on an inevitable path towards separation from our old lives and our own relationship beginning.

I left my husband and children to be with Paul following a very difficult and painful period in the summer. At the same time Paul's wife requested he leave the family home. All at once we were thrown together. Part of me was elated. I truly loved Paul and it was like a dream come true to be in a close relationship with him. We planned to have a family together and there were many joyful experiences. But part of me was virtually destroyed. I had left behind everything I had built up over the years, my children, my home, even my relationship with my husband in which I had invested so much time and emotional energy. I felt a failure.

We set up home quite some distance from my children and although I tried to see them regularly, the distance and time involved took a heavy toll. I never seemed to be there when they needed me. My sense of guilt grew and my life seemed to be in fragments. Paul became disabled with sciatica and life became very demanding. Gradually I became more and more exhausted.

I had easily conceived our much wanted child, but this also added to my tiredness and also produced fears in me about the future. Paul and I talked for many hours each night; we seemed to need to learn so much about each other. In many ways, this time was exciting and precious and we became closer and closer. But at the same time the drain on my emotional, mental and physical strength was severe. I was drawn more and more towards my children and my need to be with them. My ex-husband was hurt and angry and caused me much emotional distress by his actions. He skillfully manipulated situations and created opportunities to cause me mental and emotional turmoil. Many times, I felt deprived of the contact that I wanted with the children.

As Christmas approached I was beginning to be unable to cope with all the different pulls from every direction. I needed some space. My yearning to be with my children and my guilt at having left them was overwhelming. Inside me, there was a pain and fear that they would never forgive me for what I had done. One morning, I felt that it was enough and decided that I had leave so that I could be closer to them. Closing my heart to Paul, I took some belongings and went to stay with my mother.

Initially, I felt a huge sense of relief. Now I could be closer to my children. Since I left the family home, I had come to realise how much they loved me and I was desperate to be with them. Also, I wished for my mother to take care of me a little and have a rest instead of constantly having to address the needs of others.

This illusion of a safe environment in which I could be cared for rapidly disappeared. My mother was even more dictatorial and unsympathetic than I remembered. For days on end, I argued with my ex-husband about my relationship with him and my contact with the children. At times I felt extremely isolated, hurt and rejected.

One day, with the arrival of an assessment form from the Child Support Agency my remaining fragile strength snapped completely. I was feeling that nothing could work, because I held this very strong belief inside myself that my husband always wins. With the Child Support Agency involved, I felt that I would have to give all responsibility for the children's welfare over to him. This felt unbearable. I wanted to care for my own children.

Feeling suicidal, I confronted my husband with my anger and distress. I wanted his acceptance and acknowledgement for my needs, but he refused to give that to me. He was so concerned about money, but I knew that I had never stopped contributing a penny to the household. As I started trying to hurt myself, he began to recognise that he had gone too far. As I started trying to hurt myself, he began to recognise that he had gone too far.

Seeing that I was suicidal, he tried to restrain me in the house. I escaped when he was distracted and having bought pills and alcohol and with all my remaining money in the world, I headed towards a nearby posh hotel to end it all in comfort at least. I rang Paul, but he was not at home. I rang my husband to say goodbye to the children. Unknown to me he had already begun a police search for me and had the phone call traced. When I had been talking to him for some hours, he eventually convinced me that things could work after all - that he would stop causing me such mental anguish and that we would find a fair settlement to ensure I had enough money to live on.

My family came round with the police to the hotel and my eldest daughter stayed with me to keep me company. I still felt very strange. For some days afterwards I felt disconnected from life as though I really were dying. I desperately needed to grow strong again but I could only think of my children.

To begin, I stayed in the family home, sleeping on a sofa. I needed my children to be close to me, needing to feel as though I could still help and serve them. I had to believe my husband would help me. With the plight I faced, I had given him all the power, feeling unable to control the situation myself. And so, it was only him who could help me at that time to believe there was hope for the future. I realise now that giving him so much power in my life was wrong, but at the time it was the only solution I could see.

My husband had controlled so many aspects of my life by a variety of means. Even though I was attempting to build a new life, with a new partner, I still believed that my husband alone had the ability to decide whether I should be happy or not.

My relationship with Paul also needed to change. Although we had learnt a great deal about each other, in many ways we were both still clinging to old ways and patterns. We needed time to learn about each other and adjust. It was a painful experience for both of us that our initial time together had not worked out. I found a place to live on my own closer to my children and slowly I allowed Paul to increase his contact. I had to be certain of my own needs and frequently needed space to allow myself to find some peace. At the same time I needed to maintain a close contact with my children. I was so afraid of losing them.

I needed to see Paul as he really was and he also needed to learn how to interact with me and give me the space that I needed. I had not stopped loving Paul, but I had created a false and quite critical image of him, because of my desperate wish to be with my children. Due to the circumstances, I had come to believe that I could either have a loving relationship with Paul or the children, but not both at the same time. This was a wound that had to be healed. I needed Paul and my children, if only I could achieve that.

Looking at things, I know that Paul found my continued contact with my husband to be difficult. Whenever I became involved in arguments or emotionally draining struggles with my husband, Paul would feel very distressed by this. He would rather that I did not have any contact with my husband at all. However, because of pressure applied by various members of my family, there were questions about whether I had the right to live with Paul at all and how I wanted the relationship with him and the relationship with my children to be. As a result of the strong inner commitment I had made to my husband when younger, I also did not want him to suffer because of me, even though I was certain that I no longer wanted to live with him. These were things that I needed to work out. With Paul, I wanted him to support me and for him to let me make my own decisions about these issues even though it was hard for him.

Gradually, as I opened my heart again to Paul, it became clearer to me about how much I wanted to be with him. In many ways it was a new beginning, a time of discovery and of working through painful memories. It was not an easy process and there were times when it looked as though we might fail. However there was one fundamental fact that helped us through and that was the truth of our love. We both were willing to learn and grow through the experience and with the support of Spirit continue to take our faltering steps forward.

POSTSCRIPT
In the months following from Eleyna writing out her story, some very significant developments occurred in her life.

Firstly, her former husband began a new relationship with another woman. I suppose that for Eleyna, she considered that he was so obsessed and possessive of her that she was not certain that he was actually capable of forming a relationship and attachment with someone else. Because of her thoughts in this direction she felt that she was responsible for him in some ways. She felt that her actions and way of relating to him affected his happiness and inner state of mind.

52

However, now that he had formed this new relationship, she felt released from this responsibility, and the guilt of not meeting his needs that was associated with it. As a result of this, Eleyna made several steps towards making her separation from him more complete, including filing for divorce. Emotionally, Eleyna became aware of enormous anger arising from within her at the way she had been treated over the twenty-two years of their relationship. It actually gave her considerable satisfaction to express some of this anger towards him. She felt a need to do this as an act of balancing.

Around this same time, Eleyna asked me if I would choose for her a new name. She told me that as a baby when she was born, she was given the same name as her mother. Then when she was adopted, her new mother had wished for a boy and had chosen the name 'Lee' for this eventuality. 'Lynne' was a name quite close in sound to `Lee' and so she was called that. However, Eleyna did not feel that she had been given the name 'Lynne' with love, and so, she wanted a name given to her by me, her closest companion, with love.

My first reaction was to refuse her request. It felt like a great responsibility, and besides, I felt that if she meditated and asked for the right name, then it would come.

Some weeks later though, I was in Finland leading a workshop. Eleyna was not with me and I was missing her. One morning I awoke and the name 'Eleyna' floated into my mind for the first time. Suddenly I felt inspired to give her a name, and this name gave me a warm feeling in my heart.

Later that day, I phoned Eleyna and told her. As soon as I spoke the name, she felt a shivering feeling go all through her body. This repeated itself every time I spoke the name during those first few days. She loved the name and wanted to accept it. So this is how 'Lynne' became 'Eleyna'.

She knew that she would need to call herself 'Lynne' for her children and in other situations for some time to come. But 'Eleyna' represented her new self, a woman who was learning to believe that she was loveable and wanting to express herself more fully. Our group conducted a naming ceremony for her that was very beautiful.

I sensed that the name 'Eleyna' had some ancient connection, and I wondered if she might have been called something like that in a past life, perhaps ancient Greece. Whatever the connection though, it felt like it was coming from a place where we were very close.

Within a couple of weeks of accepting her new name, Eleyna discovered her natural father. She had had the yearning to meet her real father for as long as she had known she was adopted. However, because of what her natural mother had said about him, she had not believed it would be possible. She knew his name though, and she was aware of the town where he and her mother had met. But this was all she had to go on.

While she was at school teaching one day, one of her colleagues offered to look up on the internet the names and addresses of all the people with her fathers' name in the country. He gathered this list quite easily. There were only eight names, and one of them had the address and telephone number in the town where her natural father and mother had met.

When she came home to me, I urged Eleyna to phone this number and find out. She was nervous. When she phoned, she got a voice on an answer machine so she left her name and phone number. Minutes later, the phone rang and a man spoke with her. With a wavering voice Eleyna told him the few details she knew, about her father, her mother and where they had met. Before she finished, he interrupted her and told her that he was her father. The tears poured down Eleyna's face. I believe that it may have been similar for her father too. He told her that her contacting him was the one thing for which he had wished all his life, since she was conceived. He repeated to her that if he had had the chance to either win the lottery or find his long lost daughter, he would have chosen to find her. It was the happiest day of his life. They were both overcome with emotion.

Within days, Eleyna and I went to meet her father and his family. It was a happy meeting. He was a very emotional man, quite different from her natural mother who was more mentally orientated and fixed in her views. Eleyna asked him about the circumstances of her conception and he told a very different story to her mother. He suggested that her mother and him had been in love and that once her mother confirmed that she was pregnant, there was a day when she told her family. They reacted badly to this, and without even having the chance to meet her parents, he was told to go away and never come back. He said that he never got to see his baby daughter and it filled him with sadness. Somehow, Eleyna was more inclined to believe her father's version of events than what her natural mother had told her. He was a humble man and quite prepared to admit that he may have made mistakes along the way. This was very different to her natural mother.

For Eleyna, meeting her father helped her to understand her heritage better. It was like a missing part of her identity was in place and she could feel more whole.

It was within a week of meeting her father that Eleyna and I moved into our new home a lovely stone cottage, which we were going to rent in the countryside. It was somewhere big enough for children on both sides of our family to come and stay, homely with gardens, trees and an open fireplace. We needed such a home as a base for the imminent birth of our child. Although we'd been looking for many weeks, we felt that we were blessed in finding a place so suitable for our needs at exactly the right time for us.

Two weeks later, our daughter Grace was born. She has brought much happiness and joy into our lives. Children on both sides of our families have been regular visitors and Grace has felt like a bridge, helping to bring people together. Gradually, Eleyna's new life was beginning to grow more solid ground under her feet. With her adopted parents, the birth of Grace brought with it also, the rekindling of warmth in their relationship with Eleyna. She felt happier because of this.

Progress was being made, but the road is long ahead. At times there have been difficulties. At this time of writing, she is struggling to learn and accept something, which is quite obvious to me, her value and worth as a mother.

My Dream

While Eleyna has been going through her dramas in the course of building her relationship with me, I too have had my learning and challenges.

Recently, I had a significant dream, which seemed to indicate to me an important way in which I had grown through my experiences with her.

In my dream, I was partially living with Eleyna in a flat, but we were both also partially still living with our ex-partners and families. There was a prospect of going to a camp for a holiday, but it would be a situation where Eleyna would be with her ex-partner and family and I would be with mine. Thus, we would be separated. This arrangement did not suit me because I strongly did not want to be apart from her. Consequently, I suggested to her to inform her ex-husband that she would not be going with them. With some difficulty, she did this. Then, I needed to inform my ex-partner similarly.

Going up the steps with Eleyna into my family home, it was a large house and quite different from anywhere I have actually lived. My feelings told me that I did not belong there. When I saw my ex-wife, it felt more as if she was my mother, and I felt like a youth meeting with his parents. At this stage of the dream, I had fleeting memories of my actual experiences as a teenager and the feelings of inadequacy I felt then. My ex-wife had a partner, who, in the dream was my father. However, he was not at all like my actual father. As I spoke to this man, I noticed his listening eyes, and so I explained to him my wish to be with Eleyna and live with her. Quite easily, he accepted this, and gave me his blessing. Now I could go and be with Eleyna and leave this big house which felt so alien to me behind. With great relief, I went.

That was the main essence of the dream. Some irrelevant details, I left out. What I gleaned from the dream was that in my actual relationship with my ex-wife, I had related to her in some aspects as my mother rather than as a partner. There had been a part of me that had never grown up while I was with her. At times I had felt the need to ask permission from her to do things rather than feeling empowered to know what I wanted.

In the dream, I asserted my independence and my need for self-determination, and I acted to achieve this. It felt like a rites of passage dream telling me that I could leave that fearful, inadequate teenage part of me behind, that I no longer belonged in the house where this part of me existed. With my father's blessing I was able to move on so I could live my own life. This man who appeared to be as my father in the dream seemed to me to be a symbol of the strength and understanding of my adult Self. With Eleyna featuring in the dream, she seemed to represent my female self, and because she accompanied me throughout, and I accompanied her, this seemed to indicate that my male and female sides were co-operating together. On another level, because she featured in the dream as my partner, it felt to me that in real life, she had been instrumental in helping me to achieving this inner change within myself.

Chapter 8 -
The Ending of a Marriage

For anyone going through a marriage break-up or the ending of a long- term relationship, this will tend to be a traumatic experience. Whether we feel that we are the victims of the other person walking out on us or if we are the ones initiating the separation, or even if it is a joint decision, there will arise strong feelings as part of our adjustment to new circumstances.

At the outset of a long-term relationship, there will be the wish for safety, security and permanence with that other person. The loss of this will provoke feelings of failure and usually also guilt for mistakes and feelings of inadequacy where things have not worked out. There will be temptation to blame the other person and look for all the faults outside us. However, doing this, we will be attempting to hide from our own feelings and this strategy is unlikely to work in the long term. The other extreme will be to take on all of the blame as our own, that everything is our fault.

Typically, there will be reasons on both sides for the breakdown of the relationship, and it could be, that at heart, the relationship has run its course and needs to finish.

The ending of a long-term relationship can engender many self-limiting beliefs and challenge people's sense of self-worth and value. Patterns, for example where people feel not good enough can be felt, and if these feelings mirror other situations from earlier in life, then such limiting beliefs may be confirmed and etched more deeply upon the inner consciousness.

From my own experience, I know that people are going to be very vulnerable and need a lot of support during these times. If they don't have some people to whom they can turn, then the experience surrounding the break-up of a marriage can be very hard and damaging. If they can, I believe that it may ease feelings of suffering if people are able to reach out and share their emotions and not just build a wall around themselves so that all of the difficult feelings stay locked inside. Anybody creating these inner barriers will find that the difficult feelings will tend to swim around inside creating havoc, until sooner or later, they will probably find an outlet that is quite destructive.

Therefore it may be a useful and necessary challenge for people at these times to further their own communication skills, to find assistance so that inner feelings can be expressed. People need to receive much love to overcome their feelings of loss, so that in time, they may reach a more balanced perspective on the whole situation.

Sometimes, people may choose to stay in a difficult relationship and try to work things out, even though, in their hearts, they do not wish it. They may be afraid of the consequences if they decide to do anything different. Subsequently, people may live in fear and misery for a long stretch of their lives, if they are not being true to their hearts. On the other hand, it can be the case, that by sticking to a relationship, the two people may learn to love each other more fully and the relationship could renew itself in a worthwhile manner.

Each relationship will have its own pattern and its own needs. On an inner level, when a relationship comes into crisis - any relationship - there will be a test involved, about how to cope with it. There may be urges going in different directions, and the challenge will be about how to respond in a way that will be for the best.

In my own situation, I am convinced that Eleyna came into my life as a test for me. Inwardly, my love for her is so strong that sooner or later, I was bound to feel that I had to be with her. But how was I going to get to that point without hurting others tremendously?

Eleyna has shared with me that as a young teenager, she had an experience one day when she was feeling very lonely and unhappy, that a voice told her that later in her life there would be a man who would love her and accept her completely. She now believes that this voice was speaking of her meeting me. But Eleyna has had to release many very strong ties to be with me. She has met with stiff resistance from members of her family who have not wanted the change. It has been a big test for her.

I am sure that there have been times with both Eleyna and I, where we have each made mistakes, where we may have provoked more pain in others and for ourselves than was wise. Dealing with a marriage break-up can be very messy at times. So I cannot honestly feel proud of myself about everything that I have done, even though the outcome in terms of being with Eleyna has felt right to me.

One of my biggest lessons has concerned dealing with other people's expectations. In creating the situation where my relationship with my former wife broke down, some people have had very strong opinions quite against my own inner feelings, and I struggled to know what I should do. Every time that I listened to other people, feeling that I may let them down, instead of going within myself, I felt more lost. I have had to learn to stand firm with my own truth. The more that I have been able to be true to my own heart, then expressing this has given me peace. When such a lot of feelings are involved from various people, this can generate much turmoil.

As we consider the break-up of a marriage or long-term relationship, it is not only the two adults involved who are the only ones affected. Especially for children, the break-up of the family home can have an enormous impact.

The Choices our Children Make

As a parent, there is a temptation to feel guilty for any suffering which our children go through. We want them to be safe, to feel loved and accepted and to have a happy life. At the same time, we know that our decisions and behaviour can influence our children a lot. We are their models and they look up to us for support and guidance and protection. Of course, we are not perfect. We may get angry or impatient, or feel that we have been neglectful. There may be occasions where we feel we have hurt our children. For many families, as in the case of Eleyna and my situation too, the parent's relationship may break down. So where does that leave the children?

From a Spiritual perspective, a child may come into incarnation, knowing as a soul, say, that the relationship of the parents is likely to break down, or that one parent may die, or that there may be abuse in the family, or whatever other difficult scenarios may arise. When such situations happen while the child is still young, then this presents a challenge, and the child has choices about how they will respond.

Children tend to react in a more instinctive fashion rather than using rational thought and reasoning. The way they react may also be affected by the temperament of the child. For instance, some children will necessarily be more extrovert or perhaps assertive and others more inward looking.

Whatever the circumstances, children will naturally want their parents to be together, no matter how horrible the parental relationship has been. It will be a big challenge then for a child to accept the new situation as it is, even when arrangements have been handled amicably. Parents may try to give their children as much consideration as possible, but for the child, it still may not feel enough.

Yet, when difficult situations confront children, no one will be able to make them respond in a certain way. Their inner reality and perception of the situation will be their own creation, and what they create may have a considerable impact upon the moulding of their life.

Children may go into an inner state of darkness entirely through their own choosing. They may decide that nobody loves them, that the only safe way of being is to be cut off from others, or other similar thought impressions. However much the parents may implore otherwise; children will not necessarily be swayed by their parent's arguments unless they want to be.

It is similar for children as with adults when challenges come along. There is a need to ask for help, and really seek within and listen as to what may be the best way forward. Children may not have very good models to teach them to do that, but this may be part of their challenge.

In a situation such as the marriage break ups that Eleyna and I have been through with our former partners, the children in circumstances like these, are certain to suffer because they will feel torn, that the family unity has fallen apart. But how will the children react? They may feel through loyalty, bound to one parent and rejecting of the other, rejecting probably also all that this other parent represents. They may make moral judgements about what is right and wrong and develop attitudes to reflect this. It is possible that they may listen to the charged views of one parent but not the other so that negative beliefs or prejudices gain a foothold in their mind.

Ideally, they may open themselves to receive love from both parents and try to accept what has happened. In so doing they may learn much about the frailty of human nature and this may help them to become more compassionate. Additionally, they may gain a new perspective of both parents as individuals and manifest life experiences that they would not have had otherwise.

As an outcome to such a major life challenge, people may feel bitter and resentful or appreciative and grateful. For children as well as adults, the choice will be theirs. Sadly, they will have to nurse their wounds to come through this.

Obviously with children, if they are loved, then this will help them decide more positively. Needless to say, we have a responsibility to our children to nurture them as well as we can. If we can observe them closely and learn about their temperament, we can develop skills to be in harmony with them in terms of our own responses to things. This then is how we can be attuned to them. But we cannot decide for our children. If we can listen to them and communicate with them our acceptance and love, then that may be the best that we can do. They may feel things towards us that are not very nice, especially if they feel that we have disrupted their lives. I believe that if we can support them to express these feelings when they are there, then it will be much better for them.

Recently, my younger son, Johannes, volunteered to write a piece for this book about what it felt for him to go through the upheaval and trauma of his parents separating. I helped him a little with his writing, but basically he wrote down his own thoughts. I insisted that he be honest. What follows is his expression of his experience through this period of his life.

There was a great change in my life when my parents split. I felt very sad and distraught as my parents fought. Their fighting gained nothing. I thought that both parents tried to pull me so that I would be more with them. Because of this, I felt as if I didn't have any rights about what I wanted to do.

This all happened at the point when I was leaving Primary School and losing contact with many friends. This was the most down part of my life so far and I was feeling very lonely.

Slowly, I got used to it as I bonded with Eleyna's children. But initially, I felt very angry with both parents for ruining an important time in my childhood. I felt angrier with my Dad because he left the family home to live with Eleyna.

Gradually though, I have learned to accept the situation and I could forgive both parents. Now, I feel happier and I know that both parents would come to my aid if I needed it. I feel that my life is different now, not better or worse.

Chapter 9 -

Obsession in Relationships

It is clear from Eleyna's story that she has found it hard to extricate herself fully from the relationship that she shared with her husband. Part of the reason for this may be because there was an aspect of obsession in the relationship. Obsessions are different from normal feelings because the will has become involved, and instead of feelings being allowed to flow spontaneously, they will be directed by the person concerned to be focussed in a particular direction only. Where two people are involved in a relationship where this element is present, then the struggles involved may produce much unhappiness.

There may be times in our lives when we want something or someone very much. We may want to please someone, gain his or her attention or approval in some way. As we get caught up in particular relationships, we may bargain with the other person through our behaviour, modifying what we do with the expectation that the other person will give us something that we want in exchange. We can play all sorts of subtle games that are not spoken but where the power in the relationship is determined.

Once our personal desires are activated, we may find that it is very difficult for us if we do not get what we want. If we feel that we are being prevented from getting what we crave by the other person or by circumstances over which we wish to have some control, then we may bring in our will to try and make things go more our way.

If through our bargaining, we may feel that we should get some reward, but then if we don't, then this may bring a strong reaction in us. It could be quite complicated really. We may feel that we deserve to gain something, but then another part of us may doubt that we are worthy of it. Our reaction may be to push for the result we want so we don't have to suffer the pain of feeling that our doubts are true.

As a child, we may be given messages that we are useless, or incapable in some way. These messages may not be true, but if someone whom we consider to be an authority tells them to us, then these thoughts will affect our confidence, and the subconscious part of us that listens will expect those messages to be true. Thus, even when experiences come to us that contradict the messages we have received that are undermining us, then that subconscious part may still not accept that we are any different to what we have been told. Yet, other parts of us may rebel against that reaction and wish it to be different. There may be the makings of an inner battle about the subconscious beliefs we hold about ourselves.

Over time this struggle may be externalised when we form relationships and the people with whom we form these relationships may confirm for us different views that we hold about ourselves. Therefore, when we have struggles with other people we may really be struggling with ourselves.

We may quite easily wish to over-ride those thoughts in us that tell us that we are no good. If we are in close relationship with another person, to the extent that the other person expresses qualities that we feel inadequate about, we may wish to dominate them and find fault with them. We may not necessarily recognise that this other person could be manifesting qualities and behaviour that represent inner aspects of how we feel about ourselves.

For example, someone may have been a sensitive child wishing for love and told by a parent that he was a nuisance, that he shouldn't be so soft. Then over time, that person may alter his behaviour with his will so that he will appear harder and able to cope. He will try to hide his feelings of hurt at not feeling safe to express his sensitivity. More likely than not, that person may become involved in a relationship with a partner who will express qualities of sensitivity and softness. Then, he may try to suppress his partner's sensitivity and softness, finding fault with it at every opportunity, relating to his partner in a similar fashion to how his

65

parent related to him all those years before. He may feel both an attraction and repulsion to qualities of softness and sensitivity at the same time. But until he is able to work out his inner relationship with this parent, his feelings about these qualities will continue to be a problem for him, and probably cause others to suffer as well.

When we feel inadequate in some way, perhaps due to messages we have taken on from others, then we may decide that the only way that we can deal with that is to conquer those difficult feelings with our will. We may try to block our emotions so that we can achieve what we want without feeling bad about it. If we want success or popularity for instance, we may compromise our behaviour to realise our goal.

Perhaps if we were told as a child that we were no good, then we may have within us deep seated feelings of inferiority. We may then try to block those feelings and present an image to the world that we are confident and assured and better than others, thereby trying to compensate for the feelings that we don't want to know about. Our will can then take precedence over our feelings and the feelings of others.

Once our will is involved, we can summon its drives and determination to try to get what we want and achieve our goal, even though it may seem difficult. There may be signals for us to stop, but once our personal desires have been initiated, it may be hard for us to back away. We may not wish to feel defeated. Then, if we continue to feel frustrated, we may try even harder to get our will. With so much energy going into our goal, we may not be able to think of anything else and we may become very angry with anybody or anything that appears to try and stop us. We may not be open to the potential opportunities of other facets of our life, but only to the fulfilment of our desire.

If our hidden goal is to suppress or even destroy that part of us that we do not like, that part of us that believes things about us that causes us to feel pain, then it may be impossible to fulfil. We may need to embrace that part of us, not try to destroy it. However, it can be very hard to change, once our desires and will

66

are very strongly focussed in a particular direction. If we stay stuck in this mind orientation, then this can become obsession.

Commonly, obsessions can feature in relationships between people, but also in other aspects of our lives. If we look at the relationship side of things though, one person may not be prepared to give what the other wants. If the other person cannot accept this, then a power struggle may develop. People may decide that the only way that they can get what they want from that other person is by overcoming the will and resistance of the person concerned. Aggression and pressure may lead the other person to feel dominated and controlled, being unable to express his or her own personal desires. This person may feel like a victim, feeling wronged by the other person, and consequently want to blame that person.

However, the whole situation may not be so simple. The person who feels as a victim may be withholding love that the person with active desires wants or needs. There may be many inner struggles going on that are not at all visible. Both people may feel that they are victims of the other, that they are right and that the other one is in some ways causing psychic injury to them. It is common in such situations that each person may be locked in their own perspective without being able to view the larger picture or the feelings of the other.

On a soul level, two people may have chosen to be in a relationship to learn. However, they may have quite different inclinations. There may be lessons for both personalities about accepting each other's actions and choices, which are made. People in a relationship need to try to be true to themselves as much as they can. But this may be difficult. How one person acts may precipitate reactions in the other. These reactions may range from love, devotion and loyalty to anger, fear, jealousy, possessiveness, envy and many more feelings.

It may not be easy for people to control their reactions, especially once they are involved in a close relationship and that is the challenge where people need to learn. There may be a need on a soul level for those people to build a lasting and loving

67

relationship, or there may be a need for those personalities to disentangle themselves from each other so they can be more free and happy. This is where people need to listen carefully inside themselves to know what they need to do. People may make very unwise decisions for themselves when they are involved in relationships that are going contrary to how they really need to go. Where there is a lack of love for the other person or a lack of self-love, decisions may be made that cause pain and anguish. Their lives may become quite dark.

Someone who wants to dominate and control another may feel that they own that other person, that they possess that person in some way. They may want for that other person to behave in a certain way. This expectation may be a reflection and projection of their inner struggles. But if the other person does not behave as is being demanded, then this may produce a violent reaction in the one that is trying to control. To behave in this manner is abusive because it will not be respecting the wishes and needs of the other person.

Referring to Eleyna's story and her relationship with her husband, it may seem at first glance that she was the innocent victim of his obsessional behaviour. But she had her part in it as well. At an early stage in the relationship, Eleyna dedicated herself to share her life with him and try to help him to reach his potential, trying her very best to do what is right for him. She then applied herself to fulfil this task with utter determination and will, whatever the personal cost to herself. It was like a vow that she made to herself at a very deep level, and therefore it was very difficult for her to break the vow without feeling severely broken and a failure.

Therefore, even though to my observation, the relationship was fatally flawed from the beginning in terms of the possibilities for them to be happy together, she continued to invest much of her energy into the relationship because of her desire and determination to make it work. Even as she became desperately unhappy, her lifestyle self-destructive, and she felt on the verge of suicide, she still did not relent.

Several times Eleyna has said to me that I saved her life. I believe that it is more that she saved her own life, and that I was there to listen, love her and support her to be how she knew she really wanted to be. I felt that she needed a space where her feelings and emotions could be validated and heard. When she came to me for therapy, she had to be shown that her life was worth more than what she had made of it. There was no point in being destroyed in a relationship just for the sake of trying to make it work. She needed to direct her energies towards people and projects where she could feel happy and successful, and where she could make a positive difference. She needed to learn that she was worth more than submitting to another person's will and doing what she felt might please him.

It has been a long and painful struggle for Eleyna to be able to let go of this vow that she made. I imagine that it will always be there to some extent. She will want her former husband to be happy. But he is fading in importance for her now as she has realised she can invest her love in other people and interests where the reward and appreciation is much greater. She has had to fundamentally rebuild her life, and this has not been easy. Sometimes, this process may be necessary in a person's growth if they are to survive.

Shortly after Eleyna separated from her husband and started to live with me, he said to her that once I really got to know her that I wouldn't like her or want her anymore. These words had a cutting effect upon Eleyna. They cut into her doubts about whether she could ever make anyone feel happy with her. She felt that she hadn't succeeded with her husband so how could it work with anyone?

Over the years she had received many messages suggesting she was useless and incapable in various respects. Part of her had taken on the belief that these messages were true. Over the time that we have been together, she has asked me many times if she is alright, and she has been astonished at times to realise that I really do love her, even more deeply as we have grown closer. She has repeatedly come up against situations where in the way I have related to her that have contradicted what she expected in terms of her past conditioning. Gradually, the negative beliefs have diminished and she is growing in the belief that she is loveable.

Desires can be like psychic binds between people. When they get too strong or rigid, they can restrict the capacity of both people to function and feel free. The more one person expects from the other, the tighter these binds may become. It is obvious that in such circumstances, the two people will try to struggle against each other. They may each feel that their desires are not being met. Consequently, the situation may become very destructive between them with the possibility of anger. Their responses to each other in familiar situations may get stuck and repetitive and they may feel less alive than they want to be. Also, from the messages they to give each other, they may reinforce negative limiting patterns and beliefs within themselves so these become fixed and harder to alter.

Love can help. From within, may come peace and love. As that energy is channelled through those binds, they may loosen and freedom can return. People may need space from each other so that they can allow love and perhaps try to forgive each other for past hurts. Love flowing through the psychic connections will nourish the people concerned. The destructive power of desires and expectations will lessen.

Meditation can also help. Through listening within, it may be possible to determine what the relationship really needs. One person may need to let go of the other, or there may be a need for greater communication, for the relationship to become more co-operative and constructive. Courage may have to be embodied by both parties so that the relationship can really be open to what it needs. The two people may have to become aware that the relationship needs may not be aligned to the personal desires of either person. But it may not be an easy thing to find the truth when strong desires and drives are operating. If people facing these dilemmas can ask for inner help and release their expectations of the other person, they may gradually find a way forward. Of course, not all people may be willing to make this choice.

70

When we want something very much from another person and we think we are not going to get it, there may be a fear inside of what it will be like if this desire is not realised. This fear may be very dark and not realistic, but when a person believes it to be true, then this will have a very powerful effect upon that person's being. The fear may relate to desolation, loneliness, rejection, humiliation or many other emotions.

By using their will to try to get what they want from the other person, people can concentrate upon this rather than feel the fear inside of what they imagine it would be like without fulfilling their desire. They may imagine all that person's shortcomings without acknowledging any of their own, blaming the other person when they are not happy in themselves. People may want to hang onto an awful relationship because they are afraid of the abyss of what it would be like if the other person were not there anymore.

We can easily project onto other people lots of faults and weaknesses as a means to avoid feeling vulnerable. It is a very great tendency for us to put up barriers to try and protect ourselves rather than let the other person see where we are vulnerable. When we are vulnerable we can be hurt, because our heart is open and we are really listening and needing love. Therefore we really need to feel to be in a safe environment to allow ourselves to be vulnerable. Yet, when we are vulnerable with another and they can be like that too, then there is the greatest chance of healing within the relationship. In those moments we can be receptive to the truth about our own needs and the needs of the other person because we are open. However, we know that there is a danger that we can be greatly wounded during these moments too. So there is risk.

To help ourselves, we need to understand and acknowledge the fears underlying our obsessions. We may need support to be able to do this. Generally, people do not want to face fears on their own. This is because they mostly relate to isolation. Therefore the best help for these situations is love.

Even when fears are understood, it may not be easy to redirect drives that have been in play. This may only take place gradually, and in a relationship, much patience may be needed to allow healing and realignment of the relationship onto a more peaceful and stronger footing. The most important step may be for the people concerned to be willing to change and the change needed could be quite fundamental.

Some people may not want to change or even to admit that there is something wrong when they have their attention fixed on somebody else, to the exclusion of all else. This behaviour may be a source of comfort or security to them and they may not want to give this up. Underlying their actions, these people may be terrified of loss.

I have talked about Eleyna and the obsessions in her relationship with her former husband. There have been some occasions when I have suffered with feelings of obsession towards her too.

Throughout our relationship, I have loved Eleyna very much and wanted to be with her. I know that she has also loved me. However, there have been times when her attention has been more elsewhere. As she has written in her story, there was a time when she was full of love and need for her children, and she wanted them to come first for her in terms of time and attention before anything else. I found this difficult and wanted her to place me first rather than her children. This was something that she was not prepared to do then. There was a little boy in me afraid that she might not want me anymore. With these fears, my behaviour altered so that I was pushing myself more upon her, I suppose in an attempt to be noticed by her. However, she felt that I was interfering in her choices and she wanted me to give her space. Consequently, we became involved in some quarrels together, which had a damaging effect upon our relationship.

As a result of these, she made it clear to me that she wanted some distance from me. Then, even though I had to force myself, there was a point where I made a decision not to contact her anymore, but to leave all the contacting to her. Making this step, I felt that

I was coming into myself again. It was not easy because I had very strong desires for her, but I kept affirming about the need to let her go and release her to her own life.

Soon I began to feel stronger. My friends helped me and they supported me by letting me share my feelings with them. While I had been so occupied with her, I had felt quite weak. Now though, by letting her go, I began to give attention to my work, friends and projects that interested me, and I could perceive my life more broadly again. With each passing day, I felt stronger and more whole. But I would be lying if I did not admit that I was missing Eleyna terribly.

Within days though, something must have shifted in her. I suspect that she was missing me a lot too. She asked if she could be with me, and very soon we were closer than we had been for a considerable time. During that time when I had not been in contact with her, she felt that she was able to rediscover me. She could feel the love flowing for me again. Our actions must have broken a pattern that had developed between us. For me, the whole process felt like a very important lesson and an important step in the journey of our relationship. I realised that as far as her children were concerned, I could not compete with them for her affection, but more, there was a need for me to embrace them as vital elements in her life. Since then my vision has been that there could be an adequate place for all of us in her life.

Much patience, compassion and detachment are needed to help people suffering from obsessions and compulsions. People can create their own fantasy worlds to support the reality that they wish. They can construct false images and be convinced that what they have created is the only truth. If people are desperate in their wish for some situation to be a certain way in their lives, then they may view people and circumstances surrounding that situation in a narrow and distorted way to support their wish. Only when there is a sincere wish from the person concerned to open to further perceptions, an asking for help for truth to be revealed, can any of this shift.

In a relationship situation, if we open ourselves to learn about the other person's needs and give those needs as much importance, but not more, than our own, then this may help. We can create new patterns and correct misconceptions so our relationship may be more alive and we can move forward again. But it does take two to tango. If the other person is unprepared to change or challenge his or her attitudes and behaviour, then any possible renewal of the relationship will be very limited, and this may affect the choices that can be made.

When we are in a fearful state, our perceptions will tend to be distorted, and we need help ourselves. We may know that our thoughts and feelings are inaccurate and destructive, but feel little able to control them. This is where we need a friend or counsellor, where we can find an outlet for these feelings and thoughts - not to reinforce that they are right, but to let them go.

Chapter 10 -
Michelle

Background

When I have worked with people who have had drug problems, I have often found their inner life to be rather confused. I have had to be gentle and nurturing, but also very honest when dealing with their difficulties and issues. The most important step, for these people, has been for them to begin to take more responsibility for their own lives and what they create of it. Obviously, while they have been taking drugs, they have not been doing that.

People who have been affected by drugs are usually in a weakened and damaged state energetically. They need a lot of love and support to build up their strength again. I have found Spiritual healing to be a useful aid towards this.

Because of the allure and comfort that drugs give to addicts, usually they need to reach a desperate condition within themselves before they want to stop taking drugs and start on a path to try and make their lives better. make their life better.

Drug addicts may feel dejected and miserable about their plight and feel a drastic need to improve things. To achieve that though, they may need to be confronted with negative beliefs they hold about themselves and look at their destructive patterns of behaviour and the consequences of exercising those. But most of all, they would need to face their pain and be supported to do that. For a drug addict, that would not be very easy. The temptation would be there to opt out and escape as they had done with the drugs all the way along.

With all these thoughts in the background, I was anxious and uncertain how my work with Michelle would proceed.

It was Michelle's mother who introduced me to her. She was very worried and concerned about her daughter's health due to her being a heroin addict. When I first saw Michelle, she looked very pale and withdrawn. Her energy field felt 'limp' to me. As I talked to her, I could tell that she was an intelligent young woman and sensitive. There was a lot of anger in her and despair about what had happened in her life from the past.

I was surprised and delighted about how receptive Michelle proved to be to all my ways of working. She was not really afraid to try anything. Over the next months, Michelle did considerable work with me. She received healing regularly, attended my classes and Psychotherapy workshops. Generally, I felt that she was trying hard to tackle her inner problems. Before long, she had stopped taking heroin and was on the methadone programme. Perhaps naively, I imagined that my work with Michelle would turn things around for her.

I learnt though, that Michelle is quite a complex character. Although in her personality, she tended to be very frank and open, I discovered that she could present an image of herself to others that did not represent the whole truth of all her thoughts and feelings. It was very important for her to feel liked and accepted and so she could hide things that she did not want others to know about.

As she reduced her intake of methadone, the craving for heroin emerged again. Once more, she started 'using'.

It became clear to me that the major challenge for Michelle at this stage of her life was about whether or not she could overcome her addiction to heroin. There were suggestions that she had attempted a similar challenge in other past lifetimes, perhaps unsuccessfully. The temptation of drugs was an enormous dilemma for her. In order to succeed, Michelle would need to confront her dark side and deal with it directly and honestly. Much as I wanted to, I couldn't fix things for Michelle. Neither

76

could anyone else. This was something that she would need to do for herself.

There was so much potential in Michelle. She had a bright, sparkling, intelligent, sensitive personality. She could live a wonderful life. On the hand, her life could be gone in instant through an overdose, or ruined if the addiction went on much further.

Here in what follows, is her story. I know that it was very difficult for her to write it, but I feel that in the end she has given a very graphic, brave and forthright account of herself.

Michelle's story

My life began twenty-three years ago in Lancaster and in early life, I know, my parents and all the other adults around me viewed me as a child with 'the' most promising future. Being constantly praised for my precocity and intelligence, I was told that with my brain I could undoubtedly be anything I wanted when I grew up. I was so full of promise and brightness that at the time I was four, a friend of my parents was moved to comment that I was by far the most intelligent child he had ever met. He added that my parents must be very proud of their gifted offspring, and of course, they were.

My intelligence came from my father, who was apparently also incredibly bright in his schooldays. However, he had dropped out of university after just one term, and as in his eyes I was even brighter than he had been, he envisioned for me the brilliant academic career he had turned his back on. We therefore had a very close, special relationship and he delighted in the fact that despite my tender years we could have very adult discussions on all sorts of issues - literature perhaps, or politics, or wildlife, anything that took our fancy. At this early time in my life, I adored my father and loved to be with him.

Despite my academic abilities, however, I was in most ways a normal, well-adjusted child. I had a very happy, loving, in some ways almost idyllic childhood, and I was close to both my parents, though in different ways and for different reasons. Also, I had a sister, with whom I got on well enough, although we had the usual childhood squabbles. My parents both worked as nurses for mentally handicapped patients, and when they were not working one of our most common and favourite pastimes as a family was to go on long countryside walks.

So, very early in my life, I developed a love of and affinity with nature. I knew all the names of the wild flowers and creatures, and enjoyed nothing more than finding a rare orchid or spotting early spring violets and wood anemones. My dad also used to take me mountain walking, sometimes with a friend of his, sometimes just the two of us, but never with my mother or sister. By the time I was seven I had climbed Scafell Pike, the highest mountain in England, and when I was eight or nine we went to see the golden eagle's nest in the Lake District. I found fell walking difficult and tiring, but it was also very special to me because it was something my dad and me did together, just us.

As far as I knew, my parents' marriage was a happy one. In fact I was so certain of this that I remember feeling very sorry for the children in my class whose parents were divorced, whilst confidently thinking that this would never happen in my family. I was wrong.

My father announced that he was leaving my mother when I was eleven and my sister was nine. To my childish eyes he gave no adequate reason, he just said that sometimes people stop loving each other and that he needed time on his own. I felt devastated. This might have been easier had there been any warning and perhaps there was if I had known what to look for, but to me at least the news came totally out of the blue.

My poor mother fell apart. I do not know how much had been going on behind closed doors before my father left, but I am fairly sure the news was almost as big a shock to her as it was to us. Her own parents had died within six weeks of each other when I was a baby, so she had no one to lean on, although I tried to help her as much as I could. She cried almost constantly and often talked of suicide. When our cat died of feline leukaemia she said that she wanted to go and be with him and her parents and it was only my sister and I that stopped her.

It frightened me to see her like this and although all I wanted to do was make her feel better, I seemed unable to do so. She was totally destroyed; she had lost a fifteen-year marriage and was left with two children to bring up, and she couldn't cope. I began to hate my dad.

It seemed to me he had done exactly what he wanted and left us to pick up the pieces, a task that was beyond me. I was only eleven. It infuriated me that he was feeling fine while we were suffering, while my mum was constantly crying. I had just started secondary school, grammar school in fact, an achievement that was overlooked in the general misery of that time, and things had totally changed for me.

At primary school, I had been an outgoing child with lots of friends, perhaps a little bossy and over confident, but a nice child I think, and a happy one. However at my new school, while remaining at the top of the class academically, I made few friends. I was very unhappy and had become withdrawn and insular as a result. Also, I started developing early and as I approached my teens I already had puppy fat, large breasts and periods, all of which were to cause me great embarrassment and discomfort one way and another.

Soon, I became an easy target for bullies. One girl in particular bullied me very viciously. She made comments about my weight and appearance, about my family situation, she said my breath smelled and that I was ugly. On one particularly horrendous occasion, my sanitary towel leaked and some of my blood fell on to the school floor. This was bad enough in itself, but the relentless taunting that followed was nothing short of hellish. I suffered from agonising period pains anyway, but my visits to the sick room became more and more frequent, especially during games lessons. This girl made sure I was never picked for a team and tormented me if I missed or dropped anything, and it began to seem easier just to escape.

The bullying finally came to a head when I stood up for myself one day. We had just come out of a lesson, an English lesson I believe, and emerged into the cloakroom. Kerry made some nasty remark, which I do not even remember now. All I can say in explanation for what happened next is that something rose to the surface in me, something inside me finally decided that enough was enough, because the next minute I had turned around and punched her very hard in the face, causing her nose to bleed.

That day when I went home from school, I finally told my mother the truth about what had been happening. Up until this point I had deliberately kept the bullying from her because I did not want to add to her worries, but I thought it had now come to the point where I must tell her. Naturally, she was very upset and concerned, not least because the situation had now escalated into physical violence. We had a long talk and my mum decided on two separate courses of action.

As the first course of action, she rang the school and made a complaint to my head of year, Mrs Curtis, about the bullying. Mrs Curtis, despite usually being a teacher I liked, dealt with the situation in an appallingly stupid way. She called Kerry and I into her office and asked us both to give our own accounts of what had been happening. I told her just the barest outline because I was so intimidated by Kerry's presence and aware of her hanging on my every word for use against me later. Kerry, however, lied through her teeth. She said that the situation had in fact started with me being nasty to her. She claimed that she may occasionally have said some nasty things to me, which she now regretted, but only because she was so sick of me taking my bad moods and difficult family situation out on her and everybody else. Mrs Curtis then told us to apologise to each other and run along, no doubt thinking she had cleverly sorted out some silly adolescent squabble.

The second course of action my mum decided to take, or rather asked me to take, was as unsuccessful as the first. Her idea was this: for me to have a chat with my dad, explaining about the bullying and about how terrible things had been since he left, and then to ask him to come back because we couldn't manage without him. I was quite excited about this. I thought that if I explained all this, he would have to come back because he wouldn't want us to be unhappy or unable to cope.

My dad, as always, was very reasonable and logical and explained that his coming back would not help and in fact may even make things worse because things could never be the same as they had been before. This did not make me feel better at all and just made me hate my dad even more, and I told him so. I told him that although I continued to enjoy his company, I no longer loved him since his abandonment of us. When I said this, he began to cry and although I felt sorry for him then, I also thought it was only fair as my poor mum had been crying constantly for months. I had been trying not to cry so as not to upset my mum but sometimes I did, and I was certainly very unhappy, whereas my dad, in my view, had so far had it easy, even though he was the cause of all the unhappiness.

Of course I then had the difficult task of reporting to my mother, who had no doubt got her hopes up, that Dad would not after all be coming back. After telling her this and that I was sorry, I had tried my best, I tried to comfort her through a fresh bout of grief and dashed hopes.

As much as I tried to comfort my mum, I also had my own reactions to the break up to deal with. At night- time I became so afraid to sleep alone that I would have to get into bed with my mum. This was the only place where I felt safe and I think that it was probably a comfort to both of us.

I suffered night terrors and was very afraid of the dark, imagining that there may be burglars, bogeymen or people hiding in the wardrobe. This was something that was to return later as the traumas of my teenage years continued.

At the time my parents split up, there was a lot of speculation about what had happened because of the sudden and unexpected nature of the split. Most of this speculation came from other members of the family, principally my paternal grandparents. This was the point at which my relationship with them dramatically deteriorated. I had often noticed how my grandmother in particular treated my mother with less respect than she did other members of the family, and now she gradually began to treat me differently too, perhaps because she closely identified me with my mother. I have never been quite sure why Grandma treated my mum the way she did. However, I strongly suspect it was because my mum came from a working class family, with two petty criminals for brothers (although she herself was gentle, well spoken and wholly law abiding - she did not even drink or smoke). Grandma perhaps thought that my mum was not good enough for her son. As for Granddad, though I vastly preferred him to Grandma, he was cantankerous and could be cruel, and occasionally during my childhood I had felt very uncomfortable with him, although I could not really put my finger on why.

When my parents split up, my Grandma began a cycle of emotional abuse, which was to continue throughout my life until as an adult I decided that I no longer wished to see her.

The first thing she did was engaging in constant speculation as to why the split had happened. We went on holiday to Anglesey as normal that summer, although of course it was anything but normal. Grandma claimed to be sympathetic to my feelings and announced that I could always go to her if I needed someone to talk to. I was desperately unhappy and confused by what was happening, but at that point, I had no reason not to trust my Grandma.

One day, she and I went to the supermarket together. While we travelled there, she continued to press me to confide in her. So I poured out my woes. As I reflect upon it, I cannot remember exactly what I said. However, I do remember very strongly, my feelings. Here I was, an eleven- year- old child, who more than anything, needed some love, a cuddle, and lots of reassurances that things would not always be like this. Instead, my Grandma listened to me cry, listened to me talk about my mum, and then told me calmly and clearly that although my dad was far too honourable to say so, the reason for my parent's break-up was that my mum was having an affair.

With certainty, I knew that this was a lie. My mum loved my dad and would never be unfaithful to him. He was the one who had left. Grandma was lying. I didn't know why she was lying, but I was angry and indignant, that with all the misery that my mum was going through, Grandma was worsening it by trying to blacken her character to her own daughter. Despite my young age, I knew what she was trying to do - to shift the blame so that no one could criticise the selfish actions of her precious son.

I had heard Grandma lie before, and I had also heard her being nasty and patronising to my mum. Now I knew that she could not be trusted. Looking back, it shocks me that she could be so callous and manipulative as to try and destroy a child's image of her mother for selfish ends, although that was very typical of her.

About six months after the break-up there was news that my dad had found himself a new girlfriend. Naturally, mum was distraught, especially as this new girl friend was a person that she knew, someone with whom dad had worked. This news gave me further cause for confusion. It was never clear, although dad always strenuously denied it, whether this relationship had actually begun before my dad left my mum. At the time, I believed that it had.

I remember to this day, an occasion before the split, when dad had been on a night out with work colleagues, including this woman Lynn, seeing them together and feeling convinced, although I had no tangible evidence for it, that they were having an affair. This opinion was coloured by my feelings of absolute loyalty to my mum and hatred of my dad, and also by the fact that I was searching for explanations for events that seemed inexplicable.

From that time onwards, I hated Lynn for, as I saw it, stealing my dad, and so I ignored her or was rude to her as far as possible. This caused a lot of friction between my dad and I. On the other side, if I ever said anything nice about Lynn, my mum would become bitter and angry and accuse me of disloyalty.

I settled for not upsetting my mum rather than my dad, as I reasoned that she had been upset enough already, and anyway, the situation was of his own making and he would have to live with the consequences. Whenever Lynn attempted to assert any authority, I would respond with the familiar stepchild's cry that she could not tell me what to do, as she was not my mum.

Around this time, my dad began to criticise my weight constantly and also exhorted to me that I must wear a bra. His attitude was that breasts wobbling and braless looked vulgar. I had begun to think about wearing one, but my dad's pressure made me stubborn and I dug my heels in. I told him that I would not wear a bra, that it was my body and none of his business.

When I was fourteen, Lynn became pregnant. Dad and Lynn were obviously delighted, and my sister also seemed pleased. But my response was hysterical distress. Bursting into tears, I ran upstairs. I am not sure why I was so upset - I think that it was partly for my mum, who would be hurt deeply by this news, at a time when she was just starting to get back to her feet again. However, I was also upset for myself, because I now felt that Lynn had succeeded in taking my dad away from me and this is what I perceived to be her aim.

My attitude changed when my brother was born. I could not help but love him. In many ways, his birth improved the relationship between myself and my dad and Lynn. They were both pleased and surprised by my reaction to the baby, as throughout Lynn's pregnancy, I had been moody and difficult. Problems arose, though, in the inevitable form of my grandma.

A fawning, obsequious, mutual appreciation-style relationship had developed between Lynn and grandma, something that angered me greatly, especially in view of the contrasting way in which she spoke to and of my mother. This now began to extend to the baby, with grandma taking over whenever she could.

She took great pleasure in reminding my sister and I that we were only his half-sisters, not his sisters, and therefore not very important, and not really anything to do with him. When the baby was being named and everyone put forward suggestions, she said that it was nothing to do with us, that we were only his half-sisters. If either of us were ever holding him, she would immediately take him away saying, 'Grandmas are more important than half sisters.'

This behaviour was designed to push us out rather than helping us to bond with our new brother, and it worked. Sometimes I went home to my mum in tears, I was so hurt, and my mum, furious, told my dad that he must speak to grandma. He did, and she modified but did not stop her campaign. It felt useless trying to make dad understand the worst excesses of her viciousness. His response was always that she was old and meant no harm.

There were many instances where my grandma was cruel to me. An example was from one Christmas when she gave her other three grandchildren £50 plus expensive gifts, and to me she gave a book about nail varnish (I have always bitten my nails) with the price tag of £2.99 still on it. She was also critical of my weight. On one occasion when she had already reduced me to tears, and I went to ring my ex-boyfriend to whom I was still very close, she took great delight in telling me that he didn't want me anymore. This felt like rubbing salt into a fresh wound and hurt me very much.

The problem was that my father always stuck up for her. She made me feel worthless, with such low self-esteem, something that I have had to battle with throughout my life. Of course, other factors contributed, but grandma certainly had a big part to play, and she would still continue if I let her. In later years I have stopped caring and tried not to have contact with her. The one occasion recently when I was persuaded to phone her, much against my better judgement, I was immediately greeted with a torrent of vicious criticism before I hung up.

Everything I have been writing has really been leading up to describing how I came to be addicted to heroin.

Following my parent's divorce, I became very unhappy and this intensified with the events, which took place in my teens.

When I was fourteen, I was sexually assaulted by a boy of my own age. Because I attended an all girls' school, I did not know many boys of my age, so I didn't realise that this boy's behaviour was wrong. When I told my parents what had happened, my mother reacted with shock and horror. However, she directed these feelings at me, not the boy. She felt that I had done something that was quite disgusting. My dad dismissed it by asking me 'What did I expect when I went into a quiet place with a boy?'

These reactions to this experience led me to carry a huge burden of guilt inside me. I did not realise that it was not my fault and felt that I would be tainted until the day that I died. As a way of controlling the pain I felt, I started cutting myself.

As I grew older, my self- esteem became less and less. Because he criticised everything that I did, I grew convinced that my dad didn't love me. One family holiday, he took my brother, sister and Lynn with him but left me out.

At age sixteen, I found work as a kissogram and glamour model. This was something that I enjoyed and which boosted my confidence. Of all the jobs I've had, it was the one I've enjoyed most and stayed in for longest. I loved performing and feeling sexy, and it was also nice to have plenty of money and be able to pay my rent in cash. It didn't bother me to take my clothes off but unfortunately, my boss didn't always provide enough protection from the rowdier men in the audience. After being assaulted badly once, I knew I had to leave this job.

From developing an interest in the opposite sex, I had a succession of boyfriends, none of whom treated me well. This culminated at eighteen, when I moved to London in search of excitement. There I met Marc, who crushed the remaining Spirit and confidence that I had left. I was lonely and isolated and knew no one except him. I never got enough to eat because he drank all our money. He called me terrible names and blamed me for everything that went wrong. Even things like the light bulb going would provoke terrible rages. Often he told me that he hated me, broke my possessions or threw them across the room. He threw my writing and photos away and threatened me. Also, he made me feel that I had no home because he repeated so frequently that it was his flat and I had no right to be there.

During the relationship with Marc, I became pregnant. Although I loved the baby and wanted it very much, he persuaded me to have an abortion. This was very difficult and I felt so reluctant to go ahead with this. At four months pregnant, I was starting to show when I had the abortion. I often wished later that I had kept the baby. It was so sad and left a huge hole inside of me. I sensed that this baby was a girl and named her Zoe.

Finally Marc went off with another woman and told me on the telephone to go away. I felt worthless. Marc had this ability to make me feel that his abusiveness was my fault, and I blamed myself because I had loved Marc very much. Somehow, I felt that if I had tried harder then I could have made things right.

As a consequence from the break up with Marc, I began to be promiscuous. Somehow, I felt that I didn't have the right to say 'no' to men. I felt that it would be rude and I didn't want to hurt anyone's feelings. Besides that though, I had a desperate urge to be needed and wanted, to know that I was attractive and desired by men. I felt that my looks were all I had because I felt that I had wasted my intelligence and it was too late for me in that area. Most of these relationships were quite meaningless, but I felt that I had to find some pleasure and comfort somehow.

At age 20, I moved to Nottingham and soon met a man called Steve. As with the others, he was a man fitting the pattern of being someone who treated me badly. It was through Steve that I became introduced to heroin.

For some years I had been experimenting with drugs, and I enjoyed some of the effects that I gained from them. We started by doing methadone together. Steve made money out of this by selling it to me at an inflated price. Then Steve became very depressed and we started doing heroin more and more often.

Steve would not do anything to help himself and constantly talked about suicide. The occasions that we did heroin helped to relieve the constant misery so that for some small time things would feel good again.

Then, when I was 21, my dad died. It was very sudden and unexpected, and I didn't get to say goodbye. He had been in hospital for a short time, gravely ill, but then seemed to be rallying. Just as I was beginning to hope that he would be all right, I received news that he was gone. I felt devastated.

Despite the difficulties in our relationship, I loved my dad very much and it hit me hard. I couldn't cope to be on my own, so I begged Steve to come and be with me. He refused. Steve seemed to be too wrapped up in his depression and own problems to help me, even when I needed him most. I found this very hard.

Then three days after the death, my best friend started an argument with me, something I still don't understand. Perhaps, she didn't know what to say. Soon another girl who had never liked me joined in. They were accusing me of things that I had not done. Just at a time when I felt that I needed a huge amount of support, people seemed to be going against me. It was like I was losing everyone close to me. I felt betrayed and could not manage.

My reaction, when I returned to Nottingham, was to start using heroin more and more often. At first I smoked the heroin off foil, but after going through a rapid succession of men and being labelled a 'slag', I started seeing another Steve, an injecting heroin addict. At this point, I started stealing things and selling them to fund my habit. Steve never paid for anything, instead letting me take all the risks that stealing involved, paying for all our drugs, all our food and all our tobacco. In return, he injected me with heroin.

At some level, I knew that I was getting in too deep, that this was something that I could not control. However, it was also a time when I felt very lost and lonely, and very angry. Every time that I thought about my dad's death, and the way that people had treated me, I became enraged. Heroin took away all the pain, the tears and the depression - it felt like the answer to all my problems. I didn't have to be afraid when I was on it - it took away all the bad feelings and replaced them with happy ones. And it became a sort of obsession - life was a constant round of raising money and scoring. I didn't have to face up to any of my problems.

Eventually I became sick of Steve taking all my money and finished with him. He became very angry and abusive and showed a violent side of himself that made me even gladder to be rid of him. But I continued to steal and use heroin. Inevitably, I got caught stealing, and unfortunately, on that occasion, I also had heroin on me. The police strip-searched me because they had seen me pushing my syringes into my knickers. It was a horrible, humiliating experience and I realised that I didn't ever want to sink this low again.

This event marked an important turning point for me. By now, my family knew what was going on and my sister came to collect me and bring me home to Lancaster. My mother in particular was very supportive. However, coinciding with this, I had met someone new. For the first time in my life, I had met a man, Tee, who treated me wonderfully, and I fell madly in love with him. He was also willing to stand by me while I came off heroin.

While I waited for treatment, I continued using heroin, but I tried to keep it down to a minimum. With all the support around me, I was beginning to see the dark side of heroin - the tiredness, the depression and the lack of money. By this point, I no longer got any kind of hit. I was only taking heroin to shake off withdrawal symptoms.

After a couple of months, I reached the top of the waiting list and was put on a methadone programme. It was a long, slow process and very frustrating having to visit the chemist every day. Eventually though, I was able to stop. I was incredibly lucky - I had somewhere to go and the love and support of my family, which most addicts don't have.

My mother introduced me to Paul who started Hypnotherapy with me. By doing this, I have begun to come to terms with my past.

He has also given me Spiritual Healing and is teaching me how I could channel that myself.

I experienced a setback at Christmas when I was sexually assaulted on Christmas eve when I was sexually assaulted whilst walking home from the pub. This hit me doubly hard because it was so close to the anniversary of my dad's death and also it reminded me of when I had been sexually assaulted in Nottingham by a man I knew. Although up to this point I had been making good progress, this incident brought back a lot of bad memories. It made me feel that whatever I did, even when I tried positive things, that things would always go wrong for me. My response was to look for some way of escaping. For quite a few months after this incident I was drinking 1-2 bottles of wine a night on top of the heroin and methadone.

Upon reflection, I realise now that I took heroin to take away the pain, and remove the feelings of guilt that I was somehow 'bad' and didn't deserve anything good to happen to me. Slowly I am learning to accept that I am a good person and although I miss my dad every day, I know he loved me because I can feel his presence. Sometimes I still think that it was unfair for him to be taken away from me, just at a time when we were starting to get along again. And I think of my baby Zoe, all the time as well. But I know that both of them will always be with me and I hope that I can make them proud of me.

I managed to be clean for some months, but as I began to reduce my intake of methadone, I began to feel the cravings for heroin again. Heroin is like no other drug - it takes over your mind. You crave for it with every fibre of your being. It can cause you to become a completely different person, one who lies and steals and cheats.

I was stupid enough to think that I could just do heroin once as a sort of treat, thinking that because I had managed to beat it, I would be strong enough not to let it back in my life again. But of course, I did it once and all the old happy, peaceful feelings returned. Nothing else mattered. And remembering those feelings, of course, I wanted to do it again.

90

Every time I did it, I told myself that it would be the last time. And I thought that maybe I should talk to my mum about it. However, I put off doing this, partly because I didn't want to cause her any more pain and worry, but partly for selfish reasons.

In my thought processes, I concluded that if I told my mum, then it would have to stop. And part of me did not want it to stop, because I craved those feelings and I loved the ritual of injecting and I knew the trouble that would come if people discovered what I had been doing. I thought that my mum might be angry with me and reject me for putting her through this again.

When I had originally become addicted to heroin, I thought that my mother would never need to know, because it would never come to that stage - I could just use it recreationally, once a week. But then I began to think about it all the time, and it got more and more until it was every day.

This time around, I knew the dangers and I still did it. Heroin has a strange effect upon my mind. For periods of time I have not been able to concentrate upon anything else because I have constantly been thinking of the next hit. And I want to stop.

I hate never having any money and causing my loved ones pain. There is an immense yearning inside me to create a more meaningful life, especially now that I have started to open to my Spiritual self. By making a connection with my guide `Alex', I had begun to find real inner peace and happiness, and yet heroin has got me at its mercy again.

And now, I can get hold of it in Lancaster, something that I could never do before. So the temptation is right on my doorstep.

Sometimes I wonder if I can ever win this battle, or whether it is even worth trying, but it has to be. It turns me into someone I hate, someone I am not - a person who lies and steals and will verbally abuse and shout at people I love in order to get money for heroin. And my mum is so worried, that she has started searching drawers in my room, something that I was furious about when I discovered it. However, I understand why she did it. All the arguing and deception is a vicious circle.

In another upset, the girl who had a go at me after my dad died, is now blaming me for the death of her boyfriend from a heroin overdose, even though I hated him and hadn't seen him for months. It's a load of rubbish, but it is very upsetting to have people glaring at me, accusing me and talking about me whenever I go out. This has been causing me a lot of distress, because these people won't listen to reason or the truth - they like having someone to blame. And the unfairness of that upsets me a lot.

I have told my mother now, and in writing this, I hope that I can make a new start. In many ways, I feel very fortunate. I have taken on a part time job and I have the intelligence to make a future for myself. Also I have an incredibly strong support network, with my mother who has loved me and stood by me through everything. Tee, my boyfriend, makes me feel loved and precious and treats me like a queen. In addition, I have Paul, whose sessions make a world of difference. My wish is that I will find the strength to overcome heroin - it is not easy. But I don't want to throw everything else away.

Chapter 11 -
Addiction

Heroin addiction is just one of many possible addictions where people may find themselves trapped and struggling. Some of these may be chemical induced dependencies, as in the case of heroin and other drug taking. Others may be purely psychological in origin. However, I believe that all addictions have similar characteristics, whatever the form that they take.

Examples of addictions may include dependency upon drugs, alcohol, cigarettes, food, shopping, sex, TV etc. Addiction is commonly regarded as obsessional behaviour where people become fixed upon a certain way of being. Once this is established, then it becomes entrenched behaviour and those people find it difficult to consider doing things any differently.

Commonly, addictions will have a ritual element attached to them as a means to give the behaviour a context in those people's overall life. For instance, Eleyna, in her life story, touched upon her addiction to alcohol in the five years prior to her coming to me for therapy. During that time, every evening at six o'clock, she would have her first glass of wine, and then for the rest of the evening, she would have a wine glass filled and ready by her side. Michelle has mentioned without detail the procedures she has gone through in injecting herself with heroin. A cigarette smoker may have specific times and circumstances when he lights up.

These rituals can give a sense of order and control so that the addict will know what is going to happen and when, and this may then provide a considerable comfort to the person. If the addict feels that there are aspects of his or her life that feel out of control and difficult, then rituals and activity involving the substance of the addiction may be a stabilising factor in those people's life. Thus, the addiction will fill space and be something that those people can hold onto if they feel fearful about other things.

Rituals can be creative and life enhancing practices, encouraging people to experience life in greater depth. For example, the simple act of holding hands at the start of a meeting between people can promote a sense of linking together and the intention of unity that will positively affect the timbre of the meeting. However, the rituals around addiction can be very empty and deadening, merely serving to `fix' behaviour in a certain way.

Addiction can provide a security in people's life, filling in holes where perhaps people experience pain. It can also be a mode of escape from aspects of life in those people's consciousness that is unpleasant.

When people go into the activity of their addiction, nothing else matters anymore. It can be sustained because people will know how to do it without thinking, and they will feel that they have to do it, as everything else will feel less safe and less controllable.

Often, I have noticed that addictions come much more strongly into being following trauma. For Michelle, the death of her father provided a trigger whereby coping with everyday life became too much and it was all too easy to opt out with heroin. She already had a predisposition towards heroin from her more casual use of the drug prior to her father's death, but following this event, she wanted to escape, perhaps in some ways not wanting to live anymore. With these inner influences and her already low opinion of herself, she had no resistance to the more destructive influences of the drug.

Eleyna has shared with me of an experience she had many years before she became addicted to alcohol. There were a series of events that prompted her to want to leave her husband. She would have done so too, except that when she told her children, her eldest son who was six at the time, became very upset. Because of this, Eleyna relented and put her own needs and happiness second to that of the children. Shortly afterwards she drank a bottle of sherry until she was sick. Her response to acting in ways where she was not true to her heart was to want to withdraw and be possibly self- destructive. And drinking alcohol was already a method that she used to do that.

Sometimes I ask people what they enjoy from that to which they are addicted, and generally there is nothing. The repetition and compulsion associated with the activity reduces any pleasure and it is like going through the motions only. Often, people with addictions are very unhappy. They come to depend upon their addiction as a focal point of their life without knowing or trusting how their life could be without it. The addiction is something that is predictable in a world where nothing else can be relied upon, and where there may be a lot of pain.

Usually, people with addictions are living in the darkness and the addiction is their prop, the one thing that they can cling onto that is familiar and to which they can depend. If this is the case, then the person may internally feel quite desperate. However, the addiction may not be the dominant force in a person's life and may only involve some facet of the overall life. For the area that is affected though, it will be like living in a box. The rigidity of behaviour connected with the addiction will stultify creativity and light from entering. Somewhere inside, people will know that they are wasting their lives by doing this, but once the addiction has its hold, it can be very difficult to let it go.

It may be that at some point, people realise that instead of controlling the functioning of the addiction themselves, that the addiction is controlling them. Perhaps some trauma may be needed to alert people to this. For example, Michelle spoke of the incident where she was strip-searched while carrying heroin. When they become aware of this, then people will know that the addiction is no longer serving them in the manner that was intended. This may be the moment when people decide that they need to stop it. Otherwise, if people feel defeated by their addiction, they may just decide to wallow further in it, that nothing can happen to help them. That would be very sad.

But addictions create such deep grooves in terms of behaviour, that it is easy to slip into them, but very difficult for people to extract themselves from them, even when they want to do so.

When Eleyna came to me for therapy, she became increasingly determined to resolve her drinking problem. At first, she tried watering down her drinks, but found that by the end of the evening, she had drunk just as much anyway. In the summer of that year, she made herself stop drinking for ten days by the force of her will. However, by doing this, she found herself becoming more nervously anxious than she would feel normally. She could not cope with this anxiety and so feeling defeated started drinking again. For her, drinking was a means to numb out the pain of her existence, to dissociate from the emptiness she felt in her life, particularly around the relationship with her husband. She suffered in silence and having a few drinks would soon diminish all the feelings of worthlessness and loneliness welling up inside her. But it didn't really help because the feelings would return the next day and she had become very withdrawn.

For Eleyna, the Spiritual experience where she felt the presence and love of 'God' changed her. She had wanted to help herself and now she was ready. The faith that she gained through this experience gave her the inner strength that she needed. Within weeks, she was able to completely stop drinking without struggle. She also needed though, to confront the pain in her life, its causes and the limiting beliefs she carried within her. To strengthen her further she needed to make changes in her life so that it was really more attuned to what could make her happy.

Generally though, I feel that to gain strength to meet the problems of an addiction, there will be a need for people to confront underlying causes, and the pain which makes them feel that they cannot create and live the life that they want. Not everyone may go through such a dramatic Spiritual experience as that which engulfed Eleyna. However, if people can begin to make their own Spiritual connections and learn about their path, then there will emerge a strong determination and potential inspiration to overcome restrictions.

People will perceive addictions as restrictions in their life and want to become free of them.

Through establishing her connection with Spirit and gaining support from others to deal with the problems of her life, I feel that Michelle has made some significant steps towards inner freedom in her own life. Despite her recent setback with the relapse to use heroin again, I sense that Michelle is beginning to believe in herself. She has ambitions and a vision from within her that is growing clearer of how she wants her life to be. I feel confident that she can be successful. However, she knows that she cannot do any of these things while she continues to use heroin.

Even when people can say 'no' to the addiction and open themselves to a new life, there may always be the temptation and possibility for them to return to it as a means of escape, especially if things get tough. This will be a challenge to be endured. Our soul pathway will go on other tracks though, from where addictions would lead us to be. It is up to us whether we have the confidence and willingness to tread on those tracks where our soul wants us to go, or if we would choose the more alluring dark alternative of the addiction.

Chapter 12 -
Claire

Background

I first met Claire when she came along to attend one of my Healing classes. My first impression of her was that she that she was rather beautiful in appearance, fairly tall with light brown hair, a young woman in her mid- twenties. I was struck by her sensitivity. She seemed to have a very gentle demeanour and was polite and softly spoken. However, she also felt to me to be rather timid. Sometimes the words that she spoke were so faint that they were barely audible. Publicly, she said very little and I sensed that she did not trust others very easily. I felt that she was a very private person.

As we progressed through the class, it was clear that Claire had a great deal of ability to channel Spiritual Healing and she gained a great deal of satisfaction from doing this. One evening when she came to our Healing group, she showed me one of her paintings. The beauty and power of the image in her painting impressed me. There was a depth of feeling she had expressed which affected me strongly. I learnt that the picture related to a poignant moment from her life. Instinctively, I felt moved to ask her if she would make a contribution to this book. She agreed.

Afterwards, she began to see me as a client for therapy and I got to know her better. I feel that Claire is at the beginning of her present life's journey. Through our work together, she is starting to open her inner perception. She has much to learn about herself. However, she knows that she needs to overcome her fears so she can dare to express herself in the world and follow her heart. Her fears though, are quite deep rooted, going perhaps beyond her present life into the past. I am sure that it is one of her main life challenges to overcome these fears and to be herself and express all her gifts with others. At the moment I feel that she is still discovering about her abilities and trying to gain self-confidence so she can live with self- acceptance around others and feel comfortable in her relationships with people. What follows is her story.

Claire's story

The first major thing I had to deal with in my life was my parent's divorce. I was nine years old with sisters aged sixteen and seventeen and a brother aged eighteen. My mum was the one who left and so I was brought up by my dad. Before the divorce, my mum was at home and was always the one to take me to school and pick me up - my dad was self-employed and worked hard for the family.

My mum therefore was cast as the villain, because she had to discipline us, whereas my dad was always kind and pleased to see us. I have a typical memory of a morning before school - as usual I didn't want to go - my mum angry with me, would be inclined to lash out first and think later. My dad provided the ideal refuge, so I would stand behind him, safe in the knowledge that he would protect me.

My mum had a quick temper back then and I remember being afraid of it, as I had been on the receiving end of it more than once. But my early memories of her are by no means all bad.

My mum was and still is a very 'homely' person - the house was always full of plants, ornaments and books - comfortable rather than tidy - she's a fantastic cook, has a great sense of humour and is also beautiful. I was always proud to be seen out with her because people would comment on how pretty my mum was and is.

However, I also remember the sadness in the years leading up to the separation. One time I found her crying in the bathroom - it stands out so much, because she wasn't like that, she didn't and doesn't cry easily. I know now that the situation was making her unhappy.

My early images of my dad are often of him in his work clothes, clean on his way to work, or hands and face black with dust, when he returned - or memories of family holidays - playing football and tennis with him - he was always energetic and strong, laughing and joking. More than anything, my dad made me feel safe and loved.

From an early age, I disliked going to school. In my first year at school, I had a completely different character - I was confident and outgoing, had made plenty of friends and enjoyed playing out. However, by the time I was six or seven, I had developed a strong dislike for school, and would do all I could to avoid going. I can only put the change down to my life at home. I must have picked up on something between my parents. My parents had separate rooms for some time before my mum left. So I'm guessing that it influenced my personality quite a bit. Becoming shy and withdrawn, anxious around strangers, I wanted to be at home. It wasn't until after the separation though, that I took any real time off.

School became more and more difficult for me. Feeling painfully shy, I also always felt like the odd one out. I changed schools about age 9, but only coped with the new school for a year before I had to return to the first one, having been bullied by other girls. They teased me, and called me names like 'scruffy' and 'peasant'. This was new to me; I hadn't been treated so badly before. I guess I may have looked a bit bedraggled at the time. My mum had just left and I didn't bother to brush my hair unless reminded. My dad hadn't been used to running the house and probably wasn't all that organised, although he tried his best.

When my mum left, it seemed that the best option was for my dad to give up work to look after me, but in retrospect, it wasn't such a good idea. I relied on my dad and in turn he relied on me. We had a very close relationship, a friendship even, and we spent hours and hours talking. It seemed to help us both, but perhaps it deepened what had become 'our' depression. In the years that followed, my dad suffered from a nervous breakdown.

100

I know this contributed to my problems at school, and socially, although I don't blame him, it was just that my rock wasn't so stable any more.

In the meantime, I had regular contact with my mum and with her new partner, Paul. He had three boys from a previous marriage and it was initially difficult to accept them. They were closer to my age than my own brother and sisters, and so we became friends, but it was difficult to see my mum looking after someone else's family, when I wanted her to be part of ours.

Returning to my old school, my last year at junior school was the best one I had had. However, secondary school brought new problems with it and my sense of isolation increased. I had more and more time off, days in the first year, weeks in the second year and months by the third year.

About the age of thirteen, I was diagnosed 'school phobic' by a child psychologist. I had to answer all kinds of questions, and had to see the psychologist regularly. The main thing that came up was my fear of crowds or groups of people. Being with too many others would bring on panic attacks, and the only way to end them, would be to get out of the situation. Now, twelve years on, I'm only just realising the need to confront my fears. As a child I chose to run away from uncomfortable situations, as a child would I suppose. But by doing that, the fear stayed with me. Going to school frightened me, even the journey to and from school frightened me, and I hated to feel hemmed in on the bus.

As I had more and more time off school, eventually a welfare officer would pick me up and take me. I dreaded the knock on the door that meant I had to go. I never played truant in the sense that I'd pretend to go to school. My dad always knew that I'd stayed off. At first, I insisted that I was physically ill, but more often than not, it was just sheer panic that made me feel ill. When it became apparent that the welfare officer was not helping, I was referred to a psychiatrist who did very little. He diagnosed depression, suicidal tendencies and prescribed sleeping pills. After that, there was a child psychologist who helped much more, mainly because he listened to me - but I didn't like the fact that he spoke to my dad and I separately. It made me feel talked about. This psychologist referred me to an EBD school, a special school, for children with emotional and behavioural difficulties. Initially, it was recommended that I be residential, as the psychologist felt that my dad and I relied too much on one another. In many ways, we did. But I felt it was helpful to be with my dad and I didn't feel able to cope away from home. I refused point blank to be residential, threatening to run away. So against the psychologist's wishes, I became a day pupil.

Around this time, when I was fourteen, I started going out with a boy on my street. For a while the relationship seemed good. He was my refuge from another school I hated and where I felt very much alone. I will call him Robert. For a while, Robert made me feel good about myself, about the person I was. We spent time together every day, but it didn't take long before the relationship began to add to my problems.

Robert was two years older than I was and in his last year at school. When I had first met him, he lived with his mum and two sisters. But now at the age of sixteen, he was living alone. First his mother had moved out, taking the youngest girl with her, so she could live with a man she had recently met. Then his older sister also moved out, leaving him on his own.

Understandably, this situation began to take effect upon him and he became depressed. Many times, he tried to take his own life. His wrists were heavily scarred from razor blade cuts. He would drink bleach, and on one occasion he even tried to hang himself. It was nightmarish.

One evening, I found him sitting in a back street. He was dazed; blood was trickling onto his hands from deep gashes on his wrists and he had hidden a razor blade inside his mouth, so that I couldn't take it off him. Finally I managed to persuade him to let me have it and then I took him to my house where I asked my dad to drive him to the hospital. Until then I hadn't told him about the extent of Robert's depression and it was a shock to him that I had been dealing with this alone. However, it was not so straightforward.

Bad enough that he had been abandoned, Robert claimed that he was possessed by two evil Spirits, and there were certain events that led me to believe he was telling the truth. He told me that killing himself was the only way to end it. How much of it was authentic, and how much of it was an effort to get attention, I don't know, but I do know that the emotions we went through together at that time were very real. We sought help in various churches, and one particular minister had confirmed Robert's thoughts - even telling him the names of the 'demons' that resided in him.

There was an occasion when I called around to see him and found him lying in the darkness, growling like a dog. He was muttering to himself and hardly seemed aware that I was there. I took him to a vicarage around the corner from us. It was late, but I was afraid for us both and I had no idea what to do about it.

The door was answered and we were ushered in. After I explained the situation, we were separated. The vicar and another man took Robert into the next room where they attempted some form of exorcism. Meanwhile, the vicar's wife sat with me, asking me questions to try and ascertain how this had happened. Some of her questions disturbed me greatly. She asked whether we were involved in occult practices. Did we read tarot cards or other horoscopes? It seemed too much for me. Who didn't read their horoscope in the paper? If I hadn't been frightened before, they succeeded in scaring me then.

I was told that I had to be extra careful not to let the demons inhabit me. They told me I was at risk because I was close to Robert. They gave me a prayer of protection that I could say to give me strength and they also gave me a list of readings from the Bible to look at and call on.

That night, I was so afraid to sleep alone, that I tried to sleep outside my dad's bedroom door, waiting there until he found me and let me into his room. Even so, I spent most of the night waiting for something to happen. I was aware of presences around me, icy hands on my back. I felt that somebody wanted to intimidate me and was doing a pretty good job!

Around this time, I read my Bible every day to ask for protection, and I feel I got it. Slowly, I began to feel a different kind of presence, one that did not provoke fear in me. This was a warm and loving presence and as time went on, I believed this to be my guardian angel. As Robert began to get better, I decided I must end the relationship. We had been together about eighteen months and it was difficult, but I needed space to get better myself. I felt very selfish for feeling this way, but in retrospect, it was the best thing to do for us both. However, ending the relationship proved to be very difficult for Robert and it ended very badly.

There were days after I told him of my decision when he would arrive at my house, dripping blood, having cut his wrists and saying 'look what you've done to me'. I felt responsible, but I persisted.

One morning, I came outside to wait for my lift to school, to find that he had written my name across the path in blood. Somehow, I managed to remain calm, until I got to school. But when the first person I saw asked me how my weekend had been, I burst into tears.

Spirit was certainly supporting me at that time. I can recall one particular incident that strongly affected my faith and reminded me that I wasn't alone.

For a while I went to stay with my mum so that I wouldn't have to pass Robert's house every day. But he knew where I was staying and would still turn up there. One day however, something happened that I believe was more than a coincidence. Sitting in the front room of my mum's house with a friend, we were listening to loud music when suddenly, I had the urge to close the curtains and switch the radio off. My friend thought I was going mad, but I insisted we should be quiet. Within a couple of minutes we heard footsteps outside and then a knock at the door. Creeping upstairs I looked out of the bedroom window just to make sure it was Robert. It was. Before long he went away.

My friend couldn't believe it. `How did you know?' she said. I didn't, but somebody did, and that reassured me that I was doing the right thing.

For a couple of years after, I continued to go to some kind of church or another - I was trying to find a place that suited me. I tried a Pentecostal Church, Church of England and Baptist. I had been brought up as a Catholic and had attended church every week until about the age of eleven, when I decided not to go anymore. Then about the age of seventeen, I gave up church again; becoming interested in other things such as Tarot cards and rune stones.

In many ways my life improved. Then, in my last year at school, I thought I'd done it. I got good grades in my exams and I was due to start college in the following September. However, when I was taking my final exams my father moved out of the family home to live with his new partner. I was sharing the house with my brother and one of my sisters at the time. He offered to stay until I finished college, but two years seemed a long time - I didn't want to ruin his chance of happiness and I felt that I could manage, so I told him that it would be OK for him to go.

I started college, but a few months into the course, I realised that I'd have to do presentations and be required to talk about my work to groups of people, and I fell apart. Soon I began to have counselling and I realised that I wasn't ready for college. My tutors made allowances for me and I was able to do the written work for classes that made me uncomfortable, without actually attending them. I passed my first year by doing that, but if I were to finish my second year, I would have to be prepared to participate again. I wasn't and so I left college and got a job.

For a while things seemed OK, but six months later, I became ill. Feeling very tired and listless, I had some blood tests, which showed me to be anaemic. But it was more than that - I was becoming depressed again.

I had started a new relationship with Jason and this was difficult. He had his own issues (and it was really just a case of bad timing) but I felt rejected by him and this stirred up in me how I felt about my dad leaving home. I began to feel resentful towards my dad, angry that he had abandoned me. I felt also that I had let myself down, having left college instead of facing my fears. I had left a perfectly good job instead of facing my anxiety too and all in all, I felt a failure.

For almost a year, I was out of work. This meant that I had a lot of time to think about myself and the situation I was in. I began to drink a lot, to escape and just to pass the time. I was feeling suicidal but also afraid to die. My thoughts drifted that if I killed myself, I would go to hell, but would it be worse than the life I was living?

So much of the time, I spent alone and in pain. I felt lonely but also uncomfortable in other people's company. Inside, I feel I blocked any Spiritual help. In the mornings, I just didn't have the energy to get up.

In the meantime, I was seeing Jason, but the relationship wasn't very helpful to me. He had come from a similar background in some ways - worse in some respects. Jason had also suffered from low self-esteem. In many ways, what had attracted us to one another, was now what was causing us problems.

Both he and I needed reassurance, but for a long time, I felt as though I was the only one giving in the relationship. Although I may have had support in other places, the one person I wanted it from couldn't give it to me. In many ways I blamed Jason for adding to my misery, but I felt as though I couldn't live without him. In this early period, our relationship was dramatic and intense, and we repeatedly went through a pattern of breaking up and then making up again, sometimes for hours, sometimes for weeks.

To cope with this, I drank a lot. When Jason stood me up, which he did frequently at first - I would drink until I fell asleep. There were many dark days and nights where I would swing between angry independence and inconsolable tears.

106

While I was going through this, I was living with my sister. It was difficult for us both - one minute we were great friends and the next we were enemies. Michelle thought Jason was a waste of my time and energy, and she tried to persuade me to give him up. However, this attitude only made me more determined to carry on.

This period was the darkest trough of my life so far. I can hardly believe that I managed to get through it, but there were a few events that really made a big difference to me. One day my sister accidentally told me that there had been a family meeting about me. My mum, dad, stepparents and sister had been discussing what they could and should do about my depression. When I reflect on it, my sister, Michelle, was only twenty-five at the time and it can't have been easy for her to deal with me by herself. Initially I was angry - how dare they discuss what was best for me? How could they know? No one was talking directly to me. However, I know now that I was only hearing what I wanted to hear, and all of it was bad.

What followed next was that my dad came to see me. He found me clutching a bottle of vodka, sat alone in my room. In his hand, he had a letter he had written in case I wasn't there. It said simply that he hoped I would feel better soon and that he loved me. It made me cry then, and it still brings a tear to my eye now. Such things were not what he could say easily.

After that, I cried myself to sleep again that night, but about two or three in the morning, I woke up suddenly, convinced that the house was burning. Jumping out of bed, I raced downstairs to see what had happened, but nothing was out of place. Then the image of my grandmother came to my mind. She was engulfed in a violet light and her arms were outstretched to me. She was telling me that things would work out all right. I was afraid then to go back into my room, and I pushed open the door cautiously. The room smelt sweet like incense, and it seemed a little hazy - but otherwise there were no apparitions awaiting me. I cried again then, but this time tears of relief. I felt comforted and I knew that I had not been left alone.

This experience felt like a visitation, more than a dream. I took comfort from this and it affected me in a way that words from a living person had not been able to.

Out of this I feel I made a decision that life could be good if I tried. I began to see that I had strength inside of me that I could call on, almost like an inner core. I believed it was something I was born with, but I had lost sight of it. All these events were signs to find my way back.

I always believed in the Spirit world, and more so after my nanna died. I would pray to God and speak to my nanna, as a way of saying all that I had to say. I believed that if I asked for help, I would get it.

As usual, things got worse before they got better. Over the years, I had stored a lot of rage and anger inside of me, and this began to come out with Jason and with my sister, sometimes physically with Jason. Several times I hit him in anger, or I'd throw a drink at him. I hated myself for it, but I felt unable to control it.

My sister and I fought verbally, but that was bad enough. At one point I went to stay with my brother for a few weeks until I could stand to be in the same house with her, and I went back then only because my dad had insisted we sort out our differences.

Gradually things settled down and once I began to work again they improved more rapidly. That was by no means the end of the dramas, but it was a turning point.

I knew really, had always known, that I had some work of my own to do, that I could be of help to others, if I could get through my unhappiness. Somehow I looked on the difficult times in my life as a preparation for the life to come.

I feel as though I have learnt a lot from my experiences so far - they have made me a kinder, more compassionate thoughtful human being. I do what I can for others and try my hardest to avoid hurting people. But I feel this isn't enough. Still, I have inner shadows to face, and there are fears I must confront so that

I can be free of them. Perhaps if I had been content to stay in a mundane job, I wouldn't have been so determined, but I need to develop my confidence and self esteem to move forward. I have to keep reminding myself that I've come a long way already, and so I can go further if I persevere.

There was a time when going into a shop was a frightening experience, as was calling people on the telephone or making a journey alone. Now I can do all these things without too much effort (most of the time anyway).

In many ways, I feel lucky. My life could have been much worse. But then perhaps, if I hadn't had to struggle, I might not have been in the position I am now, in a place where I feel there is hope.

I feel I have things to look forward to now. Jason and I are finally being honest with one another, and with ourselves. For a long time I convinced myself that only Jason had a problem with commitment, but I realised only recently that it was always me that threatened to leave when things weren't working. In the past, it was easier for me to blame him rather than admit to my own reservations. It's really the fear of things not working out in the future, that had been holding me back from enjoying our relationship in the 'now'.

For years now I have been trying to discover or recover my Spiritual self. However, I'm still aware that I deny it or shut it out when I feel particularly low. Despite my effort though, Spirit has remained close and I now know that I only have to ask, for Spirit to be with me.

The way my life has been changing over the last few years is proof to me that someone is working with me. I seem to have been meeting the right people at the right times.

Academically, I've been able to study for my 'A' levels and pre-degree course whilst working and managed to get a place at university. Moving away from my family has been difficult but necessary for me to gain more independence and faith in myself.

It has also meant that Jason and I have been able to work things out in our relationship without interference.

I am optimistic about the future. I feel that so long as I work at it and continue to ask for help from Spirit (and give it where able) I can continue to grow.

Postscript

In the months since writing this account, Jason and I have separated. It has been amicable and mutual. We both accepted that we had grown apart. Our relationship had matured and changed over the seven and a half years, but ultimately, we weren't compatible.

Six months before we made the decision to split up, we became engaged. On reflection, we knew then, and had for a while, that our time together was coming to an end. Our engagement was a last attempt to make our relationship work.

To separate was by no means an easy decision to make. In those last months, there was a tense atmosphere between us and communication was difficult. However, in my mind, I couldn't have imagined life without him. But I had reached a point of no return where I felt that I had no more left to give. Physically, I couldn't try any harder. Mentally and emotionally, I felt drained. Resolving the situation was all that I could think about. I couldn't concentrate on my work and didn't care about my health. Something had to give.

It has been very sad, but necessary to say goodbye to that part of our lives. But life goes on. Jason has finished the course that he was doing and has found work in another town. I know that he'll be OK.

Meanwhile I have moved onto the university and am giving full attention to my studies. This represents another important step where I have felt my strength to make my own decisions. More than anything, these changes have made me realise that you never know what is around the corner. Life keeps on throwing things at you, but in the end it is the challenges that enable you to grow.

Chapter 13 -

Choosing to be here

In her story, Claire has indicated several moments from her life where she has struggled to face what she needed to do. Her tendency has been to back away when things became difficult. This problem of being afraid to commit one's self to life is quite common, and I know that it was a problem for me when I was younger.

Although souls may be very brave and want to put themselves through all kinds of tests, once they are born into the physical and they have arrived into incarnation on Earth, it may feel very different. Life on Earth can be very painful and fear can distort people's perception of what is possible. People can easily decide that they do not want to be alive and they do not like it here. Such an attitude and decision can go very deep and may affect fundamentally people's reactions to circumstances that come to them during their life.

Claire mentioned times in her life where she considered suicide. Certainly, suicide is the most extreme reaction to an attitude of not wanting to be here. People may draw back from suicide but still engage in self destructive behaviour as a protest against life or as a gamble to discover if their life will be taken or not. Even when it is not an addiction, people may smoke, take drugs or alcohol as a way of not being present and avoiding life. Others may drive fast cars, fight in wars or take bizarre risks just as a means of dicing with death, acting with a lack of care and not being bothered about being alive. The adrenaline rush of these experiences may tempt people to go closer and closer to the edge. There are other ways that people can also avoid facing up to life. They may retreat into a place on their own or even take refuge in a relationship, where the other person can be the strong one.

People can feel they are living their lives through another person rather than feeling that they need to have a strong sense of their own self.

All these means of avoidance though will feel deeply unsettling for people. They will be in conflict with their own souls, because basically, we do not come on Earth to avoid life but to live it. At the end of a life where we have avoided facing our challenges and tasks, we can only feel dissatisfied and know that we have failed.

From a reincarnation perspective, it would mean that we would have to go through the same kind of thing again - so the attempt to escape and avoid what we knew inside we had to do would feel totally futile. Also, if through our wish to avoid and refuse life, we have become self-absorbed and insensitive to other people's feelings, then we may think that we have managed to close ourselves to how we have caused others to suffer. However, I do believe that somewhere inside we will be aware of what effects our behaviour has had on others. Somehow, I feel that it is often those who are most sensitive who may be most inclined to avoid life. Such people will feel pain most intensely, and will need extra support.

Referring to Claire's story, she is someone who is obviously very sensitive. There are people she mentioned in her life, who at various times have been like a shelter for her against the world- especially her father, and her most recent partner Jason. When she has felt abandoned by any of them or rejected, she has struggled to cope - as she did when her parents separated while she was very young. She described how she drank or became suicidal when she was left on her own. In her early teens she ran away from school or refused to go, seeking stability in the closeness of her relationship with her father.

It is clear that Claire has a task to find her own strength as a free and independent being. She is learning to face the world standing on her own feet, so that her love, creativity and vulnerability can be expressed to many and she can really serve in the way she wants. Also she needs to learn not to keep herself hidden from all but her one close relationship and the other friends and family who may be within her innermost circle. It is a challenge for her to learn to trust that there are times when she can expose herself to others without being destroyed or hurt very badly. There are fears that restrict her, but she recognises that she needs to get out in the world and express her self to be happy, and she feels pleased to be making progress on this.

She talks about her faith in Spirit and this is very important to her. From Spirit, she feels that there is a fundamental support for her and her life, which gives her strength. As her faith has grown, her ability to confront her fears has improved as well.

Still, I feel she needs to consider how much she really chooses to be here. I sense that there are days when her drive to be alive is stronger and other days where she feels more resistance. The decision of how much she can say 'yes' to life is up to her. It will be interesting as she grows older and tries to find her place in the world to observe the extent to which she is able to express her feeling, loving sensitive nature to help and care for others. This is what she wants to do. Because of the fears and suffering she has experienced in her own life, she would be in a very good position to empathise and help other people with their fears too. She only needs to overcome her own fears a little more first.

Chapter 14 -

Suicide

Recently I had a client visit me for some intensive sessions. She had travelled from some distance to work with me. Three months earlier, the man who had been the love of her life had committed suicide.

The effect of this loss upon her being had been devastating. Since then her life had been like hell. She had hardly slept. For much of the time for those months, she had gone over and over the events of the last moments of her partner's life, punishing herself internally for mistakes that she felt that she may have made, vainly trying to find meaning and understanding for what he had done. Although it was clear that it was other elements of his life that had not been working rather than his relationship with her, she still questioned herself. Why wasn't she more aware of the extent of his depression? Why did she let him go on that last fateful day? How inadequate she felt that even though she loved him so dearly and she knew that he loved her, it wasn't enough.

Most of all, she missed him. He had been the love of her life and she felt incredibly lonely without him. As she poured out her story of woe to me, I strained to know how I would be able to help her.

During the week, we went to visit my friend Marjorie for a session with her Spiritual guide, 'Sojah'. My client was looking for answers on the Spiritual side. She longed to contact her partner and communicate with him.

Sojah pointed out that although she may consider whether there was anything more that she could have done to save him, it was his decision to end his life in this way. No one could be responsible for this decision except him. Therefore, she must let go of guilt about what had happened because it was not her fault.

Sojah suggested that her partner had been received in Spirit with love, as were all people who committed suicide. The only punishment he would confront was connected to the knowledge of what he had done and the suffering that he would have caused to others.

My client was able to enter into meditations where she felt that she could meet her partner in Spirit. This was very comforting to her, even though it felt like a poor substitute for having him with her. She was also able to meet her Spiritual guide. Her guide was a possible support to my client independent of her partner. It felt important that she open herself to feel the strength of her guide and not just try to lean only on the energy and presence of her partner. She would need her guide's strength to be able to build up her life again.

From the time that she had met her partner, her energies had been wrapped up with him. Now she couldn't do that anymore. She would obviously need a long time to recover, as she had been severely damaged by what her partner had done. It would be necessary for her to learn to stand on her own now, perhaps more fully than had been planned. But she had no choice about this, if she wanted to survive. This dilemma about whether or not to live was one of the main problems that she faced, because without her partner, her life looked so bleak.

I believe that it is never part of people's soul pathway to commit suicide. It is more an opting out and an attempt to escape from problems that may seem too enormous to endure. My client's partner felt pressure from many directions and the thoughts appeared to race around in his head so much that he could not bear it any longer. He may have been mentally ill, but did not have within him the emotional resources he needed to seek help, trying instead to cope with it all on his own.

When my partner, Eleyna, was suicidal, she had built up the belief inside her that people would be better off without her, and

116

that she was just somebody to cause trouble to others. Try as she could, she was not able to get her life to work the way she wanted. Therefore she considered that the only solution for her would be to leave. Inside, she felt very lost and her heart closed down because she did not want to feel.

The beliefs she held about herself were totally false. Had she committed suicide, it would have caused far more trouble and suffering to others, those who loved her, than her not doing this. Her loved ones, such as her children, valued her much more fully than she realised. What she didn't do, was to value herself. But in the turmoil of her mind, she believed that all of the problems around her were due to her. This was reinforced by others who blamed her, I believe, unjustly.

What Eleyna needed desperately, was help, to sort out the confusion of her mind. Over the last year, since the time after her marriage break up when she first considered suicide seriously, she has been receiving counselling. Gradually she has been trying to sort out for herself what she really wants, what is important for her, sifting through her negative belief systems and letting go of the ties of the past. It has been a long drawn out process that has needed patience from those close to her and may still need some considerable time to complete until she is well and happy. Because of my own involvement, I have not been able to help her in the way that I may have done previously, but I have tried to offer my love.

Both Claire and Michelle have also had moments where they considered suicide. For both of them, these times were occasions where they suffered from extremely low feelings of self-worth. They wanted love, but felt that the person or persons that they were fixed upon to give them that love and acceptance was not there for them. For Michelle, her father was very significant in this, while in Claire's case, it was various people who did not seem to be there to meet her needs. With Michelle and Claire, the response, especially in situations where they felt they could not cope, in a similar fashion to Eleyna, was to blame themselves and feel that they were failures.

For people contemplating suicide, I would urge them to find somebody with whom they can talk about their problems. There is a natural tendency when people become very depressed to seek to isolate themselves. But often, when people reach this state, the kind of self-image that they have of themselves is unrealistic and unnecessarily negative. Thoughts may swirl around inside those people's head, and by trying to cope with things on their own, they will tend to make their situation worse. In these circumstances, we can be our own worst enemy by closing off from others and creating turmoil inside.

When Eleyna has become very depressed, I have tried to hold her, love her and listen to her, when she would let me. I have had to learn to respect her choices and wish to make her own decisions and not to interfere. Ultimately she has had to find an outlet for her feelings, to feel accepted and cared about. For people outside her immediate living situation to talk with her and counsel her has assisted her so that she could assert her individuality, testing thoughts she has had about herself, and feed herself with new messages. What is true for Eleyna could be true for many people.

Once we have established belief systems within us, especially when they are negative and destructive, it can be very difficult to remove them completely. These beliefs may have been reinforced many times and be layered very deep within our consciousness. But change can take place, I believe that we are never given too much in life and we can cope, provided that we reach out and within for the help that we need. We may require assistance for a long time until we are strong enough to stand on our own feet. However, I believe that it is better to seek for support rather than let ourselves crumble to nothing on our own.

Chapter 15 -
Denise

Background

I first met Denise when she attended a Past Life regression class that I was leading. Although most of the participants in this class seemed to me to be either sceptical or somewhat blocked, making the process of teaching difficult for me, I noticed that Denise's response was much more positive. I felt that she was drinking in every experience from that class as if she was extremely thirsty to do that work. She was eager to learn and very open to gain inner awareness regarding her past lives. When I needed a model for demonstrations, she was prepared to step forward to do that. She felt safe in the group, and I felt that she was quite courageous in what she allowed to be exposed to others.

Soon she had joined our healing group, was attending further classes and workshops that I was leading and she was coming to see me for individual therapy. I sensed that she was ambitious to learn about Spiritual life and her own Spiritual path. She wanted to learn as much as she could, as soon as she could. From our individual sessions I observed that she was very conscientious. In between sessions, she would consider in great detail various aspects of the inner process that she had been through. She would make notes and glean from these as much as she could.

At an early stage, I became aware of her passion for crystals. Already, she had quite a considerable collection and this was growing all the time. When she made contact with her guides, she began to practice crystal healing on members of the group. She did not need any suggestions from me, but she was quite determined and it was clear that her love and innate knowledge of crystals was extensive. For her, they were living beings that she cherished with her heart. As her skills developed, when I received healing from her, I felt a great deal of power and love coming through her hands and the crystals that she used. She had much ability. When we held our public healing evenings, she was very much in demand from people who wanted her services.

Another side to Denise's character was her caring. She seemed to gain much satisfaction through giving to others. Often she would give to others as a healer, or through her work as a nurse, with little thought for her own needs. She could work until she was exhausted.

There was a period after my marriage break-up; a phase when Eleyna was very occupied with her own problems, when I felt that I desperately needed help. I could phone Denise at any hour and she would listen to me and offer me support. I felt very safe in her care. By this time we were friends and colleagues and I felt able to share my problems with her.

Although Denise could easily give of herself to others, what she has found more difficult has been to receive for herself. In the therapy work we have done together, she has released much grief, tears and anger relating to loss that she has experienced at different stages of her life. Somewhere inside though, as a result of these experiences and possibly others coming from past lives, she has engraved a pattern of thought into her consciousness, which has communicated to her that she is unlovable.

Generally, Denise makes herself very busy with various tasks to do. When she stops, she can sometimes become upset, if she dares to consider her own needs and how little she has been prepared to meet them. Because of this lack of self-love, she has spent much of her life in isolation, giving to others perhaps, but keeping herself barren. This pattern has begun to shift. However, with the strong wish in her heart that she wants to change career and become a crystal healer, she knows that she can only succeed at doing this when she can love herself much more fully than she has done until now.

I believe that it is the main challenge of her soul pathway, to resolve this dilemma. In order to love herself more, she has had to confront the blocks that are preventing her from doing so. This is scary for her and demanded a lot of courage. It has been a big task for her and I am sure that there is still work to do. What follows is her life story.

Denise's Story

In recent years I have been engaging in intensive therapy work to try and find more happiness in my life. During this process I have uncovered many painful memories and tried to release some of the suffering I have held in my life. I want to be open in my heart to love people and feel loved myself, but I do not always find this very easy. For much of my life, I have felt lonely and isolated, having shut myself away on my own. I know that circumstances in my life have not helped, but I do not wish to feel that way any more.

As a child, I was one of five, although I never felt that I belonged fully, as one of them, feeling lonely even in that crowd. Mother was unmarried and chose to bring her children up herself. This was difficult in the 1950's. Our grandparents, my mum's sister and her husband lived with us. I don't remember much, if anything about the grandparents, but my aunt had three children herself, so there were nine of us in a two-bedroomed house. All the children slept in the back bedroom, which always seemed dark.

One incident I have recalled in my therapy work is from when I was about 18 months old. I was standing crying in a cot wanting someone to be with me. No one came. My reaction was to leave my body, so from then, I seemed to have spent my life feeling on the outside looking in, always feeling out of it to some extent. To compensate for my loneliness, I tried to make myself useful by doing errands and helping in the house where I could. This always got a smile and a kiss from mum. I know that she loved us, but it was hard with five. My eldest brother had a heart problem and youngest brother was deaf. I was in the middle. The one closest to me was my sister, and we got on well.

I had brief contact with my father while I was very little, but since that time he has been completely absent from my life. I have tried to think how I could possibly trace him, but I just do not have enough information.

There is one image I have had repeatedly during my therapy work. In this experience I have sensed myself to be a child of about two, clinging to the legs of a man. This man picked me up and told me he loved me, and that he would be back for me. My reaction was to scream and cry because I knew I wouldn't see him again. I am sure that this is a memory of my actual father, and the last time I had contact with him. My feelings tell me that this was the beginning of my fears of rejection in this life, that I couldn't trust people, that they would betray me and let me down

The most difficult person for me in my childhood was my uncle. I have never liked him, nor wanted him near me. When I was much older, I learnt that he was the father of at least some of my bothers and sisters, but not me. I don't think he cared about me at all. He used to sexually abuse some of the children, and I have recalled one occasion when he tried to abuse me.

One day, I was alone in the house with him, and so I was not able to avoid him. At some point, he took me up to the bedroom he shared with my aunt and started to put his hand up my dress and into my knickers. I didn't like this, and tried to get away. His response was to push me down onto the bed. Then he tried to have sex with me. However, I wriggled and kicked and attempted to make it difficult. Thankfully, someone came in, and he had to stop. He made me promise not to say anything and I went and hid, crying in a cupboard, somewhere dark and safe. Nothing had happened. He had just tried to touch me. After that, I never liked being touched, particularly by men, and this must have contributed to the problems I had later on.

Because we didn't have an acknowledged father, this meant we spent our childhood being called names, by children and adults alike. Other children called us 'bastards' and even when we were called Gladys' children by some people, it was said in a very derogatory way. We were prevented from playing with some of the other children by our situation, and were seen as 'wrongguns', or as a 'bad lot'. These reactions to us hurt me and I became more withdrawn. Within the village, I never had many friends. If anyone asked who my daddy was, I always said he was dead.

One person who was supportive to me was the village nurse. She was to become very important in my life. When I was little she used to let us go for walks with her and her dog. She'd brought some of my brothers and sisters into the world. From walks, my time with nurse developed into days out and then holidays for my sister and I. She asked mum if I could stay with her on the weekends and soon this became a regular thing. Sometimes when I'd arrive at nurse's place she wouldn't be in, so I'd sit in the garden or go to the neighbours. When I stayed with nurse, I had my own room and I could watch TV. It was so different. I was about six years old when all this happened.

Two years later, I had come back from a holiday in Silverdale, and while staying with mum, I became very poorly. In the end I had to go to hospital and was only released from there about three weeks later. However, when I left hospital, I spent my convalescence at nurse's house and not with mum. After that I stayed with her all the time and just visited mum on my way to and from school. This was always a very precious time for me to share a kiss and cuddle with her.

For some time this routine continued in my life, until one day when I was eleven years old, an event happened to completely shatter my childhood security.

One night I called in to mum, and when mum kissed me goodbye she seemed well. The next day I went down to see her before school and I was told she'd been taken to hospital and died. They simply told me she was dead and sent me to school. Nobody tried to comfort me. Nothing was said. No one asked if I was all right; how I felt or anything - I was just left to go to school. I didn't know what to do. Sitting in lessons and in the playtimes, I felt so much on my own. Sometimes I was crying, but I didn't want anyone to see me. I think someone asked if I was all right and I said 'yes'.

Finally I was able to go home, but when I arrived, there was no one there. Standing in front of the garage, I cried a little and tried to talk with mum. It was as if I could feel her presence with me.

At first I asked her why she had left me. Then I felt that she had not really gone. I affirmed over and over again that she would always be with me. But I wanted her physical comfort. Eventually nurse came and she could tell what I was feeling. She held me.

I think it was my uncle who was mainly responsible for deciding that I wasn't allowed to go to the funeral, so I never knew where she was buried. I was never able to see her grave or say goodbye. Why didn't they let me go?

My uncle and aunt officially became our guardians, but my uncle didn't want me, so he asked nurse if she wanted to adopt me. I had started to call nurse 'Auntie' and this is a name that stuck. Nobody asked me what I wanted or how I felt. All I knew was that I didn't want to be with my uncle. But I didn't want to be separated from my brothers and sister either. They were the only family I had.

About a year after my mother died, I had to go to court for the adoption. It was a very frightening experience in a big crowded room, with lots of police, lots of noise and shouting. I went to another wood-panelled room with three people there. They talked about me but not to me. The only thing they asked me was whether I wanted to change my name or not. Because I knew that my aunt and uncle didn't want me, I was desperate to be accepted by Auntie. She was the only one in the world who could look after me. I said for them to change my name to her surname. If I didn't do that, I was afraid that she would turn against me too. So, a new phase of my life began, divorced from my family, living with Auntie, who was then 55 years old.

At first I was happy enough. Now I was nurse's girl and not Gladys' girl. Then when people talked about me, it 'sounded' and felt different. I had my own room, and because she lived in the next village, I could still see my brothers and sisters. With my sister, we attended the same school and shared comics so I hadn't really lost my family, just lived in a different house.
This changed dramatically when I was fourteen. Auntie retired and wanted to move to Silverdale, which was over 80 miles away. It felt again that my life was being driven by events and decisions

made outside my control. From my holidays, I was familiar with Silverdale and liked the place, but I would miss my sister and the few friends I had terribly. It wasn't what I wanted.

When I moved there, I felt very lonely. It would be years before I would meet any of my brothers or sister again. My only solace was to spend time in nature. At least the trees did not call me names and I could feel a lot of peace in these places.

With Auntie getting older, I was taking more and more responsibility for her affairs. It was as though my childhood had been cut short in some ways. Then when I was seventeen, I met Arthur.

All through my teenage years I had never really had a boyfriend. Then one evening I went to a party - Arthur was there, and that was the beginning of my one and only relationship, if you can call it that. We never really got intimate in a sexual way, because I didn't like him touching me.

When we'd been going out for a while, we kissed and Arthur wanted to fondle me. For a while, I hesitated, but finally, I let him and I cringed inside. I didn't like it. I wanted to end the relationship there and then. However, other people seemed to conspire to keep us together, and it felt again like people were running my life without me being in control.

Arthur had a boat and he took me sailing several times. Once I had a frightening experience when the boat capsized. At the time I couldn't swim and I had to hold on to the edge of the boat for dear life. This incident was like a symbol of feeling out of my depth with him.

At some stage we got engaged and Arthur wanted sex, but I refused, only letting him fondle my breasts. To him I pretended that I was enjoying it, but inside I felt revolted. Afterwards, I went hiding in a tree in the wood and cried. I wanted to avoid people and shut them out.

A little later, I went to meet his parents but when I came back, Auntie gave me a strange reaction. She wouldn't speak to me, hid from me and called me a 'whore'. As nothing like that had happened or was likely to happen before I was married, I ran out of the house to get away from her.

This was the end though for me. All these things together made me break off the engagement. It was the last time that I let any man get that close to me. Somehow, whenever anyone tried to get close, a barrier would go up, and I would take a mental step back, closing off. I was not very aware of doing this, until much later when someone pointed it out to me. One night when we went out, she said to me that I had just 'left' them. I knew it was true, though it hurt.

As my career path, I chose to become a nurse. Starting nursing when I was sixteen, as a cadet, led to a profession which gave me considerable satisfaction. But, beginning this work coincided with a period in my life where living with Auntie became more and more difficult. She started to become confused and her reactions to situations were more and more irrational. As time went on I struggled to look after her.

When I started working I had bought a house in which we could live together. This house backed onto the woods. At times I felt I had to get away from Auntie so I went outside to our garden or even into the woods. This was my only refuge. There were occasions though, when she would even follow me there.

For years, Auntie would alternate between periods of being normal and times when she would be confused. She would get upset, knowing something was wrong. However, it was hard to watch someone I loved so much deteriorating and becoming lost in a world of her own, sometimes not even knowing me, and on other occasions, getting angry. When she was more passive, she would need to know when I would be back and how long I would be out, if I went out. I felt like a prisoner. The only time I felt free was when I took the dog into the woods.

As she declined further, she became forgetful of recent events. At times she did not remember how to feed herself. On occasions, I'd come in from work to find her in an awful state. She may have fed the dog with the food we were having for our tea. I'd get calls to say she had locked herself out and was with a neighbour or that she was stuck inside and we had to break in to get to her. I never knew what I would find when I came home.

My work became the only stable part of my life and my colleagues were like a surrogate family for me. However, work was also demanding and so I never really got a break. I felt as though I didn't really have a life of my own. The only place where I could find peace was in the woods amongst the trees and nature.

After a while the stress started to take its toll. I made mistakes at work, had to struggle with staffing problems. Often I was finding myself in tears or getting angry, finding it more and more hard to cope. There was one colleague with whom I could talk, but most of the time I kept things to myself.

Eventually, it all became too much. I had to move to a bungalow closer to my work so I could be more available to help Auntie quickly, if needed. In the meantime, Auntie didn't know where she was, or even whom I was, living in the past, often not remembering to eat. Our new doctor helped so Auntie could go into day care. But when that didn't work, she suggested that she would need to go into a home or else I would collapse.

This was the most heart breaking decision I had to make. This woman had taken me in, looked after me, and now I was giving up on her.

The home where I chose to place her was in Silverdale. This was where she'd grown up and she knew the place.

Letting Auntie go into this home was like losing her all over again. She was not the person anymore that I knew and loved, and now I'd turned her out. Finally she died in 1986, and I felt that I lost her for a third time. Her death disturbed me a great deal, though I knew inside that it was a release for her. I sensed that she was with my natural mother, and I have continued at times to talk to them both, as though they are with me.

I hardly had a chance to mourn Auntie's death and recover from that before the next blow came. This nearly sent me over the edge, I felt so awful.

Following the sale of my property in Silverdale, I had been making some investments through a financial advisor. He was someone that I trusted.

Initially, these investments seemed to go well. I was getting some return as an income. However after a while, these payments stopped and there seemed to be a problem that I couldn't chase up. I was heavily committed with these investments. One day, a police officer called and told me that my financial advisor was in prison for fraud. All the money I had invested was lost. He had destroyed the records so it would be very difficult for the police to recover it. For years, the crown prosecution service tried to bring a case against this man. They used evidence from various clients that he had had. In the end, they didn't use my evidence and I thought that I would get nothing back at all. It was the most harrowing time, and I felt completely devastated. However, after much struggling, I finally felt justice was done - I did have some money returned to me.

I felt ashamed of what had happened to me, and I didn't talk with anyone about it. I kept my feelings bottled up. How could I be so stupid? I had trusted my financial adviser and now I was finding it so difficult to keep up my payments on debt and mortgages. My life fell in ruins.

Inside I went numb and I just kept on appearing to be normal in my work, dedicating myself to be a good nurse, but I was completely closed. Talking with no one, I just existed in my work and in my home, without seeing anyone. My very few friends could hardly comfort me. It took several months before I even broke down and cried about it.

More and more, I became very insular. After work, I started drinking wine, while watching TV. I was trying to escape. To be able to pay the bills I had to sell jewellery and other items. It didn't seem fair. For years I had worked so hard.

At times I would get very depressed and weepy. I had one friend with whom I would talk a little, but I tried not to show how I felt, because then I would end up in tears or angry. I didn't want people to see me like that. After some time, I decided to stop drinking because it had become a habit. My life was a mess, and by drinking I was only making it worse. I felt a determination to make my life better, but I didn't know how? I wanted some answers and to learn more about the meaning of my life. Surely I could find a way to be happier. I wanted to find a way out of the trough I was in.

The places where I found the most peace were in nature. I felt the trees were my friends, and I felt a growing love for stones and crystals. They seemed to be living beings to me, not things. I read books about past lives and lost civilisations. All these things fascinated me.

I also liked animals and my dog and cats were very important to me. But I could not trust people, and I could not let them close. They would only hurt me or leave me if I did. It was safer to be on my own. Sadly though, my life felt very empty. I couldn't talk to anyone about how I felt. This made me feel like a prisoner in my aloneness.

After some years, I started to regain some strength and equilibrium again. But in my life, I was still so isolated, and I felt desperation to want to change without being able to admit it.

One day, I saw an advertisement for a course in healing and I felt strongly that I wanted to do it. On the way to the course, I had problems with my camper van and went into a ditch. I felt as if I was being deliberately restrained from going to the course. Something in me felt that it wasn't quite time yet. Was I being guided? I felt both frustrated and excited at the same time.

Eventually, I did manage to attend a later course in healing and it was really what I had been wanting to do. By that time, I had started having individual sessions of therapy with Paul, and attending his personal growth workshops.

The first workshop I attended included some work about healing the inner child. I became aware of an image of being a child in a cot - screaming. Paul guided me to experience this memory directly. This memory released feelings about how I'd found myself always helping in my own way - wanting to get attention and to be seen. In that cot no one came to me when I needed them. This process brought up a lot of tears, tears I'd never expressed, and anger, the feeling of wanting to be seen and appreciated for being me, not the little helper who would always do a job. I wished to be loved for being me, not a projection of who people thought I was. I was surprised at how violent my emotions were.

When I broke free of the 'cot' we'd constructed, it explained many things from my childhood, like my need always to be good, doing the errands that no one else wanted, even why I'd kept a photograph which was a double exposure with a shadow me. That shadow was how I had felt during a lot of my childhood.

This was the beginning of many experiences and memories, which came up during workshops and personal sessions with Paul. My first workshop brought me in touch with my inner self, with very strong feelings of rejections and loneliness. This was difficult. However, during those three days, I also felt a cloud lift off me and suddenly felt how wonderful it was to be alive. That realisation was very powerful and has driven me into more and more explorations of my inner life. I have felt this helping me to break out of my shell. It hasn't been easy. At times I have felt very afraid and upset.

There have been many traumatic sessions with Paul where I found past circumstances linked with present, where old habits had become habits of the present. Repeatedly, I found my fear of rejection had kept me apart, stopped me from allowing people close.

Somehow, I knew that I needed to change my life, so that these patterns would not operate any more.

In the time leading up to the healing class I became aware through my inner consciousness of a lady who wanted to help me. Soon, I identified this lady as my Spiritual guide, Helena. I have since felt Helena to be a very comforting and supportive presence in my life. During the Healing class, I learnt to channel Helena. She has taught me that the love of Spirit is always there for us. Another consequence of this class was that my love of crystals increased. They were my friends and I could use them to channel healing. I started to collect more and more of them, feel their energies and learn about them.

But it was still difficult with people. With Spiritual healing, I knew that I needed to be able to give and receive love, being able to accept love and to love myself. Whereas I felt I could care for others, I found it hard to accept that others could love me, that I was worthy of love, that I didn't need to always do something to 'buy' love.

I became aware of some very deep-seated beliefs that I was unlovable, that there must be something horrible about me to have attracted men like uncle and Arthur. At times I felt it was even wrong to expect Spirit to help me. I could not shift these beliefs very easily.

For some years I had been in contact with my sister, but we had never really talked. Finally though, I was courageous enough to begin a conversation about our childhood. We talked for a long time. She told me that she also had not been allowed to go to mother's funeral. I had missed her so much after moving to Silverdale. Talking about these things lifted a barrier that had existed between us until then.

My house was a symbol of my isolation. For many years I had not even had any visitors. This was gradually changing, but I had got used to my ways without sharing. Then, after a workshop in Scotland, I was in tears, because I didn't want to come home to an empty house. The pets were no longer enough. I felt lonely, just being there by myself. This was a new experience. I'd been lonely in a crowd before, but not on my own. I felt that I liked my own company, but now I didn't.

However, that evening, Eleyna came to my door in desperate need of somewhere to stay as a place of sanctuary. Despite her distress, it was welcome company. We talked for hours as I tried to help or just listen to her. There were times during her stay when the house was full to overflowing with people and children - and I loved it. The solitude I normally felt on my own was well and truly shattered. She only stayed for two weeks though, and then she moved on.

Initially, I could still feel her energies in the house and I would go into the room where she had been and lie there feeling the energies. But after a week or so they diminished and I was beginning to feel very lonely again, wanting company. I didn't want to live on my own anymore.

Within a couple of months though, another friend came to stay with me. She was also going through a personal crisis and needing shelter. I was happy to share my house with her, and she has stayed and we have become very close. This has been a major step in my life.

The biggest commitment of my time energies has continued to be my work as a nurse. I was only sixteen when I started training as a cadet, so I have been a nurse now for 32 years. For many years, going to the hospital was like a refuge for me - my security and my life. I feel I succeeded in doing my job well, and gained a lot of respect from my colleagues. But it was also a safe place. I could not love anyone or get too close to anyone while I was there, so it meant that I could do my duty while inwardly remaining somewhat isolated.

Just over ten years ago I started having problems with my back. More recently, this problem recurred. I noticed how when my life was stressful the pain got worse. But I couldn't allow myself to take time off work. I had to be there, because there was too much work for the others to do already. I had to look after things. My identity was so much tied up with this job. It was only when I nearly collapsed from pain and nervous exhaustion that I finally agreed to take sick leave.

My recovery took a long time. Perhaps if I had rested earlier it wouldn't have been so long. But I realised that my heart wasn't in nursing any more. I didn't want to be there. I wondered if my inner conflict about continuing nursing had contributed to the flare up in the pain. It's not surprising I became run down. My learning was about looking after myself more and letting others help me. That was not easy for me.

In my heart my passion wanted to work with crystals and healing. This is where I wanted to put my energy. However, I had a lot of resistance and fear about giving up a job that I had held for such a long time. There were still aspects of the job that I enjoyed. Yet, there had also been many changes where I felt that being a nurse was less satisfying to me than it once had been.

Finally though, after many months of wrestling with the fears and problems associated with it, I have decided to leave my work. I feel now that my unit will function OK without me. I do not know how my life will be once I leave, but I feel that for my Spiritual path, I have to move on and I want very much to learn and teach about crystal healing, and to serve Spirit.

I am becoming a different person through the therapy and Spiritual work I have done. It feels more like the true me, and I don't want to hide anymore. Each time I take another step, I encounter more fears, thoughts and feelings that would want to limit me. So I need to be patient in order to cope with these feelings. But then, to follow my path gives me joy and I know it is right, no matter how hard it feels sometimes. Through my Spiritual work I have become sensitive to energies. The more sensitive I become, the more I feel, and whereas previously my feelings were largely blocked and buried, now they come out very easily, and I want to use this sensitivity to help others.

Chapter 16 -
Rejection

Denise has acknowledged that the fears of rejection that she has suffered have influenced her life a great deal and affected choices and decisions that she has made. For instance, it has meant that she has never had a fulfilling long-term relationship with a man because she has been too afraid of being hurt. Now, with it being some months after she wrote her story, she has still not made any decisive steps about leaving her nursing job, even though in her heart she has no doubts that it is the right thing for her to do. Being in that job is safe for her and she does not know how her life would be without it. Denise is struggling to overcome these fears so that they will no longer limit her. She knows that it is one of her patterns, indeed one from many lifetimes, to take refuge in safe places rather than expose herself to the rough and tumble of the world where she may get hurt.

It is possible to look at each of the life stories that have been presented so far and see that experiences and fear of rejection have affected all the people concerned quite painfully.

Certainly, one of the most unpleasant experiences we can face as human beings is when we feel that someone, whom we love and want very much, does not want us. The effect of feeling rejected like this can be devastating. It is easy for us to be very attached to other human beings, so that if we feel we are not wanted, this can place our whole survival into question.

Our bodies can react to the experience of rejection in quite a dramatic way. We may feel tightness in our chest, loss of appetite, violent emotions, lethargy and depression, or even thoughts of suicide. It is sad that such strong reactions can occur, but for the people experiencing them, these reactions may feel to be outside their control.

Sometimes the fear that people have that they may be rejected, even if this is not the case, can bring just as significant symptoms and responses. The imagination can act resolutely to create adverse bodily and nervous reactions. When a person believes that they may be rejected, there can be much feeling of hopelessness, helplessness and powerlessness as a result.

The experience of rejection can also provoke feelings of rage and anger. If we give ourselves in love to someone, we may feel that this person should give love just as much to us. If they do not, or if they turn away, it may feel unfair and unjust to us. We may want to make them love us or acknowledge us sufficiently to match what we have given to them. But we cannot determine how another person will love us or even if they will do that. If another person chooses not to love us, there is nothing we can do about it. What is in our hearts is for each of us to determine by ourselves. However, our anguish if another person does not relate to us in the way we want, may indicate deep feelings of unworthiness or fears that we are unlovable. Beneath that may be overwhelming fears of loneliness and separateness, which can make people feel very small indeed.

As human beings, it is instinctive for us to seek out companionship and for that to be very important to us. Therefore, the problems of rejection are very common. Even for those of us who may feel very strong and self- contained, if we are open to our feelings and emotions, and if someone we love turns away from us, then this is likely to affect us profoundly.

Of course, it is possible for us to shut down our feelings so we will not allow ourselves to feel when someone we love has turned away, but this will not stop the feelings from being there. By suppressing those feelings, we may feel empty or numb - and the feelings locked away inside may eat away at us and eventually make us ill if we do not acknowledge them.

Because the experience of rejection is so difficult, many people will go to great lengths to avoid having that situation happen to them. They may try to please others, and do all sorts of things that they may not even feel like doing, just to placate other people who are important to them, and make sure to keep on good terms. If the fear of rejection is strong, people may feel that they have to conceal their true feelings and put on a kind of front, which they hope, will be acceptable to others. They may make themselves appear nice and pleasant when they feel anything but that inside.

I do not feel that this strategy is likely to be successful in attracting love. We cannot open our hearts to someone's mask, but only to someone who is able to be true to us. When people feel that they need to wear a mask, in the way they behave towards others, they will generally feel unhappy and empty inside. Sometimes people may feel they need to be like this with everyone or there may be one specific person who provokes this response in them. Either way, people who want love, but who are not willing or able to express their true feelings, are not likely to be understood, and other people will pass them by. This can produce expectations of rejection that become very entrenched in that person's life.

Once people have established habits for themselves where they regularly try to conceal their true feelings from others, this can be very difficult to change. People then may be very afraid that if they exposed themselves, then they may not be liked or wanted. If there are memories of this kind of experience having happened in the past, people will be even less inclined to reveal themselves to others. Consequently, they may live in some half-alive state but their fears will prevent them from living any differently. It will feel safer to stay with what is familiar rather than to try anything new, even though the existing situation may feel to be very unsatisfactory.

Referring to Denise's story, she faced strong instances where she felt rejected from a very early age. First there was her father who had some contact with her while she was very little, but then disappeared without trace. Next, there was her mother whom she loved very deeply and who died suddenly when she was only eleven. No one seemed to want to help her or support her, so it felt like a double rejection, profoundly affecting her sense of self-worth. Then with the adoption, this completed a picture where it seemed that everyone, who meant anything to her while she was young, either died or was separated from her.

The fact that she has now, in current time, started to rebuild a rapport with her sister has helped. But there is a lot to make up.

Due to feeling so overwhelmingly rejected by so many of her loved ones, even though in some cases, this was not intentional, Denise doubted more and more that she was loveable, and the reality of being separated from those she loved was deeply painful. She formed a belief that people she loved would go away and therefore because of the pain and hurt involved, it was better not to love at all. Then she could avoid this pain.

When she grew up, Denise developed a life of increasing isolation, but with this isolation, she felt more and more unhappy. Without loved ones, her life was very empty. When she started therapy, it became clear to her that what she wanted most was to love, to give and receive love. However, for her to do this, she would have to dismantle all the inner barriers around her heart that had accumulated over the years. And she was afraid. But the alternative was even bleaker. She had to do it.

Denise's soul test was about whether, after early setbacks, she could allow herself to embrace people in her life or face a life completely on her own. She feels that having made the choice to embrace people has led to her life feeling much richer and fuller even though she has cried bucket loads of tears along the road of learning how to do that.

It is also possible that people can feel isolated inwardly even when they are with others. When people believe that others do not see them, then they will feel disconnected from people whether they are with them or not. People with these feelings may also feel inadequate and afraid to express themselves. I am sure that Denise has felt that way at times. Such people need a lot of gentle support to feel safe and comfortable with others.

'I know from my own personal experience that in the past I have stopped myself from speaking with others because I was afraid that I might stumble when I expressed myself and be embarassed or ridiculed by others. When people feel like this, they can be very fragile inside. It wont take much to lock them further away in their shell.These people need confidence, but it will only come as they dare to take risks in terms of their self - expression.

But some people do not seem to want change. Many people in our present day and age appear to lock themselves away in their homes and rarely relate to anyone outside their family group beyond the most superficial of conversations. These people may really just want to be safe and not put themselves at any risk with others that may seem to them to be strangers. Their homes become like a fortress. In this case, these people are rejecting others, and may have inner reasons for doing this.'

Another instance of rejection can manifest when people become locked into a belief system where they feel that only when a particular relationship is right or functioning well will they be able to be happy. They may feel afraid that nobody else would understand them, and they may feel ashamed of their own fears and anxieties, fearing that if anybody knew what they were really like, they would not want to know.

Even though love can come from many various sources and in a multitude of forms, people may not be open to receiving this. They may be fixed on one person, feeling that this person has to love them in a particular way or their life will fall to bits and pieces. People can feel very fragile in themselves if they fear that they could be rejected. Being fixed on one person like this can give the other person much power and control which they may not be able to use wisely. For people in this situation, their worst fears may be realised. Michelle's relationship with her father and Eleyna's relationship with her former husband could be examples of this kind of fear and fixation.

It is never easy to cope with rejection. However, our inner beliefs can make a difference. People with a Spiritual faith may feel that it is through God or Spirit that they receive the love that they need and that there is an abundance of love for everyone, if only we can open to it. With faith of this nature, we might be less affected by other people's more negative responses to us and more open to possible inner help that is available to us.

If we do not have a Spiritual faith, then when someone that we depend upon rejects us or turns away from us, we may find it very difficult to cope with this. Psychologically, the only response we may feel we can make is to become very self-centred. However, we all need companionship, and to close in on ourselves can feel very lonely. If we feel that there is no support from the universe or from `God' then we will feel that we have to control everything in life ourselves to make it work. In such circumstances, if we depend upon somebody and they let us down, the effects may be overwhelming and we will have nothing to fall back on.

When we feel lonely or rejected, we need help. If we have a Spiritual faith, we may pray or ask Spirit to help us, and through this we may find peace. If we ask the universe to help us, there may be someone with whom we can talk coming across our path; there may be thoughts and feelings coming into our minds, prompting us to act in a constructive manner. All sorts of circumstances or events may play themselves out in a helpful way. These situations may not have occurred if we did not ask for help, or otherwise we may not recognise their value. The person we meet may not be a person we expected to meet, and help that is given to us may not necessarily be by a route that may have considered as viable. But the more open we can be, then the better the chances are that help can be given that will make a positive difference.

If we have suffered from feeling rejected, and it may be a situation where we feel we did nothing to create it, then this may need time for us to recover. Instinctively, when we feel we have been wounded like this, we may need to withdraw and take stock of our life. It may be a time for us to go within and reassess the direction in which we are going. If we allow ourselves to do this, rather than lashing out at the person we feel has deserted us, then we may find renewed strength and a greater assurance about being true to ourselves.

We may find that we can manage quite well on our own. However, in the end, we will want to open to companionship, because as human beings, I believe that we want to experience love more than anything else. Hopefully, where one door closes, another can open.

Chapter 17 -
Guilt and Self-love

It is obvious to all of us that love is an energy that we need both to give and receive. However, many of us fear that we are not worthy of love and that others are more deserving than we are. It is a very common tendency to judge our own mistakes much more harshly than we would judge the mistakes of others. So, if we have made a mistake in some area of our lives, we may remember this for a long time and not dare to do anything similar while we feel the pain of this, for fear of making the same mistake again. Thus, we can restrict our activities and our willingness to interact with the world because we cannot accept our own weaknesses or what we believe to be fallible in ourselves.

As I have written in the chapter on obsession, because we do not like to make mistakes, we will also not like that aspect of our being where we feel we tend to make mistakes. Consequently, we may then try to close off our awareness and acceptance for that kind of behaviour, which we feel has produced those mistakes. If we perceive similar sorts of behaviour in others we may also condemn it. In our minds, if we start thinking about it a lot, we may become very angry about these faults because they disturb us. We will not wish to be reminded of them. If we don't want to be angry with ourselves, then we will direct this anger at others, precisely for what we do not like in ourselves.

Many people try to ignore what they consider to be their faults and will concentrate their attention more upon what they consider to be their strengths, building up a life around this so they can feel comfortable and good about what they do. This will not be so easy to maintain. If we try to avoid some aspects of our being, then we will be neglecting that part of ourselves and in a way, keeping it in the dark. Inevitably, that part of our personality will not grow and will not be able to learn from experiences because of our act of will to keep it suppressed. Fundamentally, we want all aspects of our being to grow and learn, so that act of suppression will be in direct conflict with our inner desires. Therefore, our inner self will ensure that we keep meeting situations to prompt us to give this part of our personality some positive attention until we either decide to do this or we close off further.

When I was a child, I was very nervous about meeting other people and imagined all kinds of difficulties about how they may judge me. In social situations I was quiet and shy. Then when I was a teenager, there was one occasion where I was asked to read out a story I had written in front of my English class. I felt very nervous and afraid. When I held the paper with my story written upon it, my hands started shaking so violently that I had to put it down. All the other children were looking at me. Feeling very humiliated and ashamed, I did not ever want to expose myself like that again. As I grew older, my shyness continued. By the time I was eighteen, I could hardly dare speak into a telephone for fear of what others would think of me. I had my own small circle of friends and family with whom I could relate and that was all.

I didn't like myself being like this, and inside, I felt very isolated and unhappy. Try as I would, I could not escape from situations where I would need to relate to other people. Dimly I was aware from deep inside that I wanted to be able to relate easily with lots of people. The act of which I was most afraid was that which I most needed to do.

Eventually, I plucked up the courage to attend some communication workshops. During these weekends, I could hardly say a word, but I watched other members of the group and listened. I discovered that others could be nervous like me. Once I stopped having my attention fixed so much upon myself, but widened my awareness to include others, I started to relax a little. When other people could break down in front of the group and be very vulnerable and not be judged harshly by the group, this opened my awareness to the possibility that I could do likewise. This was the beginning of my healing around this problem.

142

The example, which I have given from my own life, is not so much one where I felt I had done wrong, but more one where I felt inadequate. I am sure that some basis for how I felt with others came as a result of messages that I picked up from my mother. I believe that she tended to feel anxious and afraid about how I would be with others and as a result, she was very insistent in telling me what I should and shouldn't be doing, and what terrible things may happen if I did not do what she said. However, I was temperamentally quite highly-strung and sensitive to other people's reactions anyway.

Now I believe that this problem came into my life as a soul challenge I had chosen within to overcome, because there was such a strong inner urge for me to learn to be able to relate easily and deeply with other people.

The messages that we receive from others can have a substantial influence upon how we feel and what we believe about ourselves. It is up to us though how we react to the interactions that come to us via others. Our self-beliefs are not determined by others but by our own decisions about what we feel is true and about what we want to be true. It is though our self-beliefs that we decide about what is right and wrong. When we feel that we have done wrong, then we feel guilt.

Guilt is a condition that comes about when we feel that we have created some hurt in other people or some other living being through our own actions. We may feel that we have made a mistake or fallen short in some way of what was expected of us. In truth, we may not have actually caused any hurt, but if we imagine that we could have done so, then this will be sufficient for us to feel guilt anyway.

If we have taken on messages from others, perhaps messages of judgement about what is right and wrong, then if we accept these judgements, we may feel guilt if we do anything except what these judgements tell us is right. Yet internally we may feel a sincere impulse to perform some action that goes contrary to these judgements. Then, if we act according to our impulse, we will be contradicting the judgements we have accepted, and feel that we

143

are doing wrong. If we do not respect our own impulses though, we will be placing ourselves in a situation of inner conflict by not being true to ourselves. We need to be very careful then about what judgements we accept as guidelines for our lives so we do not twist ourselves into inner knots.

When we feel guilt, it will be as if we are judging ourselves to be 'bad'. We may have set guidelines for our own behaviour, guidelines, which we have broken. Therefore we will not be very happy with ourselves and may want to punish ourselves for being so foolish. As we think about what we have done, we may wish to undo our actions and make things right. We may then feel regret and anger towards ourselves.

However much we may wish to alter what has been done though, we cannot do so. What has passed is over and cannot be lived again. We can only move forward. But when we feel guilt, we may not want to move forward.

People feel guilt when they are sensitive to other people's feelings and are very conscious and concerned about how the result of their actions may affect others. Some people may be so anxious in case another person will be hurt, that they may tiptoe through life without making a sound for fear of causing some damage. Unfortunately, when people are like that, they may find it quite difficult to be happy because their fear may hinder them from being able to relax in the company of others and also prevent them from generating deep and meaningful relationships.

At the other extreme, there are people who appear to make attempts to stop themselves from feeling guilt about any of their actions by deliberately concentrating completely upon satisfying their own urges without any thought for any other people involved. Even if they try to hide from or deny their feelings about their actions though, they may feel still uncomfortable and uneasy about what they have done. But if any feelings of hurt from others are brought to their attention, they may be inclined to deflect criticisms and blame the person who has been hurt for creating an upset so they do not feel wrong. Such people may like to create an illusion that they are OK and it is everyone else that

144

has shortcomings.

This attitude may result in feelings of isolation and an inability for those people to accept themselves beyond the self-image that they have built up to protect their position. They may feel that they have a right to do what they want. As these patterns become more ingrained, it will be very difficult for these people to listen to anyone else. They will only want to hear their own views confirmed. Such people can be very abusive to others without consciously realising it. To survive, they may feel that they must shut themselves off from how the other one feels, and so the pattern goes on.

The effect of people deciding that they do not care about others' feelings will be for them to close their hearts. They would not be able to open their hearts and still maintain the illusion that they are right and everybody else is wrong. With open hearts, people perceive situations much more truly. Therefore, while their hearts are somewhat closed, as well as not being able to love and care for others, they will not be able to love themselves either. I believe that we can only feel good about ourselves when we allow the love that we feel in our hearts to flow outwards to others and then open ourselves to receive that energy as it returns.

To love ourselves, we need to be able to accept all the different aspects of ourselves, not only the parts of ourselves that we like and want to present to the world, but all the other parts too. That means that we need to be able to accept our mistakes and the experiences within us where we may have been hard and cruel or neglectful towards others. This is a soul challenge for all of us. So, to be able to love ourselves, we need to be able to overcome our personal feelings of guilt.

The first and most important step for us to be able to do this is to be able to acknowledge our feelings. Too often people want to hide from their failures and where they feel that they have gone wrong. We want to be in control of our lives so that we can feel safe. To admit the experiences where we feel ashamed or regret can make us feel vulnerable and not in control of our reactions. It is understandable, therefore, why many of us prefer to leave these experiences alone.

When we do express our vulnerable feelings though, especially if we are able to share them with somebody who listens and does not condemn us, it releases a burden from us. Once our feelings about some area of our life in which we feel guilt comes out into the open, it allows a space for us to gain new perspectives about the situation that we have dwelled upon. If we have a Spiritual outlook, and we are open to inner help from our guides or from 'God', then bringing these feelings to the surface can create a passage for light to enter into what previously may have been a very dark place within us.

One barrier that needs to be overcome initially though, is the resistance to receive help for this problem in the first place. Very often, people decide around areas of their life where they feel guilty, that nobody can help them. They may have been thinking around the problem themselves in so many ways and have decided that if they can't solve it then no one else can either. This really is just a pathway to further isolation. It is a method whereby people create inner walls to shield off those aspects of themselves that they don't like. By doing this, they place these vulnerable aspects of themselves beyond anybody's reach.

It may be unrealistic to suggest that while we are human that we will be able to accept all of ourselves. But the more of ourselves that we can accept, then the more connected we will feel with the wholeness of who we are, and we will feel strength available to us to help us so that we can meet the various challenges that come our way.

While we are focussed upon our weakness or avoiding facing feelings of guilt from inside of ourselves, then we will be prone to depression or to adverse reactions in situations where we want to be in control. We may be afraid that if we began to expose those parts of ourselves where we feel `bad', then we may be overwhelmed by the difficult feelings it would bring up. Therefore, because of these fears, many people choose to do nothing and hope that they may be able to avoid challenges that would disturb them.

146

It is only when people feel an ache or longing that they want to improve their lives, that all is not as fulfilling as it could be, that change is possible. People need to have the will to alter their inner patterns before they can do so. But once people have made a sincere inner commitment to try to live their lives as well as they can, with a willingness to make inner changes, then help may come in unexpected ways. For people to confront the inner elements of their being that they do not like, this may not be as overwhelming as they had feared. It may happen in stages as a healing process. People, books and inner experiences may come along that help guide and direct the process gracefully.

When people feel that they are not worthy of love, it can take a long time to turn this around. Attitudes that result in an absence of self-love can stem from child-like responses. If people treat us badly, we can easily feel that we must have been horrible for them to treat us that way. This may not be the case at all. But when people are lacking in self-love, then they will tend to feel that any difficult situation that arises is their fault. This response may be one that has been conditioned through the messages of others. When people feel like this, they need help from others, to learn other perspectives and for their own fragile feelings that honour their own needs to be validated.

Chapter 18 -

Helga

Background

During the final years of my marriage, I felt a sense of dissatisfaction in my relationship to my wife. We had both developed separate interests, and although we were happy in many ways, there also felt to be gaps in how much we could meet each other's needs. Both of us began to make contacts with people outside the marriage as a means to try and fulfil what was missing in our relationship. One of the things which I did, was to join a pen friend club. Helga was one of the people with whom I then became associated through this club.

My correspondence with Helga was quite rewarding because we were both interested in each other's inner thoughts and feelings. As we gradually both felt our way forward, I discovered that I could be unusually frank with her in describing various aspects of my life and she could be the same with me. Our writing became intense as we could share some things with each other that we did not share with our partners. It was quite strange really, developing such a friendship with someone that I had not actually physically met. But I feel that as time went on, the contact became more valuable for both of us.

There were gaps of course, some months where both of us would be occupied and we would not correspond, and other times where our correspondence would be more frequent. I came to understand that Helga trusted me in a way that was not normal in her life. She was a sensitive woman who obviously thought about her own life very deeply. I felt very drawn to want to meet her and to introduce her to my work, but I also felt nervous about doing this.

Eventually we did meet and Helga came to attend one of my workshops. It was a difficult meeting. On the one side, I felt an attraction due to our knowledge of one another. Yet there was also a part of me that did not want to be too close to her. For most of the week I concentrated my attention upon leading the workshop and kept her at a distance. I think that for her, she found this to be quite frustrating and disturbing.

Then at one point in the workshop, she accessed a past life where I was the father she had then who killed her. Inside myself, I felt such strong feelings that I knew that her identification was accurate. Now I was aware of why I had felt cautious of being close to her - I was afraid. Although afterwards I tried to help her process her experience, I found myself inwardly backing away from her. This continued over the next months. Consequently, at a time when I think that she really needed my support, because she was facing enormous difficulty and felt unable to talk to anyone about it, including me, I was not available to her and I feel that I let her down. Perhaps though, she needed to find her own way through this very dark period in her life.

Since then, my relationship to her has altered considerably. I have had to go through quite an involved process with her to sort out our relationship. During the course of this, I have needed to own with her, weaknesses in my character, so that now I feel that my friendship with her is a lot stronger. In the meantime, there is much that she has discovered about herself and she has been challenged to make shifts in the way that she relates to others who are important in her life. Here in what follows is her story.

Helga's Story

As a child, I was quite happy until I had my first near death experience, when I was eleven years old. It was the first time that I had been exposed to the forces of death and happened like this.

During a swimming lesson, I went under the water and lost control so I could not return to the surface. Inside, I felt very strongly that if I did not get help soon, then this would be the end of my life. While my physical body was still trying to escape from

149

the situation, my consciousness felt pulled towards an illuminated tunnel. During these moments, I saw the good things of my childhood passing by. It was like a movie, but everything was peaceful and very slow. So actually, it was a good feeling and I did not panic at all.

With my awareness, I recognised two forces. The first one wanted to bring me back into my body, while the other one wanted to bring me into a peaceful place. I felt very attracted to continue my experience and it seemed to go on endlessly. My memory of this is very clear.

However, then I was suddenly back in my normal consciousness, and found myself in the medical care department together with my rescuer. It felt very upsetting to be there.

I believe that this was the most important Spiritual experience of my childhood, but it felt strange and difficult for me to understand at that time. Although my mother was present there, I knew that she wouldn't understand this experience. Much as I tried to explain to her, she did everything she could to avoid this subject. As I reflect upon it, I think that a child cannot go through the kind of experience that I went through as fantasy. It felt real and I recognised the forces present as something very much alive, real and magical. In my private thoughts, I dwelled on this experience very often and it was strongly present in me.

However, the fact that I felt unable to share this with my mother disappointed me very much. I cannot remember that she made any efforts to comprehend it. As a result, I felt isolated, so that I needed to withhold important parts of myself from others.

About one year later, I had another experience, which was quite similar, although in different circumstances.

On this occasion, my mother and I needed to go to the dentist. Although it was a beautiful summer's day and we could have gone by bike, she decided we should drive in the car. I argued with her about this, but I could not persuade her. As we started our journey, I felt very uncomfortable. Then when we reached a guarded level crossing, my mother's car stalled and would not start again. There was a train approaching.

It was as if my mother was paralysed. She did not react and seemed unable to understand what I said to her. Clearly, she was in a state of shock. We only had a few seconds before there would be impact. The thought came strongly into my mind to pull her out before the train could reach us. Again, I felt something that 'pushed' me to react that way. Somehow, I succeeded and we survived.

I suppose that this was an incident where I saved my mother's life, but she was unable to talk to me about this incident. However, for me it was a profound experience where once again I had felt protected.

From then on, I feel that I started to live my life in depth, even though I was still a child. I felt that there were important aspects of what I felt that I couldn't express to others. Therefore, even though I considered that I had many friends and was seemingly quite a social child, I felt more and more an outsider. I had strong thoughts that when we die that this is not the end of our existence, but because I felt unable to share about this with anybody, it felt very frustrating.

During my childhood, my uncle was someone very precious to me. In the way that he acted, he was a role model for me in my growing up, even more than my father. He was a police officer and greatly respected by many people. I felt close to him and he introduced me to nature and to the sea. Very often he took me out on long walks.

While on one of these excursions when I was thirteen, I was alone with him and sitting on the grass. I noticed that he was behaving oddly, as if under the influence of alcohol, but he wasn't. He started to touch me. I remember and still can feel how his big hands moved under my clothes. I was astonished and did not really understand what was happening. It was very confusing. Finally, I reacted and forced myself away from him. I ran away very quickly.

This type of incident happened just once, but it was enough to destroy my trust and confidence in him. My contact with him became more reserved. But I feel that this experience affected my trust in adults generally, especially people who had an important and protective role in our society.

Strangely, I saw him as a victim and someone needing help. I felt sorry for him. But I suppose that these thoughts deflected from the damage that the experience did to me in that it increased the wariness I felt towards other people. Inside I felt very shocked that just by being myself he could want to use me in such a way. I felt less safe to be me.

This led to a period where I tended to act in a way that others expected and tried very hard to please people. At times, I felt very much manipulated. When I tried to focus my attention about what other people wanted from me, I felt frustrated. Sometimes people did not take my needs into consideration at all. Already there was a pattern expressing itself where I felt I needed to listen to others and attend to their needs, but I found it very difficult to express my own needs. I suppose that I doubted whether people would value and honour me if I told them too much about what was important to me.

However, I felt very driven that I did not want to hurt or disappoint people, especially those who were most close to me. I would dedicate myself to make sure that these people were satisfied with whatever was expected from me. It was my way of feeling that I was good enough for them. Often though, I felt that I failed and I could not fulfil demands people had placed on me. I know that I placed a lot of pressure on myself, but when I felt I could not meet their needs, I 'blocked' and closed down

As I try to analyse myself, there have been times when I have tried to force people to love and respect me through my good works. Even in my present job, I have wanted to finish projects before a deadline is reached, so that everyone is happy, no matter how much energy it has cost me. Perhaps I have been afraid that if I didn't try to 'make' them honour me like this, then they wouldn't do it at all.

I felt that my parents had very high expectations of me, and I had to try and please them. As a child, I went to church every Sunday because they wished it of me. My perception was that my parents treated me differently to my brother and sister. They seemed to have no limitations and appeared to be able to do what they wanted to do, while I felt very much controlled. When my brother and sister were meeting their friends, I was required to help with the housekeeping. There was no time for me to relax and do what I wanted. Eventually, as a teenager, I grew restless and wanted to escape.

Although I had many meaningful friendships, which felt important to me, these often seemed to be contacts in one direction only. Sometimes I only realised this after these people had gone out of my life. I tended to be appreciated as a good listener, but with my own needs I was left alone, with feelings of discomfort, fear, disappointment and maybe most important, emptiness. I was very afraid to feel rejected and sometimes felt very angry when this seemed to happen. These feelings swirled around inside of me and could be very destructive. My strategy for surviving these situations was to have a well determined strong will to go my own way.

However, my will did not always prevail. When I started university, I wanted to study psychology or the history of art. But there did not seem to be many career possibilities with these subjects, so my mother forced me to study science. I was not happy with this choice but I managed to finish my studies without problems.

During this period, I met a lot of interesting people. The most significant was a friendship I developed with Rita, a woman eleven years older than me. She was single, had a lot of life experience and had a strong Catholic faith. This contact changed my life and I felt very close to her. Finally there was someone prepared to listen to me and support me. She introduced me to her Spiritual world. Rita had come at exactly the right time for me as I had started to believe that no one wanted to open his or her heart and listen to me. However, just as I was starting to feel very secure with her, she decided to move to another place so that our contact would be very limited. This made me feel very sad, and I could not cope with the feelings of hurt and loneliness that welled up from within me.

Consequently, I became restless again. Somehow, I felt that I had failed, perhaps that I had not pleased Rita enough. I entered into a phase of my life where I had many relationships with men over a short period of time. Although some of these contacts were meaningful to me, I tended to be the one to finish these relationships because they did not give me the fulfilment that I wanted.

There was a great desire in my life to have someone to know me as intimately as I know myself. For this to happen, I recognised that I would need to trust such a person, very, very much, so that whatever happened I could always depend on that person. Now I do not know if such a wish is possible to be lived.

After Rita, I found it very difficult to trust people. By ending relationships in the way I did, I am sure that I hurt many people. But I had to move on to explore and experience more. I could not be still and rest.

At one time I chose to be a volunteer at the local hospital. I worked in the department where there were children with cancer. My job was to read stories for them every night just before they went to bed. This was a task, which at first I enjoyed very much because all the children appreciated it.

There was one girl with whom I became very close. She wrote poems about life and death and appeared very deeply to accept what life would bring to her. Inside she was very strong and had a strong will to survive. I felt that she had a Spiritual outlook to life. She taught me a lot and I was very afraid of losing her. Despite her condition, she had a lot of beauty in her. One day though, she died, as did most of the children in this ward. It was a sad place to be. After a while I had to stop my reading to the children because I found it too difficult to say goodbye.

While I was working at the hospital, I met Frans, who was fifteen years older than me. He introduced me to the 'New Age' world and soon we began a relationship. Frans was very sensitive and understanding. He seemed to be everything that I wished for in a man. And he took care of me. At last I felt that I could live a life that was true to my heart. It was a Spiritual love and I realised that I had been searching for this for a long time.

Unfortunately, he did not conform to my parent's expectations because they felt he was too old for me. But we continued to meet each other.

My life began to change. I found peace and experienced a strong connection with my inner self. In many ways this time was exciting and very precious to me, as we became closer and closer. This was an unconditional love. For the first time I could open my heart to a man.

Then, one day, Frans told me that he would move to Greece. This was a total shock for me. I could not cope with the separation, so I closed myself down utterly from the outside world. Inside I decided that I couldn't trust people anymore.

When I did finally venture out to meet people again, I wanted to hurt people - emotionally. My favourite occupation was to attract people to me and then to reject them. I suppose that it was a kind of revenge. If I couldn't be happy then I didn't want other people to be happy either. Again I felt this restlessness. I had to move on.

About two years later, I met my husband. Within a short time we married. I felt very much that this was the person with whom I wanted to 'ground' my life. And so this felt to be a very positive change. We shared love and passion and enjoyed being together. Although our interests did not completely coincide, we could stimulate each other and this resulted in a warm and open-hearted relationship. Soon we celebrated the birth of our first child, which was very much wanted. Professionally, I had a good job with no difficulties. Through my work I had to travel a lot and thus, I could enjoy life.

However, my husband did not share my Spiritual outlook to life. As a result, I stopped meditating and felt my life become more superficial.

The pregnancy with our second child was very different to the first. I had physical problems and somehow, I did not feel responsible for this child. When this child was born, I rejected her and did not want any physical contact with her. Although the medical staff and my husband encouraged me to have a closer contact, I refused. Perhaps I was incompatible with this soul for some reason. But it was not a happy time. Soon it became clear that she was not a healthy child. Only after a few operations did her health become more stable.

My reaction to this situation troubled me greatly. After seeking the help of one of my friends, I started meditating again. During one of these sessions, something shifted in me and I felt a release, as if something was lifted up. As a consequence, I regained energy and could now be open to contact with my daughter.

Throughout the years, I have never found it easy with this child and I have had to work to make sure that she received enough attention. At times, I have felt 'guided' in difficult situations where I felt resistance to her, so that now I feel more at peace. It has been hard learning for me.

As time went on, my life settled down. I suppose that I conformed to all the things that others expected me to do. However, there was a part of me though, that did not feel satisfied with my life. I longed for some freedom and adventure where I might express myself more fully. My husband was not always available and I was often away with my job too. I noticed that I was starting to feel restless again.

It was during this period that I came to be in contact with Paul through a penfriend club. My correspondence with him became more precious and important to me. With Paul I could share my inner thoughts in depth and he showed interest and acceptance of what I wrote. This was unusual for me in my life because I still tended to experience this one way kind of relationships where I did all the listening and could not express much of myself in return. He shared with me of his marriage difficulties and I felt that I could support him too.

However, as our correspondence evolved, I often had a strange bitter feeling in my heart. There was something frightening about relating to Paul. I could not place what made me feel like that. Very reluctantly, I finally agreed to attend one of his workshops.

During this workshop I was introduced to my first experience of past lives. The life that I experienced was very real. It was an unhappy and traumatic life, as I was a child who was killed by an older man. Just as I was finishing the experience I was shocked and devastated to realise that the man who killed me then was the same soul as Paul.

As soon as I told Paul this, he seemed to react and was unable to help me. Suddenly Paul changed for me from being a precious friend into a monster. My hate towards him at that moment was indescribable. I felt the same odd feeling in my heart that I had felt many times before. There was a very strong desire in me that wanted to beat him very hard.

I think that Paul may have been distressed too, but he now felt a stranger to me. I had lost a friend.

During the last evening of the workshop, in the early hours of the morning, I wandered out of my bedroom feeling very distressed. At that moment I met Paul who had also been wandering around for the same reason. It seemed fateful that we should meet like this. For some hours, we talked and I experienced a lot of healing. However, even this exchange was not enough to prevent me from feeling very unsettled.

This was the beginning of what was to prove to be the most difficult year of my life. I suppose that when I left the workshop a large part of me wanted to reject Paul and reject the Spiritual work that he was trying to teach. It was too painful. Several events then happened that plunged my life into darkness.

First of all there was an occasion in which I was not faithful to my husband. The man was a friend, but not someone whom I loved, and he was not someone with whom I felt that I could be in relationship. However, from this act I became pregnant. What could I do?

I could not tell my husband and consequently my relationship with him became increasingly distant. Strangely though, I felt very happy to be pregnant. I was able to love this child and had a very strong connection with it, far stronger than with my other pregnancies. The only thing that made me unsure was that it would have no father who could give his love and protect it.

At work, I informed my boss about the situation. He was a man that I felt I could trust and with whom I had developed a good contact over the years. Unfortunately, my judgement of him proved to be wrong. He started to blackmail me, threatening to tell my husband. I couldn't bear for him to do that and felt no other way out. I became subject to his will. Increasingly, he demanded emotional and sexual favours. The experiences I had with him are too perverse to write about. I can only say that I felt deeply humiliated. It was bad to undergo the physical violence. For him to do this to me while I was pregnant was disgusting. I wanted to protect this child. But on the other side, I had to undergo all his fantasies. He changed from the nice person that I knew into an animal.

There was no one to whom I felt I could turn. I felt I just had to endure this suffering in isolation. I tried writing to Paul, but he was embroiled in his own problems. This was a further disappointment to me. I could trust no one.

At the same time I was acutely aware of my children's needs. I did not want to break up my family. My youngest daughter had been unwell, needing treatment for a growth on her leg. I did not want to be the cause of suffering to them. The relationship I shared with my husband was quite strained. I could not have sex with him or other intimate contact. He must have found this very difficult.

Also, I had to be careful of my health. A few years earlier I had developed diabetes and needed to control this by keeping my life in balance. But I was in such a state that I struggled to sleep at night and felt desperate.

All these factors combined to make me feel that I would have to have an abortion. This was very difficult, but the only thing, which I felt I could do. The father of the child did not know. In one way, I feel good that it was me who was totally responsible for what happened to this child. The only other person who knew was my doctor. When I went through this abortion though, something in me died. For now, though, I cannot write more about this event.

Eventually, I received some help and advice to cope with my boss from the company doctor. This began a process where I was eventually able to get free of him. But the experiences with him damaged me enormously. They had continued for some time after the abortion. There were several occasions over these months when I felt suicidal, and I struggled to cope with my life. One day I caused a severe car accident because I wanted to finish my life.

As the situation around my boss eased though, the problems in my family got worse. My husband formed a relationship with another woman. This happened while my boss was still using me, and at first I did not care. I urged him not to tell the children and desperately tried to find ways to preserve our family. Still, I could not inform him about what had happened to me. I had to be strong. For months I had not been able to be intimate with him. So this very uneasy situation developed where he was living in the family home with me, and for the children's sakes we were expressing our lives as if we were still together, while he pursued his life with her.

I did not know where to turn. There were possibilities where I could have been offered counselling help, but I was afraid of people's judgement. Somewhere inside I felt protected, but it was very difficult.

Later in this year, Paul sent me a copy of his book 'Healing Journeys'. Reading this helped me understand him more fully, but also prompted me that I needed to open once more to build up my faith in Spirit again. I decided to attend another of his workshops. Another step, which I made, was to seek some past life therapy to try and find some understanding. This helped me to some extent.

At Paul's workshop, I had a major Spiritual experience that made a big difference to me. I felt that I needed a 'safe' place where I would feel protected and where I could tell my story and maybe ask for support. But I did not feel safe enough with any person to do this. Maybe I could ask for the help of Spirit?

During the inner processes that Paul led, I found that I could enter a very deep state of trance. So, one day I worked with Denise and she supported me so that I could feel my consciousness lifting. Now I could ask questions of my inner self. Before doing this, I wanted to go through the different crises of my life and relive the most difficult parts of them. I could do this quite easily. As I relived the 'bad' experiences, I felt quite helpless, and I was reminded of all the emotions that I had been through during these times. Suddenly, though, I wanted to move forward, and didn't want to be stuck in these experiences any more. By this decision, I seemed to go into a very peaceful place. This was my final destination, and it was a safe place to be. Many of the events of my life seemed to gain a new perspective. I wanted to stay in this place. It was only with great reluctance that I returned to normal consciousness.

This experience helped me to regain a positive belief in life again, something that I had lost. I feel that some of my inner blockages were lifted from me. These Spiritual experiences made me feel stronger and I regained my energy. To know that I could contact my inner self was a great support to me.

In the months that have followed, I have tried to gain more balance in my life again, but not always successfully. The problems with my husband continue. There are times when his female friend is absent when we are closer. But when she is around, things are more strained. My children are very important to me and I want them to be happy.

160

I know that there are still issues for me to resolve, for instance, my fears of being controlled and my inability to trust people. Also, I know that healing is needed with regards the child I had to abort. In some ways I still need to say 'goodbye'. I hope that this will be possible.

However, writing this has been a therapy for me. It is the first time I have shared about many of these experiences to anyone.

Chapter 19 -

Abortion

When a woman conceives a child, as well as the many hormonal and other changes, which happen on a physical level, there are also energetic adjustments that take place. The woman's energy field is opened to welcome the soul on a journey towards physical incarnation. This is a very subtle and sensitive process. The mother to be will naturally love this soul and want to protect it and nurture it along this journey. Strands of the woman's energy field will wrap themselves around the soul that is to be incarnated and they will share an energetic space together. On a Spiritual level, the mother to be will connect with the maternal impulse and want to provide a home for this soul to grow in. This is all very delicate, but the woman will not be able to avoid feeling these changes and links that have occurred. There will be a very strong desire and drive for this process to want to culminate in the birth of a child.

It may be very sad then, if through some unhappy circumstances the woman may feel that she cannot have this baby, or perhaps there might be a part of her that does not want to have the baby. Such thoughts and reaction will be in direct conflict with all the natural instincts within her. As a consequence, making a decision to abort the baby will be extremely painful. For a woman to nonchalantly deny that this would make any big difference to her could only imply that she has blocked her feelings and is trying to hide from the truth. Internally, she will not want to do this because it would feel like killing a part of herself. The connection she feels with the soul to be incarnated will feel very intimate and precious. If she attunes herself to it, she will feel its energy and the sacredness of the contact that has been made.

It could be though that there have been some problematic elements around the conception. If there has been conflict or negative feelings between the two people involved, this may affect the capacity of the woman to welcome the soul. Where she feels guilt in relationship to the event of the conception, or resentment or even hatred towards the man involved, then these feelings may wrap themselves around the energy of the developing embryo. So there may be a part of her wanting the child and a part of her not.

Sometimes when a woman does not love herself, she will still want to love the soul of this embryo. She may feel that if this baby could be born and grow to live a happy life being looked after by her, even if she has not been able to be happy herself, but if her child is happy, then something worthwhile would have been achieved. Just imagine how devastating it must be for a woman with these longings if she then chooses to have an abortion.

People can be complex beings and in relationship to the growing embryo, there may be many layers of feelings about this, some of which may contradict each other very strongly. Pressures may be applied from outside, by family or society. The man involved may regard a potential baby as some kind of threat. In order to protect her position and please the man, the woman may feel that she has to release the child that is growing in her.

The actual act of abortion, by physically inducing the embryo to leave the body, forces the soul to leave the woman's energy field. Even if the woman in some ways wants to keep her baby, the effect of the abortion will be like a wrenching away of this soul so that the woman's energy field is forced to adjust, whether she likes it or not. She is bound to feel an acute sense of loss, which she can try to block. However, the abortion will have a substantial psychological impact.

If she tries to suppress the feelings associated with the abortion she may feel an underlying guilt that she does not want to know about, and therefore she will have a more negative relationship with herself than she did before. Otherwise, if she chooses to try and acknowledge the ramifications of what she has done, she will wonder about the fate of the soul that has left her and suffer

163

because of the violence that she will feel has been inflicted upon that soul. For herself, she will miss this soul because of the relationship that had already been established, and feel a longing for this soul, probably for the rest of her life. There is the potential, if she opens her heart, that she may then feel greater compassion for other living beings as a result of this loss.

For the man who was responsible for the pregnancy, there can also be strong feelings of loss as a result of an abortion. When a child is conceived, there is a Spiritual impulse within the man to want to care for the woman and to provide a loving home in which this soul can grow into physical incarnation. If a man is sensitive to this, then these feelings can be significant. Therefore, when an abortion is being considered, the man may want to have some input about the decision. Where there is disagreement between the man and woman about this issue, then this may have a very damaging effect upon the relationship of the two people.

Psychologically, the process of bringing a soul into physical incarnation is akin to the impulse in all human beings to create and grow. So when a woman has had an abortion, until both the woman and the man have come to terms with this actuality, then both of these people in their own ways may become 'stuck' in some areas of their life. There may be facets of their life where they stop 'growing' or 'being creative'. However, it is the woman who will be most strongly affected because of the nature of her contact with the soul that was aborted.

The first step of healing after an abortion is to allow a process of grieving. Especially for the woman, because of her direct involvement, there will be many feelings swimming around inside her. These will need to be expressed and if she can find a safe and loving environment in which to share these feelings then this can help considerably. Ideally, if the man and woman can share together and support each other, then this may be very healing. But this is not always easily possible in such difficult circumstances.

In Helga's case, she did not talk with anyone following her abortion. None of her friends or family knew about it. She also concealed the information from the man with whom she had become pregnant. Consequently, because of this and other challenging developments, she entered a very dark phase in her life where for a time she felt completely isolated and suicidal.

Whenever anyone we love dies, it can be very helpful to honour the memory of the soul who has departed. Therefore, in the aftermath of an abortion, to construct some form of altar for that soul, can focus thoughts and feelings and provide a sacred space for meditations and prayer in relation to that soul.

In conjunction with the grieving, there may be a need to communicate with that soul which has been aborted. Through meditation, this may be possible, and I have witnessed many moving instances where people have felt themselves able to connect and feel the love of the soul that they aborted. Because the longing to do this can be so intense, it can encourage the awakening of the people's Spiritual faculties so that they can achieve their aim. Typically, people will experience the soul as a being of light and love and they will know the identity of this being.

From the channelled information received from many of these souls from various sources, it seems that when a soul is forced to leave the physical plane through abortion, usually it is protected and does not suffer nearly as much as the woman on Earth. In the early stages of pregnancy, the soul is not yet very connected to the physical plane anyway. Often it will become clear that the soul has come to help serve the woman or man in some way. The soul may have been aware that it would not reach full physical incarnation.

We may find in our lives that we are placed in the situation where we need to make choices of life and death, as with an abortion. This can be a very difficult challenge and it may be part of our soul pathway to face this. There may be much for us to learn whatever we choose.

With Helga, after her life story was completed for this book, she attended another of my workshops. During this week, she managed to share about the abortion and the story leading up to it. She was able to connect inwardly with the soul that had been with her during the pregnancy. She felt this as a very loving soul that was close to her and, after much processing, she was able to accept more fully what had happened. An important step for her was that she was able to find some inner reconciliation with the man with whom she had become pregnant. There was much cleansing and release of negative feelings. Altogether, she allowed herself to trust others by sharing her feelings in a way that she had not done so before. Hopefully this will help her in her life to come.

She told me afterwards that the experience of her pregnancy and the abortion was not something that she would be able to forget or resolve and she sensed that it would stay with her for all of her life.

For anyone in the situation of facing an abortion, it must bring up some very difficult inner dilemmas. Whatever the rights and wrongs of it, I believe that the women who have suffered through these experiences need a lot of love and care.

Chapter 20 -
Relationship Dilemmas

Breakdown of Trust

From Helga's story, it is clear that one of her main problems has been her fear around trust. She is a sensitive woman who has felt that she has had to withhold herself from others in order to survive and not be hurt. I believe that this is a common problem and that there are many people who close off from others because they have difficulties to trust.

When we form a relationship with another person, it may be very precious for us to consider that person as our friend. We long to feel a sense of belonging and acceptance for the person that we are. The more we can reveal of ourselves and feel that our friend sees us truly, the richer and more rewarding the relationship may be. To combine our energies in harmony and love with a friend can be the hope of our hearts.

However, friendship can be easily damaged if we stop caring or if we feel that our friend is not caring about us. Even the toughest of us, when we reveal the vulnerable sides of ourselves to our friend, can be very sensitive about this. We need to be honest with our friend. Yet, if we start to speak to our friend in an unkindly way, or with our hearts closed, then this can quickly create a gulf or distance between us. Such a chasm may be a wound that is not easy to repair. Likewise, we may feel affected if we perceive that our friend is not being open-hearted and concerned about us.

I feel that we need to take responsibility for what we contribute to a friendship. Our thoughts can have a big impact upon our friend. If we think critically towards our friend, even if we do not express these thoughts, our friend will still sense what we are thinking. Our thoughts are energy, and if they are directed towards our friend, then these thoughts will interact with our friend's energy field, causing a reaction.

Consequently, because we choose our thoughts, we need to be careful about what we project to others. If we are troubled by negative thoughts about our friend, we may need help to work these thoughts out, so that they will not damage the relationship. For, if we are afraid and try to withhold thoughts or feelings from our friend, perhaps things that we do not want our friend to know about, then I do not feel that we will be successful in doing this. On some level, our friend will know what we are thinking and what we are doing, even if they are not fully consciously aware of it. In a similar way, we will be aware of our friend's thoughts and actions too.

I believe that we are much more sensitive to the events and energy interactions around us than we realise. Many of us remain relatively closed to these perceptions because we centre our thoughts and feelings so much on ourselves. As we become more caring and open to others, our perceptions and sensitivity will also grow. We can also then be more easily hurt.

If someone does not like us very much and perhaps wishes us harm, we may need to try to protect ourselves so that we will not be too negatively affected. When we can be aware of our own strength and be mindful of what is true for us, from deep inside, while also keeping our hearts open, then this may be the best way for us to maintain our peace and happiness. Yet, this may also be quite a challenge for us to attain.

There can be much learning for us with friends. Very few of us can be positive with our thoughts all the time, and because of our individual desires and needs, it is not possible to be always on the same wavelength with each other. Therefore, we will tend to make mistakes and close our hearts somewhat on occasions. One of the main challenges will be for us to learn tolerance and find a peace from within to forgive hurts that have been caused, and to forgive ourselves for our own shortcomings.

168

Sometimes though, hurts can feel very big. We may feel betrayed or let down, perhaps feeling that our friend has not been there for us when we needed support. In our heart, we may feel pain and this may be hard for us to bear. We may feel that the damage cannot be repaired, that we do not want this pain. When a friendship breaks down, this can be very difficult and cause an acute loss of trust. If it was a friendship that we depended on, then we may feel lost without it, feeling very alone and cut off from others.

We may easily make the presumption that because this one friendship has not worked, then no other friendship can work either. As a result, internal barriers may be put up to keep other people separate. We can block input from other people so that we only perceive what we want to perceive. The thoughts in our minds may go along the lines that 'everyone is against me', or 'nobody wants me', and we will see that reflected in other people's behaviour towards us, whatever they do. Thus, we may shy away from that which we want most. Love may feel too dangerous to get near.

Once people start to feel that it is not safe to be themselves with their friend, then they may lock their heart away and feel increasing despair and loneliness. This is one route by which people may approach being in an inner place of darkness from where there seems to be no escape. In this situation, people will have lost trust and alienated themselves from others. When they experience this, people may not want to be helped and may not feel that they can be helped. It will be like they are in their own little shell or dark place where nothing else may seem possible.

We may notice from Helga's story how she, on several occasions, felt betrayed and rejected by others. But in her suffering, instead of seeking help from anyone else, she has tended to close herself down from everyone. It may be an attitude within her that if she cannot trust the person closest to her, then she could not trust anyone else either. In these situations, she has been determined to manage on her own, but at a great cost to herself. She has had to endure terrible feelings of isolation and emptiness.

When we know someone who is living in the darkness, the best we can offer, I believe, is love and space to be. People need to feel that they can make their own steps. They have got themselves into this situation and only they can get themselves out of it. But they need support, and there may be many feelings and confusions that they need to express to find some clarity. A person in this situation has to make some gesture of reaching out before help can be given. That first reaching out may feel very delicate, and unless people in trouble feel that their gesture has been recognised, accepted and received with love, then they may withdraw further, and use this experience as another reason to maintain their isolation.

Relating again to Helga's story, I realise that when Helga went through her recent year of darkness and crises, there were occasions when she reached out to me for help. However, because at the time I was so absorbed in my own troubles and crisis, I did not feel able to respond to her gesture as fully as I know she needed. Now I feel sorry about this, but given my state of mind at the time, I do not know if there was more that I could have done. Because she did not have anyone else with whom she could confide, the fact that I was not receptive to her needs, due to it being around the time of my marriage break up, led her to close off further from others around her.

It is only when people start to feel accepted that they can begin to trust. And if that person can open to trust one person, then it may be possible for that trust to develop towards further people as well. While we feel that there is only one person whom we feel that we can trust, then this places an enormous responsibility upon that other person. If that other person has not fully chosen this responsibility, then it seems very likely that at some point there will be disappointment and loss of trust. We may expect more of that other person than is possible for him or her to fulfil.

Trust is a very delicate quality. No one can give it to us. We can only find it within ourselves. The more we trust, the more love we will feel, and without trust, our lives will feel very empty. We need to feel protected somehow, if we are afraid that other people will hurt us. However, if we stop operating in the world because of this, then we will feel powerless and very frustrated.

From having been in an inner place of darkness, there is no simple way to fully learn to trust and love again. When we feel that friendships have broken down and that we are not capable of living life happily, much time may be needed before we can believe that even the best of friendships will support us when we really need it. For all of us, there are places of inner darkness where we are afraid and where we fear we may have gone wrong. The hand of friendship though, is so valuable and may fill the heart with healing.

To reach out our hand to another, may help our own trust to grow again. If we feel we are needed, then this may help us to believe that we are loveable. Then we may start to believe that we are worthy of being a friend. However, we need to be careful not to keep someone so chained to us, that they will feel they need us to be happy, because people will not really feel happy unless they also feel free.

In the end, we must find peace within ourselves. No person can provide us with all that we need. If we try to make another person fill up what we are lacking, then we will be living our lives more through this other person rather than being true to ourselves. We may be inclined to blame the other one when it goes wrong, when the other person may act in a way that does not feel to be attuned to our needs, but really we will have largely created this situation ourselves.

Trust, when it arises, is a quality that emerges independently of anyone else. When we trust, we feel safe and we feel that we can be ourselves. With trust we feel we have the power to create our own life.

Love and Fear in Relationships

A deeper aspect of friendship is for people to open themselves to be involved in a committed, close and intimate loving relationship with another human being. Many people cherish this as a dream of what they want more than anything else. It may be an ideal that is quite difficult to attain, even for people who are 'together' with someone else. Societies have attempted to institutionalise such relationships through rituals of marriage, for instance. However, even with all kinds of vows and promises, marriage does not necessarily make a relationship more intimate or loving. Essentially, this is a challenge for both people about how deeply they are prepared to love one another.

To be 'in love' can bring forth, beautiful feelings of happiness and union, a sense of belonging. Yearnings for these kinds of feelings, I believe, are common to all human beings. They are connected to that sense of home that perhaps we lost before we were born into physical reality.

As we love another person, we begin to know that person, perceiving the many various strengths and weaknesses that are there. When we allow ourselves to be loved, our partner may also begin to know us similarly. Often, it can be quite frightening to let another person know us intimately. We may fear that if our partners close their hearts to us, then they may use one of our weaknesses to hurt us. Many people carry memories of such hurts from present and former lives, so there can be a wariness of letting something like that happen again. It can feel safer not to be too close to another person, so those sensitive feelings can be protected and held in. But, as has been mentioned, if we keep our sensitive feelings locked away and find no expression for them, then our lives will feel empty and unfulfilled. Even though there may appear to be risks involved, we all essentially want to love and be loved at as deep a level as possible.

When we love someone more than anyone else, we may feel almost as though that person is a personal reflection of ourselves. We want to trust that person and rely on them. When we become very close to another human being, the patterns, fears and imbalances of our subconscious mind begin to mingle with that of this other person. As we become emotionally and perhaps sexually involved, we may react very intensely to how that other person is feeling. We may react negatively to some aspects of our partner's behaviour. Indeed, because we are so involved with our partner, we may perceive accurately a fault or weakness in our loved ones.

However, we can also project onto our partner thoughts, limiting beliefs and prejudices from within our own minds. These images are our own creation and may not correspond at all with our partner's intentions or attitudes. We can live out illusions where we think we know our partner, but really what we perceive is a reflection of our own minds. These kinds of projections can occur in all sorts of relationships, wherever there is an involvement between two people.

If we want to be successful in our relationships we need to be as certain as we can that we are not creating fantasies with regards the other person, but that we perceive them correctly. Nothing is going to be more frustrating for our partners than if they feel they are not being seen or perceived for who they really are. But this means work for us, learning about our inner beliefs and expectations concerning other people, trying to sort out what are our own thoughts and expectancies and what really belongs with the other person.

One clue, which may help us, concerns our reactions to others. When we react emotionally to some aspect of someone else's behaviour, then it is usually an indication that such weakness is also in ourselves, although we may not be aware of it. What we do not accept in our loved one may mirror an aspect of ourselves that we do not accept. Therefore, if we can begin to take responsibility for our own feelings rather than blaming every difficulty upon the other, then this may help our perceptions to become truer.

Working through these kinds of patterns can be quite difficult. As an example, there have been phases in my relationship with Eleyna where we have both reacted to each other, feeling that the other one was too controlling. There was a period while we were still establishing our relationship, when Eleyna felt smothered or questioned by me, whereas in my corner, I felt powerless and rejected at the same time, feeling that I couldn't get anything right. When feeling these emotions, we struggled inwardly, trying to adjust to the new circumstances of being with each other.

But these reactions pointed towards deep fears in each one of us, fears of being abandoned and unworthy on my side, and fears that

173

she could not assert herself in the way she wanted and make things work for everybody, on her side.

Once we were able to start sharing our vulnerable feelings around these issues, we could begin to understand each other and grow closer. We had to realise that basically we wanted to care for each other rather than do harm, and so we could make adjustments to listen to each other and be more sensitive to each other's needs. While those fears were operating, it was easy for each of us to suppose that the other one did not care, and this was not true. This is just one instance of many where we have had to be very honest and frank with each other to determine the truth and learn how we can support each other better.

I am sure that such processes are important in any relationship to be healthy and well. Too often, it may be typical for people to erect inner barriers or try to push the other person away rather than face up to the feelings inside. These kinds of situations are a test for how open we are to accept love. The choice for us will be whether we decide to run away and close down, or if we can dare to be truthful and expose our vulnerability, but also to really listen to the other person.

Our relationship partners can be very important teachers. If we can acknowledge our projections and disentangle what is within ourselves from what belongs to the other, then there is much that we can learn with each other.

There may be crises that will from time to time emerge within the relationship. This will challenge the love of those involved, testing the tolerance and dedication of one to the other. The challenge may come through difficult circumstances that arise or perhaps external people who become involved. Too often, relationships may split up when really there were opportunities for learning and for deepening one's capacity to love.

A relationship that is very safe and dependable may not actually be providing learning for the love of the people involved. By going over familiar ground with each other, the spark of the relationship may diminish. Situations may arise to challenge the relationship to become once more a growing space for the people concerned. If these challenges are not met, then opportunities may be lost. The people involved may lose interest in each other and not want to be together any more.

Our souls do not want us to be idle. Therefore, it is often through crises in relationships that people will grow most. The challenge for us in these situations will be that we could try to keep our hearts open so while we face these situations, our capacity to love can increase. If we feel pain and our hearts are open, then we will also become aware of the pain suffered by others. Our caring and compassion can reach out and we will feel more connected to all various life forms around us. With this feeling of connection, there will be openness to greater love and peace. If, on the other hand, our hearts close, then we are likely to feel bitterness and resentment at what has happened to us and therefore respond very negatively. Then we will not really be able to appreciate our partner's feelings. We will be locked in our own little world.

There is much for us to learn concerning love. Because of this, our personal challenges may become greater as we go further along our path. Our soul wants to be strong, so that we can keep our hearts open, even in the face of adversity.

Learning together with another person, we have to build up the capacity to trust. Both partners need to contribute to this. Trust is built upon many experiences where both partners in turn feel supported by the other, perhaps in situations where each may not expect to be supported. When someone is loved by another, in a way which that person doubts is possible, and that person really lets the love in, then the healing and learning can be tremendous.

It does not need a crisis for love to grow in a relationship. Love can flourish during peaceful and stable times. The act of working together or joining together in some mutual activity can be very strengthening for a love bond. When the hearts are open, this kind of sharing can help substantially to move a relationship forward.

Some people are lonely and don't believe that they are capable of forming a relationship. What we believe about ourselves tends to become the truth of our experience even if, really, this is not the potential of who we could be. Within each one of us there is a wellspring of love, and therefore everyone could form relationships where there is love and fulfilment. For some of us though, that pathway may be harder than for others. But our souls do not incarnate without there being many opportunities for us to learn about love. What we do about those opportunities though, is up to us. If we can believe that we could form loving relationships, and gain affirmation that this is so from our families, partners and friends, then this will help build our confidence.

Once again, the art of forming loving relationships is connected with how honest we are with ourselves, and how much we can listen to our inner truth. When we can consciously begin to sort out our confusions sufficiently so that we can become still and listen, then we may receive genuine guidance to help us.

As we listen to our heart, we may first need to acknowledge feelings of pain and hurt from the wounds and memories of occasions when we have not felt loved. Yet, underneath this, if we have faith and we persevere, there will be love.

It is important in a relationship that we are compatible with our partner, that there are shared interests and goals that can form a firm foundation for the relationship. People may need to listen so that they know what they really want, so that they will be ready for a partner with whom they can be compatible. There may be a need to resolve much confusion first. Hence, while we are not in contact with our essential selves, the partners we choose may not be those that are most suited to us.

If, for instance, we are operating with sub-conscious drives telling us that we are not loveable, that we only get hurt in a relationship, or that nobody really wants us, then we will live out relationships where those drives become a reality. We will attract people to us who will fulfil our inner expectations, and we will tend to trigger reactions in those people that will reinforce our beliefs.

I think that it may be obvious from reading some of the life stories in this book how many of those people have experienced adverse reactions and difficulties in their primary relationships. From the point in their lives where they have been able to learn about themselves more deeply and to come to terms with inner confusion they may have been carrying, then this has tended to make a difference. Relationships that did not serve those people have tended to end and new relationships have been happier.

When the time is right though, people may come into our life that can help us to learn about love. As we become more Spiritually attuned, we may be drawn to that person with whom we already have a deep soul connection. That is not to say that relating with this person will be necessarily easy. We may have a lot to learn with that person, and there may be many lessons and inner difficulties that we need to work through with them. Such a relationship will not be without its purpose, but ultimately, if we are courageous with our heart, it may be very rewarding.

Chapter 21 -

David

Background

When I first met David, I was very impressed by his appearance. He was immaculately dressed and clean-shaven, not a hair out of place. In his manner, I detected a wilful determination, but this contrasted with his eyes, which at times expressed a soft and sad vulnerability. He was an insurance salesman and I could tell that he would be good at his job.

David's main passion in life was Transcendental Meditation. He practised its techniques daily and was convinced of its worth as a solution to the problems of our human race and as a means for individuals to attain enlightenment. Often, when he came to visit me, he would appear to be crusading, telling me stories about the value of TM and how, if enough people would practise it, then it could change the world. He tried to enlist my help, and I must say that eventually I did enrol upon a course to learn TM and found it useful as a tool to help me go within.

It was because of the problems he was having connected to the relationship he had with his second wife that David came to me as a client. In his own mind, he perceived his wife to be his soul mate and felt enormously frustrated that she did not seem to share this perception or his passion for TM. For some years the marriage had appeared to go reasonably well, but had then deteriorated and now she refused to have any sexual contact with him.

The description David gave of his wife seemed to indicate a woman whose interests consisted of her job, friends and material security and that was about all. Yet for David, he sensed that there was a deeper level to her being and their potential relationship together that she was not expressing. But, as much as he tried to change her and awaken her to this, she seemed to become ever more resentful and distant.

David tried everything he could to win her over. His work with me became long term. We explored numerous past lives where David felt that he had known his second wife before. On occasions, he would inform me of some subtle experiences connected to his inner consciousness that for him were indicative that he may be approaching enlightenment. However, concurrent with this, the problems in his relationship appeared to worsen. I tried to encourage him to let her go, but he would not give up. In the way he interacted with her, it felt as though they were engaged in a battle of wills.

I feel though that David was learning. His wish to have a loving Spiritual relationship with his wife was quite sincere. The basic feeling he appeared to convey towards her was caring and so he was prepared to make sacrifices for her. Gradually, in my own interpretation of his process, he shifted from a position where I felt that he was trying to control her and make her be like him, to a stance where he was much more passive. With this approach, he behaved in a more detached manner, being kind and gentle towards her, but allowing the moves in the relationship to come from her. To do this was not easy for him, and as she continued to reject him, he suffered a lot. But he was steadfast and continued to do what he felt he could do to support her however much she reacted towards him.

Although in the end, the relationship failed and he separated from her, I feel that David learned a lot from his experiences with her to help him with his 'pursuit of love'. As a result, his relationships since then have been more flexible and fulfilling.

Throughout my work with him, I have regarded David as a man of integrity and a friend. Here, in what follows is his story.

David's story

As I have tried to remember my childhood, my first thoughts have been about how blessed I have been to have such good parents. My father was a loyal man devoted to his work, but also he seemed to love my mother. His main weakness seemed to be his difficulty in expressing his feelings, a trait, which unfortunately, I think I copied. I remember once our family watching a sad film, and my dad was coughing and pushing back the tears. He wouldn't allow them to show. His own dad was a bit Victorian so I suppose that this trait had come down through the generations.

My mother was a very special person; she had so much unconditional love for my brother and I, that even now, I still feel tremendous gratitude thinking about her. My impression is that she was always there for me, whatever my needs. She would comfort me if I were sad or lonely. I adored her, felt safe with her and was very devoted to her. She could do no wrong in my eyes. Looking back on it, I realise now that this level of attachment to her has actually caused me problems. One practical problem came about because she did everything for us, cooking, washing up, etc. Hence, when I was older and married, I didn't know anything about housework, much to my wife's dismay.

Many times during my childhood, I felt lonely, not really feeling that I fitted in and I lacked confidence. Making friends at school was difficult for me, and got worse as I progressed to secondary school. I struggled to feel adequate enough to meet other people's expectations of me.

One very awkward memory, that I carry from when I was young, was being asked by my father to look after a rabbit that had just been born. My father kept rabbits and was very knowledgeable about them. I was asked to keep it warm and then he left me to it. Trying to please my father, I diligently kept it on a woollen jumper while it basked in the heat of the fire. When it tried to get away from the fire, I kept returning it and did not realise that it was actually overheating. Then, by the time that my father returned, the poor thing had blisters and died. This whole incident affected me greatly. I felt that I had let my father down and felt very guilty for having made such a dreadful mistake.

Another incident that affected me very much took place when I was 13- 14 years old. At that time, I had a close friend whose name was Michael. I felt very insecure about being with other

180

children and so I was very dependent upon Michael. Once we were on a school trip in Switzerland, far away from my family. On the second day, Michael announced to me that he didn't want to be friends with me anymore and asked me to go away. I felt very rejected because I had tried very hard to be his friend and now he didn't want me.

This pattern where I would reach out to try and be close to someone and then find that they were not interested in me would be one that would recur in my life several times.

Although I admired my father very much, he was often very busy with his work as a milkman and therefore was largely absent from my life. Consequently, when I was about 11, I was quite grateful to be befriended by a man who wanted to spend time with me. One day he suggested that we go out into the countryside. The sun was shining and I felt relaxed lying under the sun. Soon though, he talked me into taking out my penis, while he took out his, and then proceeded to get me to play with his. I got quite upset at this, believing it to be wrong. Despite his reassurances, I stopped seeing him and he disappeared from my life. Somehow, I couldn't tell anyone because I felt stupid that he had taken me in like that. I just wanted to forget it.

As my teenage years progressed, I became more confident. My friend and I started roller-skating and that enabled us to start having girl friends. I remember once taking a girl home and feeling so elated afterwards as though I had just climbed Mt Everest or something. I was very determined to lose my virginity, but it was not until my 21st birthday 'do' in the Lake District that I managed to achieve this. After slightly too much alcohol, I went back to the tent with a girl who turned out to be much more experienced than I was. Allowing her to take control, we had intercourse. A few months later, she informed me that she was pregnant. Even though I was rather immature, I still felt a keen sense of responsibility. The only option seemed to be for us to get married. Inside, I tried to convince myself that we would have got married anyway. The wedding was a registry office service, after which we went for a game of tennis. So, there I was, married with a baby and a mortgage. I had to grow up fast and it was quite hard work. During the day, I worked as a gas fitter and then at night, I was on emergency call for my job and helping with the baby.

Soon we had a second child, another daughter. As much as my daughters and wife brought me pleasure, I felt pressures growing inside of me and I could not love them as much as I wanted. Working as a gas fitter, I struggled to feel competent and could not cope with it very well. Because of these difficulties, I made a radical change and decided to become an insurance agent instead. But this meant further adjustments and learning, as I tried to make a good impression in my new work place. In addition, our second daughter did not sleep well, and so I was becoming very tired.

The stress in my life was mounting. However, I tried to press on regardless, not really realising at the time how serious it was becoming.

Then my mother took ill and the Doctor at the hospital informed my father and I that she was dying of lung cancer. This was a massive shock and the first time I had ever had to deal with anyone dying. Emotionally, I felt numb. I had been so used to bottling up my feelings that I didn't know what else to do. My father didn't want to face up to the situation, so I had to do a lot of the caring. Her condition got worse and so they agreed to take her into a nursing home. It was here that she died.

The most shocking experience for me happened when we went to give our last respects. As the curtains went back, there was the body of my mother. Her face was towards us with her eyes wide open and they seemed to be glaring straight at us. As this was the first body that I'd ever seen, the shock was too much for me. Still, I was not able to cry and release the pain I was feeling.

Instead of having a space to deal with my grief, I was thrust into a demanding situation at work. There had been floods in the area and so I was working until midnight most nights filling out claim forms and report forms for my customers. Because I was conscientious, I didn't want to let anyone down.

Then, one evening at 1.30 am, I got up to help my daughter who was crying and found that my right side was completely numb. My speech was slurred as if I was drunk. Immediately, I feared that I'd had a stroke. However, the Doctor reassured me that I was suffering from nervous exhaustion and prescribed Valium.

This crisis marked a turning point in my life. Inside, I felt a mess and I was hardly coping with any aspect of my life. I needed help.

The brother of my wife suggested T.M. (Transcendental Meditation) and I decided to try it. Going to the first session of this, I was very nervous. My confidence had sunk so low that I doubted whether I could do it. I had an attack of Hay Fever, which I recognised as a sign of emotional stress.

Anyway, I was given a sound called a mantra, and as I tried to meditate for the first time, I remember feeling myself relaxing, feeling greatly relieved that I was able to do it. There was a wonderful sense of peace, a feeling of coming home. I knew that I had found something very important for me. Before the session had finished, my hay fever had disappeared and I came out feeling very elated. This was the beginning of my Spiritual path.

When I was a child, my mother had taken me to Sunday school, but I did not understand or accept what they were talking about. I became an atheist. I had found no meaning in life. Learning T.M. changed all that. As I was able to experience some inner peace, this awakened in me an interest to learn the truth about life. I discovered through books about Karma and reincarnation and developed a thirst for inner knowledge.

Soon, I was feeling much better. The meditation gave me both peace and energy. Within four weeks, I was able to stop taking Valium. Emotionally, I was less snappy with the children. Even though I was not sleeping more, I felt less tired. Even at work, my performance began to improve. Whereas before, I had been on the verge of being given the sack, now I could feel more secure and do my job well.

I became very dedicated to T.M. and enthusiastic for others to learn it. After six months, I learnt the more advanced programme called the 'Sidhi's', that included 'yogic flying'. I was told that this programme would help me to release stress and evolve more quickly. Along this track, my life continued quite smoothly until 1982 when I was 32.

In retrospect, I do not believe that my first wife and I deeply loved each other. We had been thrust together at a time when I was still immature and not really knowing what I wanted in life. But during our marriage we tolerated and accepted each other and I had no reason to suppose that anything was wrong. However, one day, I was told that my wife was having an affair with a Doctor friend of ours. When I confronted her with this, she had to admit it and I felt devastated. My first thought was of my two daughters and how it would affect them. Without being able to control my feelings, I broke down crying. Through her death, my mother had left me, and now this. I am glad that I had the T.M. to help me, otherwise I don't know how I would have coped.

Something about this experience greatly troubled me. It felt like a disaster in my life. Through my experiences of T.M., I had expected that my life would continue to get better, but my marriage breaking up did not feel like this. There had to be a reason for it. I was not going to give up my positive beliefs.

My wife went to live in a flat with the Doctor. Meanwhile, I resolved to do my best to look after the children when they came to see me, for I did not want them to suffer. Inside though, I felt lonely and betrayed. I wanted someone to love, someone who would love and appreciate me. I could not escape from this feeling of loss connected to both my wife and my mother.

I remembered when I was in the hospital visiting my mother and I had picked up a leaflet. There was one paragraph in this leaflet that seemed to stand out from the rest, as if it was a message for me. It talked about a carpet weaver who laboured all day on the back of a carpet, but only when it was finished and he could turn it over, could he see the fruits of his labour. This chapter indicated to me that I was not ready to see the full picture yet. I needed to let my life unfold further.

One evening, I attended a meditation evening at a friend's house and I was very mindful of the wish and intention inside of me to find someone with whom I could share love. In the rest period after the meditation, I affirmed this. The next day, I met the woman who was to become my second wife.

We dated and I could feel myself falling in love. However, when she met my two daughters, she left saying that she couldn't share me, even with my children. What a difficult situation! Should I release the woman whom I loved or should I forsake my daughters? The urge for love in me was strong and passionate. Therefore I decided to try and talk to her and suggested that I could see my kids on Saturday, while she was at work. She agreed with my proposal and so we got back together again.

In 1983, we got married. It was a glorious church affair, complete with bagpipes and Rolls Royce. We honeymooned in Sorento, Italy. It was very romantic and I felt that all my dreams had come true. Still doing my meditation and being in love proved to be an unbeatable combination. My work went from strength to strength. Materially, we were very well off, and this seemed to please her. We would have three holidays a year, two new cars a year, super house etc. For ten years we seemed to have a wonderful marriage.

A tragic event occurred in her life though when her uncle died. She had not spoken to her father for fifteen years, having had a very traumatic relationship with him, and her uncle had been like a father to her. The shock of this loss appeared to affect her personality and her attitude towards me.

There was anger in her and it felt as though she was blaming me for everything. Desperately, I tried to reassure myself that it was just pent up emotions relating to her father that she was now expressing. However, she did not seem to see it that way.

It was very painful for me to sense distance in our relationship. Inside, I had developed this strong belief that she was my soul mate and that we needed to share our lives together on all levels.

She stopped meditating and having sex with me and seemed only interested in material things. I considered this as some sort of test for me and tried all sorts of approaches to try to win her over and show her where she was going wrong. In my opinion, she needed counselling and to embrace a much more Spiritual way of life. If she did this, I was convinced that she would realise how much we were meant to be together and we would be happy.

Around this time, I decided to lead by example and seek therapy myself and that was when I started working with Paul. During our work, I went through a number of past life experiences. With most of these I felt that I was linked very closely with my second wife. There appeared to be a pattern where very often, I had been separated from the one I loved at a crucial time when I did not want it. Through these experiences, I gained much understanding of our relationship, but also the relationship with my first wife and the reason it needed to end in the way it did. There was much grief that poured out of me in these sessions. I wanted so much to preserve the relationship I shared with my second wife, for I did not want to lose her again.

As much as I tried to make her do what I wanted though, the more she resisted. She refused counselling and showed no interest in Spiritual matters and most of the time did not even want to speak with me.

My response to this was to try even harder. I attempted to keep my thoughts very pure in her direction. With my sexuality, I tried to find ways of being so that even though she was not having sex with me, I would remain faithful to her and be ready if we could resume contact on that level. However kind and sensitive I tried to be to her, she only seemed to be rude and abusive in return.

I allowed myself to soak up her anger without retaliating, hoping that eventually, it would diminish. But things only got worse. In the evenings she went out with the girls and drank Bacardi. Usually then on the following morning she would precipitate an argument. She kept on saying that she wanted a divorce from me but I didn't listen.

186

Over this time I had been losing weight, I suppose, as a result of the stress I was experiencing. There were also other changes though. I was becoming less materialistic and more concerned with living my life as purely as I could on all levels.

Consequently, it is perhaps not a surprise that in 1995, I lost my job and career. Hence, whereas in the early years of our marriage I had been the main wage earner, now she had to support me. Quickly, she got fed up, especially as her job was improving. She did not want to spend her money on me.

One day during a confrontation, I could hold my own anger in no longer. Instead of being passive, I challenged what she said. She was furious, stomping around like a dragon. As we kept going at each other, I thought she was going to burst. At one moment she grabbed a knife, so I took hold of her wrist and we jostled. Finally, I knocked the knife out of her hand and upended her. She got up and stormed out of the house. Shaken, I felt I had no choice but to ring the police and I asked them to put it on record. This was the end. I felt I had no option but to seek a divorce. Having tried for what felt long enough, I had to regain some happiness.

For such a long time I had been putting energy into a relationship where I got nothing in return, but I kept focussed on her because I really believed that she was my soul mate. Now I needed time to recover, for my self-esteem had been badly savaged. Although part of me wanted another relationship, a larger portion of me said 'no'.

There was one young woman who helped me. As I entered into a friendship with her that was purely platonic, it helped me to remember how enjoyable a relationship could be.

Inside, I sensed that I was holding onto a lot of unprocessed emotions including grief. I felt that I had done my best with my second wife, even if she did not respond to me. Over time there were a lot of tears that I shed. I decided to try some drama therapy.

187

When a partner acted out the role of my wife, I felt a huge amount of anger rising up, which I vented on my partner. I had to apologise to her afterwards, but she understood. In another inner process, I contacted my mother and was quite surprised to find that I was angry with her too for leaving me at such a delicate time. I felt the presence of my mother replying to me and telling me that she was hurting and that her time was up. She challenged me by suggesting that I would not have got stronger if she had stayed around.

As I pondered on this I realised that I was strong and much more living a life true to my essential self than I had been all those years ago. I could forgive my mother now, and even begin to appreciate the gifts that my mother and two wives had brought into my life.

In a further stage of this process, I also inwardly contacted my father who had seemed to hit the bottle once my mother died and he was not there for me. In listening to him, I sensed him telling me that he had fallen to pieces when mother died and didn't know how to cope with her loss. As I sensed his vulnerability, my anger towards him dissipated and I was able to forgive him too.

The question, which remained for me, was that if I could not get the love I needed from these people, then where was it to come from? As I asked this question, I saw in my mind's eye, a large pair of golden hands open and welcome me and I knew that it was the presence of God. This whole experience had a profound effect upon me and transformed my attitude towards life. My meditations became deeper and I felt my heart expanding.

Through these inner processes and the release of grief over time, I felt that I had let go of the hurt and pain I had carried connected to my second wife. Because I felt more settled in relationship to her, I felt I could move on.

There was a strong yearning in me to love somebody, and it was at this time that two women came into my life. Both these women were engaging in the same meditation practice as me and so I felt a Spiritual compatibility with them that I had not felt with my previous female companions. With the older one I developed a friendship where I felt able to express my feelings and emotions much more fully than I had been able to do before.

To help my body to regain its balance, I tried Herbal medicine, and visited a Maharishi Ayuravedic doctor who advised me to undertake a special diet. This really helped me, as for years I had suffered from constipation and now this became easier. Other steps which I made, included getting baptised in the church. By doing this I enjoyed an increased period of worship with Christ. Also I explored my sexuality by learning about tantra, and felt this to be a more Spiritual way of utilising sexual energies.

Previously with my wife, it had been very difficult to communicate with her. I wanted to express my feelings but either she was not receptive or I did not know how to reach her. Now I felt a great desire to communicate my feelings more intimately and honestly. With my friend, the younger of the two women, I was able to attain that. She was only half my age but I felt a closeness with her that I had never felt with any female before. It was wonderful. We started a relationship.

A month or so later, she told me that a young man of her own age wanted to enter a relationship with her and she wanted it too. How could I respond? I felt a surge of unconditional love and said to her that I would always love her wherever she was and whomever she was with and I offered to give her my blessings. She broke down and cried and it was the first time I had seen her cry. Although I felt gutted that she had not chosen me, I had to let her go. I tried to maintain a positive outlook.

Even though she was involved in another relationship, my love for her continued to grow. I felt drawn to work again with Paul and found that she featured in a past life experience where she was the woman I loved. Sadly she was killed in front of my eyes but I pledged to always love her.

After some months, her relationship with the young man broke down and I felt great desire that she may get together with me. In the meantime, I had been enjoying my friendship with my older woman friend and gaining a new outlook about the nature of relationships. Some words from Barry Long made me feel that I needed to experience the divine in relationship to any woman that I loved and I felt myself starting to do this.

I am still full of hope that my young friend is the love of my life and that we may form a relationship where we can celebrate that. I do not know if she wants that too but we are very close and seem to be improving. Time will tell if we can get back together again.

I feel that I have come a long way during the years. For many years, I have endeavoured to experience bliss and cosmic consciousness through my meditation practise, but I have realised that I have had my own lessons to learn so I could progress. My main drive is still to have an intimate and loving relationship with a woman and I do experience loneliness to be on my own. However, I feel at the same time that my life is much richer and fuller now and I am grateful for all the experiences that I have had.

Chapter 22 -

Power and Receptivity

It is very important for us, psychologically, to feel that we can direct and mould our lives, that we can create a life to a certain extent that we want. If we do not feel the capacity to do this, then it can leave us with terrible feelings of impotency and powerlessness. It is a basic need, which we all have, to assert ourselves. However, to compliment this, we also have the need to allow the process of life to unfold for us and this is more passive. In this mode, we receive inspiration and creativity, and we can be receptive to Spiritual help.

Both of these modes of operating are important for us. They traditionally correspond to the principles of the masculine and feminine, active and receptive, outward and inward. When these qualities can be functioning in harmony with each other in our actions, then we will be in balance.

As souls, we usually come into incarnation with one of these qualities tending to be more dominant than the other one. We need to learn how we can best utilise the more dominant quality as a constructive characteristic in our lives. From there we may be tested to discover how we can accommodate the complimentary quality so that it has its place in our behaviour as well.

In David's case, he was clearly born with strong masculine qualities that he was able to develop. In becoming successful in the Insurance business, he needed to express initiative, assertiveness, vision and other active characteristics. He tried to make his life successful through the forcefulness of his own will. Unfortunately, the universe was not going to let him achieve his aims by this means alone.

From an early age, he loved and adored his mother and later loved women. To me, this indicated his attraction to the feminine principle. But in adoring his mother and other women at a distance, he was externalising a quality, which he needed to learn to embody in his Self.

After his mother died, and he suffered his subsequent mental breakdown, David began to meditate. This, I feel was the first step. However, I feel that his most significant transformations came about through the trials he endured connected to his second wife.

Here was a woman who appears to have developed her masculine side at least as much as David. She wanted things to be on her terms and no other way. For David to try to communicate to her using his masculine qualities was like going into battle. He couldn't get through to her at all. In desperation, he began to change his approach, becoming more passive and allowing, waiting for her to make moves, and he tried to be patient and loving with her. By doing this, he hoped that she would change. She still wasn't interested. Consequently, when she became violent, the only thing he could do was to let go. For a man like David who had his will and heart set so much upon wanting her to be his soul mate and for her to live happily with him, this must have been a very difficult decision. He had to surrender what he wanted.

But as he recovered from the loss of his second wife, David went through various healing processes and had an intense inner experience that it was the Divine Will that mattered, not his own. If he was true to himself but surrendered to the will of the universe rather than insisting that life turn out according to his will, then he could be happy. I believe that he was learning his lessons. Since then, I think that he has felt much more peace within himself.

It is not always the case that men will develop masculine qualities most strongly or women the feminine qualities. As with David's second wife, our physical bodies are only one factor in determining which of these two modes of being will be most strongly expressed. Other factors include our parents, who as models can be very influential, but we will also be born with a given temperament that we need to learn to manage.

People developing their more masculine qualities will want to try to direct and control any situation in which they find themselves. It may be very frightening then for these people if a situation, which feels important to them, appears to be moving out of their control. People who want control may go about doing all kinds of things with their will, sometimes with little sensitivity or regard for others. I have noticed in my own life, that I have on occasions, wanted to control a situation because I have been afraid that if I did not, then I would not get what I want, and even that people may go against me. Usually these fears were without foundation and I made myself very tense by trying to hold on and do everything myself.

To overcome these fears, people developing their masculine qualities need to learn to trust. Therefore, by trusting in others and trusting in the universe to support them, they can do what they can and then let others and the universe do the rest. However, this journey of learning trust can be a very long and painful one until the person concerned can learn to reach out and embrace help.

When people develop their feminine qualities, they feel receptive, vulnerable and sensitive. They want to form unions and have contact with others. Mostly, they want to be loved, just for being who they are. Sadly, those developing masculine qualities can often abuse these people and they may feel defenceless to be able to do anything about it. They may feel as victims that they have to do what that other person wants because they feel that they need to surrender their own personal wishes to the will of the greater whole. This situation may prompt them to build up a tremendous anger towards those who are abusing them until they feel that they have to lash out in order to gain their freedom.

People who embody dominant feminine qualities need to learn to be assertive, that they have the same rights as anyone else. They need to take care that their actions are not determined by the reactions that they feel inside towards those who may have abused them. Otherwise, they may become abusive towards others themselves, seeking revenge upon those who have hurt them. They may even seek to deny and suppress that soft and sensitive nature that is so precious to them. Thus the victim can become the perpetrator of violence and abuse.

What they need to do is to sense truly what is right for them and to move forward as a loving individual according to their own instincts and feel the strength that this is OK. They need to acknowledge that they have a unique place in the scheme of things and that this place for them needs to be honoured and protected with integrity. When they stand with others, they have equal importance and a need to be respected.

Again, this journey can be long and painful and along the way there may be the need to learn much forgiveness for self and others.

Chapter 23 -
Sexuality and Intimacy

Sometimes, when I can gain a perspective on it, I notice how much I have changed since I met Eleyna. She is a person with strong emotions. However much she tries, she cannot hide her feelings from me, even when she wants to do so. Mostly though, she has wanted to be very open with me. She has also wanted to be close, physically and in other ways too.

From my past I have been used to having my own space, including when I slept. Eleyna though has wanted to feel me with her. In the early stages of our relationship, this was quite a challenge for me.

At night time, I would huddle in my corner of the bed with bedclothes tightly wrapped around me, just like I had always done. But she didn't want this. On occasions she would touch me when I wanted to sleep, and I became tense, telling myself that I couldn't relax. It felt like an intrusion inside my boundaries, and yet, I wanted to experience greater closeness and connectedness with her.

Gradually I experimented and opened myself to her contact. It felt like opening to a new level of trust that I had not experienced before. After a while, I could sleep with her holding me. I felt safe with her. But also, by letting her be so close, I was involving myself with her rather than being detached. In my life until this point, I feel that I had been detaching myself from others, keeping a distance. But now, by letting her close, life mattered more, my life with her involved me, so that with my emotions also I could not be detached.

Allowing Eleyna close to me physically was a symbol of allowing more openness and intimacy in my life. Doing this had quite an effect upon me. It meant, especially in relationship to her, that I would react emotionally very strongly to our various interactions with either pain or pleasure, depending upon what was going on between us. I felt less stable, but more alive. The whole process, I believe has been extremely beneficial for me and helped me to 'incarnate' much more fully than before. It has also led me to feel other people's feelings more strongly and keenly as well, not just Eleyna.

I believe in the same way that I have experienced allowing myself to love and be close to Eleyna , the experience of being close and intimate with another human being can be beneficial for all of us. However, it is a potentially very challenging path too. Because our emotions well up so strongly when we are close to another human being, we will be confronted with our patterns, fears and weaknesses more intensely as well. So, this experience could be very loving and supportive of our life process, or otherwise damaging, depending upon how we and our partners handle it.

With Eleyna, I greatly appreciated her gentleness and patience with regards how close I was prepared to allow her. Slowly I began to let her into my space, and she welcomed me. Because she did not criticise me, I felt supported to make these steps at my own pace. As I allowed myself to be closer to her physically, I bonded with her more closely on other levels too.

Our openness to intimacy is very linked to our expression of sexuality. This is one area of our being where much guilt may be stored. When we open to another person sexually, we naturally want to give ourselves to that person and there is a merging of energies. It feels exciting for us to be intimate and free with that other person. We reveal ourselves in a way that we normally would not do. When our sexual urges are engaging in combination with our heart, then there is the urge to create a union with that other person and a loving inner home together.

These natural inclinations can be disturbed by our inner beliefs, what we think about ourselves and how we feel about ourselves in relationship to that other person.

When we interact with another sexually, we expose our physical bodies. If we do not like some aspect of our bodies or if we are afraid that our sexual partner may not like it, then this may hinder us from surrendering completely to the sexual act. We may then wonder if we are performing well enough for that other person to like us. Our feelings can be very sensitive around sex.

On an emotional level if we fear that the other person may not like us, especially if they got to know us too closely, we may try to block our true feelings and put on some sort of act for our partner. We may be afraid that we could be hurt or rejected by the other person.

Our responses to these fears may be to shut down our heart so we concentrate only on the physical aspect of sex. We may try to dominate our partner or be prepared to engage in sex only in the way that feels safe to us, and thereby not lose control. By making our partners do what we want, we may feel that we can possess them and make them how we want them to be. Otherwise, we may also be inclined to withdraw from sex altogether because we are afraid of what emotions from within may be stirred. We may fear that if we have a sexual interaction with someone, then this may give that person power over us and we may not trust that we can defend ourselves.

While we are interacting sexually with another, we will be acutely aware of that other person's feelings and their thoughts towards us. Of course, we may be so caught up in our own fears and insecurities that we don't notice much about the other person. But if the other person tries to project thoughts and feelings that are not true, then we will sense that mixed message. We will also know when we are not being honest to that other person regarding our own thoughts and feelings, and because of the sensitivities involved, this can provoke much confusion, hurt and guilt.

By trying to withhold our true feelings or by being afraid to admit them, sexual interactions can feel to be a very empty experience. If our partner experiences this emptiness, then he or she may withdraw. This can confirm our worst fears and shake our doubts about our self-worth to the core.

People can easily feel rejected if they feel attracted to someone and that other person does not want them sexually. This was a challenge for David in the relationship with his second wife. I believe that for David, it has been one of the main driving forces in his life to search for and find a fulfilling sexual relationship. It was when his second wife refused to have sex with him that David came to me seeking therapy. David tried very hard not to be discouraged. He wished to remain 'true' to his wife sexually, in case she changed her mind and wanted him again. He tried all he could to 'win' her. In the meantime, David tried various forms of masturbation so that he would not be totally suppressing his sexual life. It was very hard for him.

When we do have a sexual relationship, the challenge for us is to try to be honest with our feelings and thoughts and be prepared to learn with each other in a balanced giving and receiving manner. This way, sex can be very healing, and over time, many barriers may inwardly be removed, helping each participant gain greater acceptance of the other and self-acceptance. By being open to our emotions during our sexual experiences, we may be able to have adventures exploring various reaches of our inner psyche and learn much about ourselves. However, we need to be prepared that the places within us where we visit may stimulate feelings and memories that incline us to feel very vulnerable. To be able to share mutually of these things with our partner may bring trust and closeness into a relationship.

There may be various opportunities for us in our lives to experience sexually healing interactions. Any experience of this nature, which serves to open us more fully to an appreciation and acceptance of our being will be healing. Such experiences may not only be confined to those that we can attain with our long term partner, but can arise at various stages of our lives, when we need that help. It is up to us whether or not we take up these opportunities. For some of us, there may be many people with whom we could have satisfying sexual relationships during the course of our lives. However, for others, it may feel important to build up that trust, safety and commitment with one person only.

198

When we can continue to generate loving and creative sexual experiences with our long-term partners, this can give us much strength and integrity that allows power and vibrancy into our lives.

For us to allow our sexual interactions to be a fulfilling experience over time, we need to care for that other human being who is our partner. We need to be tolerant and patient to build up a rapport with each other. To engage in sex is like dancing with our partner - we need to be very much attuned to our partner so that we can both enjoy the pleasure and harmony that is possible.

When we care about our partners, our sexual relationships can help teach us about love and can enable us to grow more fully from inside to express ourselves. If we feel we cannot share our feelings honestly and blend our energies in a balanced and caring way with our partner, then sexual experiences will only serve to make us feel isolated and lonely. We will feel empty and sex will be like a craving for something which we do not have.

Our sexual relationships can form a very fundamental part of our life. But they can easily be disturbed if our energies get drawn away to someone else.If we have an 'affair with someone else, or even if fantasise about having such an affair in our minds, then this can have a drastic effect upon the sexual relationship that we share with our existing partner. For most of us, we instinctively can only build a substantial relationship, especially if it has a sexual element, with one person at a time. Therefore, if we spread ourselves, even in our mind, to seek satisfaction with more than one person, then this can result in inner conflicts of loyalty and feelings of guilt. This may also manifest in problems associated with the physical side of expressing our sexuality.

On the other side though, if we have stored negative feelings towards our partner, without working these through, then this may affect our openness to sharing a sexual relationship with that person. If we feel that our partner is not open to us sexually, then this in turn may form the base from which we feel the impulse that prompts us to seek someone else.

The whole situation in the structure of a sexual relationship can be very delicate with many layers of feeling. Disturbances from the past, from previous relationships can also have an impact. Where people can be honest and vulnerable, feeling supported and able to support each other, then this may help people in such relationships to heal problems that exist. But it may not feel so easy to share about such things with complete honesty.'

In my own life, I have noticed that my sexual responsiveness can be very much influenced by how I feel about myself. When I have felt creative and in my power with my life going positively in the way that I wanted it to be, then I have felt much more responsive than the times when I have been feeling self - doubt and impotence in some situation. Sexuality is very linked to creativity, and our feeling of aliveness.

Sexually relating to another human being is an act of joining together with that person in a very intimate way. It is something for which we all yearn because we all wish to feel lovingly connected to others. This is, I believe a fundamental desire of our existence and so it is an issue on our soul pathways that we all have to face.

Chapter 24 -
Jill

Background

In the eleven years that I have known her, there are many times when I have valued my association with Jill enormously. She is someone whom I have felt to be very committed to the New Age movement, to healing and to raising awareness in general. With a wide range of interests and contacts, she has been connected to many groups and individuals, wanting to serve and help in a local and global capacity.

One of her main problems has been that there has not seemed to be enough hours in the day to fit in all the things that she has felt that she wanted to do. She has had to learn to give herself time as well as giving to all the various causes and groups to which she has been dedicated.

From close to its conception, Jill has been involved as a member of the healing group that I founded. It has been through this that I have gradually got to know her more fully and deeply.

As a personality, Jill has appeared to me as a kind-hearted, mature and dependable woman, capable of a balanced judgement even in difficult situations. She has held a responsible job as a manager of a team of Social Workers and generally, I have felt able to trust her as a woman of integrity.

Yet, as she and I have grown closer and shared more, I have come to learn that there are other sides to Jill. In an environment where she felt safe, she could be very vulnerable, expressing self-doubt and uncertainty about her abilities compared to others. She could feel lost when considering her purpose and direction.

In personal growth workshop situations, Jill could go into cathartic processes wholeheartedly. Without any resistance, she could release her emotions powerfully and be a catalyst for change within the group. Yet, at other times, she could try to relate about her thoughts of herself, and what she expressed would lack coherence, meander around and be very unfocussed.

To me, she has appeared as a woman of contrasts. When she has been operating in her strength and power, centred in her heart, Jill could be inspirational, expressing herself with vibrancy and aliveness. However, this state of being has often swung another way, where, as she has tried to analyse her state of mind, she would feel terribly weak and confused. When she has been stuck with this feeling of weakness, I have noticed how much it would fill her with despair.

Trying to cope with this weaker side of her character has driven Jill to seek numerous forms of help to try to overcome these problems. She recognises that a lot of her inner difficulties must stem from the experiences of her early childhood. As much as she has tried though, she has found that many of her difficulties are very deeply entrenched and hard to shift. Jill is not one to quit though.

In recent times, I have observed strength growing in Jill. Concurrent with this, I have felt that she has become more compassionate with herself, less hard. Her heart has been opening, and I feel that there has been a great amount of healing in her life. What follows is her story.

Jill's Story

In writing this account of my life, I find it very difficult to enter into the feelings of my experiences, especially the early ones. Although I have tried very hard to dig into these over the past 20 years or so, I still feel confused and uncertain about what was going on for me then. I sense that in my early years I gathered around me a kind of shell, which became quite impenetrable. (Interestingly, my astrological sun sign is cancer the crab.)

By adopting this shell I was able to shut out many of my experiences so that now, it is either very difficult for me to recall things, particularly my earliest experiences, or I have a very indistinct memory of them. Therefore, in order for me to understand myself in terms of the roots of my early childhood, I have had to rely on the perceptions of others. This has resulted in me gaining some very confusing and sometimes contradictory pictures of my past that has not always felt helpful to me.

It has been a pattern for me that even when I have felt a strong perception about some aspect of my being or my past, I have very easily tended to doubt it and not trust my own ability to perceive accurately and truly especially in terms of my feelings. I know that as a child, I was much criticised and I did not live in a happy home, so it is possible that my self- confidence was damaged considerably then.

Throughout my life, I have found it very difficult to believe in my own perceptions of things. I have wanted confirmation from other sources of any feeling notion that I have held. And even then, I have tended to look for other points of view that have either placed doubt on my own perception or otherwise made my own version of the truth feel less decisive. When I have tried to analyse parts of my life in my mind, I have often felt myself to be in a fog of confusion.

A good example of this is the difficulty I encountered when Paul asked me to write my "story" for Soul Pathways. The first draft was full of references to various books, tapes and other sources of "wisdom" which I felt had been sources of guidance in my life. Paul was not happy about this and wanted me to tell my own story without reference to such external sources. I found this very hard to do and kept getting "stuck". Finally Paul took it upon himself to use what I had written plus what he knows and has learnt about my life over the 10 years or so that we have known each other to write a draft. From that base, I felt enabled to complete this account of my life in my own way.

In my career, I have worked hard and attained what others may consider a responsible position in society managing a team of social workers. And yet, whilst holding that position, I have at times felt very uncertain of myself, doubting my self-worth.

I am sure that much of this insecurity stemmed from my childhood where I locked myself away from others, feeling I did not belong in my family, with nobody seeming to take much notice of me. As a child, I often used to wonder if I had been adopted, I felt so little connection with members of my family. Some years ago, after I had already undergone therapy for a considerable time, I heard a sixties song on the radio, 'A world without love'. I was driving at the time and though I had heard this song countless times before, I had to pull off the road because I was crying so much, no doubt due to feelings that I had suppressed. Hearing the song had obviously triggered memories of how I felt as a child.

I was born in 1946 just after the end of World War 2. My father had been a serviceman during the war and, after his return, took the opportunity to retrain as a teacher. I have often speculated about the effect, which the war had upon my father's mental health, because he had a very critical and physically abusive relationship towards me, often shouting at me and hitting me about the head whilst I was a child. Throughout my life until my mid-30's, I was aware of my hatred of him because of the way that he treated me. In the 20 or so years since then, through various forms of therapy, I have worked at understanding my relationship with him and have searched to try and embrace a more compassionate and understanding view of him.

My mother was less obtrusive in my life but I felt her to be largely absent due to her work as a teacher. I have a deep wish and longing that she had loved me more and embraced me as someone precious to her because as a child I did not feel that she did this. Consequently, I felt starved of love, as if nobody really cared about me.

Sometimes, at night-time I would try to shut out the sounds of my mother and father arguing, as their interactions sounded rather violent, so I never knew quite what I would wake up to in the morning. There could be an atmosphere of fear in the house, especially where my father was concerned.

I sense that there were three very significant events in my early life. These are events which I know must have affected me a lot, but about which I have no conscious memory now.

The first was a period of hospitalisation for surgery for an umbilical hernia during, I think, the second year of my life. This surgery was in the area of the third chakra, the site of our personal power.

The second was the birth of my sister soon after I had turned two years old. She and I were only informed as adults, that she is in fact my half sister and that her father was a Polish prisoner of war to whom my mother was teaching English and with whom she had an affair. This would have been during the time that my father was away at training college. I have wondered if I had any form of relationship with this Polish man or if I never met him. It is possible that the circumstances of the birth and conception of my sister contributed to the souring of the relationship between my mother and father for I sense that things were different after her birth for me.

The third event was having my hair cut when I was possibly around four years of age. In photographs of me before this, I have lovely long blond hair. I distinctly remember having my hair cut as we were on holiday in Dover with my maternal grandparents when my sister and I were taken to the hairdressers in Bobby's, a Department store in Folkestone. This was presumably the first time I had ever been to the hairdresser because I cried throughout the experience and could not be consoled. The hairdresser said that if I stopped crying, she would turn on a tap and black water would come out but even though I was curious about this (and still am!), I would not stop crying. I still have my hair in a brown paper bag after all these years.

In photographs, I seem happier and more content in the very early photos than how I appear afterwards. I do not feel that I received much love after my sister was born, feeling that my sister 'stole' the affections of my mother from me. Between my

205

father's temper and my mother's apparent lack of interest in me, I felt little space to be. Consequently I was very jealous of my sister and we shared a difficult relationship as we grew up. Regrettably, we were therefore unable to be much comfort or support for each other.

It has only been in more recent years that we have been able to speak about this and that I have discovered that she was also very unhappy during her childhood. My perception had been that she was the child who was loved and I was the one who was not. However, she did not feel loved either and she also felt rejected by me, her older sister. She tells me that I was horrible to her and there is much truth in this unfortunately.

From the age of two I had to wear glasses. Initially and for quite a long time, I wore National Health spectacles with elastoplast over one lens to try and make the other eye stronger. Sometimes I had to wear an eyeshade, which was pink on the outside and green underneath. You can imagine that when I went to school my appearance made me an object of ridicule from the other children. This only reinforced the feelings I already had of not being wanted and of not being someone who was loveable. I wonder now if in some way I may have manifested a weakness in my eyes because I did not want to 'see' what was going on around me. There was an air of secrecy within our home environment, so I often did not feel that I knew what was going on and perhaps I did not want to know.

As my mother had returned to teaching when we were both still quite small, we had to go to childminders after school which neither of us really liked. However, it is possible that, at least with some of them, we may have been looked after with more care than when with our parents. As I grew older, I wanted to spend less and less time at home in order to escape from the situation, which I perceived to be so miserable. I had a series of best friends whom I would visit, integrating myself into their families where I noticed that life could be rather different, not so much a battleground as in my family.

On one occasion I was sitting at the piano with my friend in her home, when her father came into the room. He raised his arm slightly to rest it on top of the piano while he talked. However, I flinched, expecting that he was going to hit me.

Because I did not want to listen to the endless abusive criticism from my parents, I sense that I tried to cut myself off from this but I sometimes wonder if this has affected my memory and concentration as I do seem to have problems with both of these at times.

From the age of about 12 onwards, my father rarely spoke to me unless in anger. On numerous occasions I remember passing him in the streets of our small town where he would totally ignore me or he would walk out of a room in the house if I entered. I feel that this hurt me very deeply, and it is only in recent years since undergoing therapy myself that I have been able to release some of the distress and grief I have held about this.

My relationship with my father remained difficult throughout his life. When I was a teenager, he had a mental breakdown that resulted in ECT treatment and other forms of therapy. I was hardly aware that this had happened at the time and I suppose this is an example that shows how little meaningful interaction and communication took place in our family then.

As a teenager I rebelled. Going to Grammar school, I was constantly getting myself into trouble. I was never able to meet my parent's expectations academically. From an early age I started to smoke. This was not allowed of course. When I finished school, I attended secretarial training rather than studying to be a teacher as my parents would have wanted.

By the time I was 20, I had married my husband who was 6 months older than me. We spent our honeymoon sailing to Canada, finally escaping from my parents, as I had always wanted. However, I was still to learn that we do not escape from our problems so easily but tend to carry them wherever we go.

In Canada though, I did start to make some steps towards improving my life. As a teenager, I had suffered from various health problems, which I realise now were probably due to all the stress I was under. I started attending a yoga class, even though at that time, yoga was something I had not previously heard of. I found this very helpful, possibly due to the emphasis on relaxation.

During the first two years I was in Canada I smoked very heavily, partly because cigarettes were so cheap, but then I suddenly realised what a horrible habit it was. Fortunately I was able to give it up without too much trouble and I have not smoked since.

In my career, I was employed in a number of clerical positions and managed to achieve some promotions. However, I also experienced blatant discrimination whereby men, who were very much in the minority in the organisation, were favoured for senior positions over women. I suppose that this was a seedtime for me in which I began to understand about oppression and feel a need to try and make society a better and fairer place for people to live.

Before I got together with my husband, I had been through a phase of my life where I was quite sexually promiscuous, passing in and out of a series of largely meaningless relationships, which I think were due to my feelings of low self esteem and self worth. With my husband though, it was different. We were bound together, in some ways, very closely and spent a lot of time with each other. However, from within myself, there were still many problems that I had not worked out. These affected my relationship with him.
One problem concerned communication. When I was troubled by something, I would keep it to myself. I did not place a high value upon myself and did not tend to volunteer information about my inner feelings, thinking that nobody would be interested. By doing this, I remained quite closed at times and this created distance in our relationship.

In our intimate life, I did not like being touched, finding this deeply disturbing. I suppose that this was a throwback to the abuse I suffered from my father. This problem affected the quality of our sexual life together.

From a young age I decided that I did not want to have children. I was still disturbed by the way that I had been brought up and did not want to be responsible for bringing another child into the world to suffer in any degree like I had done.

My husband and I shared decisions together and depended upon each other heavily. Our families were in England and we had little contact with them apart from one visit from each set of parents during the 4 years we spent there. We did make some friends both individually as well as together though, and I still maintain one or two of those links to this day.

In 1971, we returned to Britain. My husband was a time-served electrician having completed his apprenticeship in his father's business before we immigrated to Canada and he had worked mainly as an electrician during our time there. He thought that by returning to Britain that he could improve his education.

His father owned an electrical firm and wanted my husband and other members of the family to join him as partners in the business, to which we agreed, in what we expected to be an interim measure. My secretarial skills were also needed, as there was insufficient cash flow in the business to afford to employ someone else. Consequently, we both found ourselves thrust into working full-time for this very demanding business, living and working together even more closely than before.

Although, initially, my husband had not wanted children either, by this stage he very much wanted to have a child as so many of our friends and work colleagues had young families. Although I still had reservations about myself in the role of mother, I felt that this change in our lives was the time to try for a child and our daughter Victoria was born in 1972.

Being a mother to Victoria placed me in a dilemma. I did not want to be a working mother where I would be physically and emotionally absent from Victoria in a similar way to how my mother had been with me. On the other hand, I was under intense pressure to continue my work with the family business. To be able to accommodate both these needs, I would work at night or at other hours when Victoria would not need me. Thus I tried to place Victoria's needs first. This arrangement though did place a strain upon my marriage and produced a lot of unhappiness.

1980 was a watershed year for me, a year in which most of the structures of my early life fell apart. So many traumas occurred during this year that I am amazed that I managed to get through all the various events with my sanity intact.

First, my father in law died, leaving a business with six shops and 30 employees in the hands of my husband to sort out. Then I became ill. Within a month of my father in law dying, my own father died. After several more weeks, it was discovered that I had had an ectopic pregnancy which necessitated surgery and then, one day whist I was still in hospital, my husband came to visit me and informed me that he had begun a relationship with one of the employees from the business. Although I did not realise it at the time, this signalled the end of our marriage.

It was only in the last months of his life that I found that I was able to talk to my father a little more. He wanted to spend time with Victoria, my daughter, who was a young girl then. In fact, strangely enough, the very last time I saw him was probably one of the best days I ever spent in his company. However, when he died, I felt it to be more of a relief, or even a release, than anything else. I think that both my mother and sister felt this also and it was almost as if we had been locked in some karmic situation with him that had ended with his, very sudden and unexpected, death. It was also from this time on that my relationship with both my mother and sister started to improve.

From the time I lived in Canada, I had been very concerned to preserve my health. My father and two of his sisters had suffered from mental illness, and I did not want to follow in their footsteps, so my preoccupation with health was not only the physical aspect of being, but also mental and emotional and later, Spiritual.

Some years before my father died, my mother had become interested in other religions, in past lives and spiritual matters and in the life of Edgar Cayce, the healer, in particular. She introduced me to some of these ideas, which I suppose was the start of what has become a lifelong interest for us both. She has also been very generous, supporting me in various ways, particularly following the break up of my marriage, to enable me to get my life back together and for many years we went on holiday together, mainly to France, which she loves, but to other places also. Regrettably, she now feels unable to go on such journeys any longer.

As a result of the breakdown in my marriage, I sought help firstly from the Samaritans and then from a marriage guidance counsellor. I desperately needed to sort myself out. My husband refused to engage in this process with me. Although I discussed with him the need to be as honest as we could with Victoria who was then aged 7, he told her that the reason for our separation was that he was leaving home so that he could live closer to the business. I then found it difficult to know what to do about this as not a great deal was said about it at all but I also felt that to try to tell her a more truthful version would make her father into a liar. It was many years later before we did talk more about this and even now there are many things which still need to be said, I feel, though I think now that the questions have to come from her.

For some months I continued to work part time in the business but finally I could tolerate it no more. I was glad to get out, even though it was a decision that carried financial risk. What could I do with my life?
Exploring one option, I applied to go to university because I wanted to study and give my life some focus and somewhat to my amazement, my application was accepted. I started my course in October 1981.

Then in 1982 came the significant turning point in my life that I had needed. I discovered Rebirthing.

Until this moment, I had been living my life fairly much on the surface, trying to cope with all the material and practical challenges life threw at me, just going from one day to the next. Rebirthing helped me tremendously. The therapy of connected breathing enabled me to begin to release emotions and thoughts from my past that troubled me from within. At times I felt quite stunned by the force of the emotions that would rise up from inside of me. Understanding that I was not alone in feeling unloved and unwanted also helped as I heard other people sharing their "stories" in workshops. Through affirmations I learnt to assume a much more positive attitude, understanding how much our mental beliefs affect us. This all helped me to feel stronger and more able to cope with life.

During one of the early workshops I learnt about the importance of making life goals as a key to manifestation. I realised that I had never had a plan for my life until then, not bothering to think of what I wanted at all. At that time, I was still in my first year at university without any really clear idea of what I was doing there and where I was heading.

One of the women I met on these workshops was an inspiration to me. Her name was Margaret and she taught me a lot. She wanted to help people gain a sense of their personal power, to be courageous and yet compassionate. She worked as a social worker and this led me to a decision to undertake the same career path, for I wanted to be like her.

In the same year, I started receiving regular sessions of massage. This was incredibly soothing and healing for me. Gradually, all the knots of pain and hurt that I had endured physically from my father were being eased out of my system. I began to enjoy hugs and other forms of physical contact.

Later on I would experiment with many forms of therapy and complimentary medicine trying to find what would help me the most. I suppose that my introduction to Rebirthing also corresponded with my awakening interest in religion begun some years earlier by my mother as well as trying to find a path of Spirituality that would suit me. I explored both Buddhism and Christianity practically as well as academically through my studies as part of my degree was in comparative religion. The place of worship in which I have felt the most comfortable was the Unitarian church as it seemed more of an enquiry and so much less dogmatic than other things I had tried. However, I have not attended a church for many years.

After finishing my studies at university, I began my job as a social worker, filled with an idealism of wanting to help people. Soon I was disappointed though because the reality of the job was quite different from what I had hoped. I felt that often I was expected to exert a form of social control upon people, which I did not feel was necessarily of any help to them. My disillusionment with my work prompted another inner crisis for me whereby I sought psychotherapy to try and come to terms with my inner conflicts. I now think that this crisis was another manifestation where I had to deal with oppression.

In the end I felt that I had to compromise my idealism because of the need to earn money. I decided that I would do what I could to be true to the values I believed in and this led to a change in direction. I left fieldwork to become the manager of a day centre for people with physical disabilities. Here I felt more able to have a more direct impact on the lives of people, not only those attending the centre but on the staff as well.

During these years I had been divorced and my ex-husband had remarried and had more children. We had both moved house away from the village we had lived in together and Victoria had spent time living with both us. However, by 1987 he had sold the business and moved to France. He wanted Victoria to go with him and she was very keen to join him there. For another year I had her with me. Then, following an extended summer holiday in France at the end of her GCSE year (1988), she came home saying that she wanted to return and carry on with her education in France, which she did. This happened very quickly and was quite a shock in some ways. However, this was cushioned for me by the fact that after 8 years or so on my own, I had met someone else.

After the break up of my marriage, I had had a few brief relationships, but nothing substantial. However, after 8 years on my own, I was beginning to feel that I wanted to embark on a more meaningful relationship again. Over the Christmas/New Year period (1987/8), I was with my sister, her husband and our mother at my sister's home and I spent a lot of that holiday planning my ideal relationship. So when I returned home and found an ad in our local paper, which really jumped out at me, I knew I had to answer it. Although at our first meeting, I was not so sure, our feelings for each other quickly grew and soon I felt that we had been brought together in some way.

By the autumn, Victoria had gone to France and Bert had moved in with me. We were both in our early 40's by this time and decided we did not wish to marry and have kept our lives quite separate in many respects. I think that, underneath, I have not wanted a man to be in a position in my life where he could control me again. My first need with Bert has been for independence and this has suited him as well. At times I have wished that we might have had more in common, but overall it has been a strong and stable relationship in my life. Although we see life very differently at times, we each have a great respect for the other's point of view and we have never really argued.

In the meantime, I missed Victoria and regretted that our relationship was not as close as it could be. However, in 1990, she had a bad car accident. I went to try and be of support to her, and during this time we talked. I believe that some of the barriers that were in place between us broke down during this period and my relationship with her has been much better since then.

From the mid 1980's, the Spiritual aspect of my life grew stronger. I became very interested in the new age movement, in the notion of a planetary consciousness and the need for peace in our world. One of my passions was with networking and helping to bring people together, raising awareness of Spiritual needs. I fell in love with dolphins and some of my most precious moments have been swimming in the ocean with wild dolphins.

Through meeting Paul I became interested in healing and contacting our Spiritual guides. I discovered that I had a guide called Swift Eagle, whom I felt as a strong presence wanting to generate peace. Many times when I have felt confused I have asked for his help, though perhaps not as often as I might have done. I became dedicated to Earth healing, wanting to try to help the Earth Spiritually through meditation and prayers.

Concurrent with these Spiritual aspirations, I felt my old doubts and lack of self-confidence surfacing again. How much could I believe in these Spiritual realities? On occasions my own inner perception felt so vague, I did not know if I might be making it all up. Other people seemed to have more skills and be able to do more than me. I wrestled with a lot of self-criticism and doubts about others. In the end though, I felt that doing this work was what my heart wanted to do, and this was sufficient reason for me to dedicate myself to it.

As my heart has opened, I have felt an increasing yearning to be true to it, and this has lead to an increasing feeling of dissatisfaction with my work. Then, in the year 2000, I had a major breakdown where I could no longer cope with work anymore. Although I had achieved a managerial position through various promotions, it had become a very stressful and punishing job. Now, emotionally I was very fragile and tearful and I experienced many bodily difficulties. Consequently, I needed to take several months away from work.

During this time I recognised that I needed to live my life more true to my heart and be gentler with myself. I discovered interests like sound healing and a personal need for space that I had not been honouring sufficiently.

In the end, partly due to financial pressures, I felt I had to return to work. Although I have approached this as positively as I could, my physical and emotional body is reacting again and causing me difficulties. I feel an inner conflict between my commitment to this work and the other aspects of my life, which I have been developing, in more recent years. I know that this job is not what my heart wants me to be doing, but in my mind I do not yet understand how I can leave it. As I write this, I have made some plans and put some training in motion, so we will see how things evolve.

Looking back, I feel that I have had to endure quite a difficult life, especially in the early stages. My inner awareness has gradually awakened, as I have become older. More and more I am coming to understand that in some way I chose this life that I am living now for myself and that therefore no blame attaches to anyone, that everyone was playing their part.

As well as the difficulties, I have had some very positive experiences, particularly in more recent years. Internally, I know that I am still affected by my early conditioning. I still carry the scars but in many ways I feel that these have strengthened me as I have come to understand their roots. During moments when I feel that I am floundering, I despair about those times. But then, from the base I was given by my parents, I have had to be very determined to build a life for myself that would be worthwhile.

Reflecting on this recently awakened in me feelings of `impotence' that part of me had been 'frozen in time' since I was little. These thoughts released feelings that my mother had not wanted me and not really cared for me during my childhood. Such notions disturbed me greatly and I pondered what I could do about it. My strong instinct was to talk to my mother directly and confront her about it. However, she was now 85 and had recently been ill.

One day shortly after these thoughts had come to me, I was travelling to her home to collect her and take her out for lunch and, during the journey there, I earnestly asked for guidance from within so I could find a way to address these issues. As I walked into her house that day, my mother did something fairly unusual for her - she gave me a hug. This was something that I do not recall her doing when I was a child although in more recent years we have overcome this barrier. She then stepped back, looked me in the eye and said, 'I just want to tell you how much I love you. I have never told you this before and I can't explain why that is, but I think it is about time'.

Feeling stunned by this, I could not speak, nor could I cry. After a while, I spoke and told her how amazed I felt by what she had just said. I told her about these feelings of being abandoned by her as a child, and how unloved I had felt. I was then able to say things to her that until then had seemed impossible. She listened to all the difficult impressions I had felt of her relationship to me and then confirmed that I was right! My mother told me that she had never wanted children and that she had been too self-centred and full of her own concerns to care for me properly. This admission, validating my experience so clearly, did allow my tears to flow. Later we went on to our lunch appointment where we talked about many things we had never discussed before.

For me, the fact that she told me that she loved me on this particular occasion seemed like a miracle and a few weeks later I asked her why she had chosen that particular time. She told me that the reason that she had shared this with me was because she had felt a strong urge to complete things with people who were important to her as much as she could before she died. She felt that she had not done this with her own mother.

I have felt very blessed that my mother has shared these feelings with me. For some years I have felt that my later life would be the best years of my life so I am looking forward to more opportunities to develop and heal myself as well as helping others. I feel that I have travelled far, but I still have a long way to go.

Reflecting on my life, I am now aware of a strong theme of oppression as a context for my life. I have certainly experienced oppression as a child and as a woman living in today's society. I have also dedicated the last 15 or more years of my life to working with people who are oppressed in various ways, particularly those with physical disabilities. For some years I was involved in co-counselling which helped me to more fully understand oppression and its insidious nature. Nowadays, I feel very strongly that this affects us all in some way. I believe that we have the task, both individually and collectively, to free ourselves from all the many forms of oppression so that we can reclaim our personal power. Only by doing this can we build a better kind of society and world, before it is too late. I feel that my purpose for incarnating in this life has been to free myself and, as I do this, help other people to free themselves. I hope that in whatever time I have left, I will continue to play my part in making this dream a reality.

I have found writing this much more difficult than I ever anticipated when Paul first invited me to make a contribution. It has taken around nine months and has felt, at times, like a pregnancy and giving birth. I feel that it has been helpful to me to think about my life in this way and my purpose in writing has also been to express the hope that others may find something of meaning in my story to help them make more sense of their own lives.

Chapter 25 -

How We Experience Our Families

For many of us, the family bond is sacred. It is a space and fundamental unit where we feel that we belong or where we feel that we should belong. There is something very intimate about the uniting of two people to conceive a child and the sharing of 'blood ties'. Yet, being in a family does not always provide the caring and loving, safe home that it could do.

In Jill's case, we have a situation where her parents were arguing frequently, her father was violent to her and her sister had a different father who had no other contact with the family. This was hardly an ideal family model for her. As she was growing up though, she had no other models with which she could compare her own situation, until she started visiting her friends. Therefore, a lot of her conditioning and learning about how people relate to each other would have come through her interactions with her family. I am sure that each of the members of her family was doing their best to survive and live as well as they could, and within this culture, Jill would have made her own decisions about how she needed to be in order to survive too.

The kind of family setting in which Jill grew up would not be unusual in our present day and age. Families can be quite unhappy places in which to be. But people appear instinctively to want to cling onto their families, however unpleasant the relationships may be between the various members within it. For people to lose a member of their family can cause them a huge distress.

I suppose that we all have within us, an instinctive urge to be part of a clan or family group. We may be afraid deep inside that without belonging to such a unit, we would be lost or very lonely. So a family can be like a comfort to us, even if we are unhappy within it. There can be strong pressures to be loyal to our family, a collective pressure that is hard to break. People may be very afraid of being outcast if they act contrary to any of the family patterns.

Often, I observe that people within families regard anyone that does not have a blood link with the family as an `outsider', someone not to be considered as having any significance. Therefore, the family bands together and there is much force applied to ensure that each family member conforms to family expectations and traditions. Thus, family traits can easily be passed from one generation to the next as each new generation assumes the habits and prejudices of the generation preceding it.

A lot may be unsaid in family situations whereby agreements between family members are presumed and instinctively known. Habits and family rituals may reinforce these agreements and make it very difficult for anyone who feels that they want anything different to make a stand and demand that. Because of these assumptions, communication may be very poor within a family, unless there is a more open atmosphere where people's individual needs are taken into account.

In my own family background, I remember, for instance, when I was a teenager, how empty I found the family rituals around Christmas. Yet, this was what was done, and I just did not feel that I had the power to question how things were organised or do anything differently to try and meet my own needs.

As souls, we may choose to enter into such a family set-up for very definite reasons. The personality characteristics of various family members may suit the kind of grounding we need, to learn the lessons that we have chosen for our lifetime. Also, we may have been connected with the soul of one or more of the other family members in many previous lifetimes. The relationship from the past may not have been particularly harmonious. Therefore, to meet those souls in the pressure cooker of a family situation may provide an intense opportunity to work that relationship out.

220

The main challenge though for all of us in such situations is for us to be able to remain true to ourselves, to assert our independence, even in the face of opposition and pressure to conform to group behaviour that may not be right for us. To achieve this may require great courage and inner attunement. Whenever we feel that, in our decisions, we may go against other people's wishes, especially the expectations of our family or group, then this can be very testing for us. We need to be very clear about our own inner truth.

The first indications that we may need to make some adjustments in this regard to our family could be vague feelings of discontent in relationship to our family. If we look in our heart about what we really want in life, we can consider our hopes and dreams and how we want to express ourselves. And if we then measure that against the expectations and pressures applied by our family, the places where there are differences, will be the areas that need our attention to enable us to assert our freedom and individuality.

Without having realised that we have done so, we may have become very enmeshed within the family culture to such an extent that it is difficult to extract ourselves from it. To act contrary to this culture may risk disappointment and disapproval from other members of the family. But also, when our identity is wrapped up with the family, it may be very difficult to imagine who we could be without it.

The best way forward may be to seek psychotherapy and unlock the inner patterns of our minds. From experiences early in our life, there may have been crucial events where we felt forced to act contrary to our own inner truth so that we would conform to family wishes or perhaps the will of one particular parent. In as much as these experiences were not digested within us, the energy associated with these experiences may have subsequently have caused us problems.

If we compromised ourselves in our reactions so that we could perhaps feel accepted, even though we were not being true to our own needs, then we may not feel good about ourselves for this. Internally, we may have struggled to know how to cope and therefore tried to shut down from our feelings connected with particular events. All we would have succeeded in doing though would have been to move the feelings and nervous reactions associated with these events out of our ego control and into the realm of our subconscious minds. Here, elements of the experience would have become part of our inner belief system and be incorporated into our typical nervous reactions to specific types of situations.

When we compromise ourselves to make ourselves acceptable to others or the family group in which we feel we belong, then this can build up resentments within us that sooner or later will have to be addressed for us to have a healthy life. If we have shut down from those feelings then what we have internalised may eventually prompt negative reactions or even depression.

In my experience as a therapist, I have found that it is quite common for people to have reacted to situations by trying to shut down their feelings. When people do not act with complete integrity and internalise more difficult feelings that they don't want to know about, then this can set up patterns of inner conflict. To help people to locate these memories and to live out the energy of these experiences again so that their responses express more truly their instincts and needs can be very healing. Methods for achieving this can be achieved include psychodrama and Hypnotherapy.

Bringing to the surface subconscious energy blocks and restrictive patterns can be very freeing and help people to feel more whole and in control of their own choices and reactions to events now. If, however, people become aware of how they may have compromised themselves in the past, it may be difficult for them to come to terms with that. In fact, we all do make mistakes, and all we can do really is to try and let go and release this past so we can do our best now.

From Jill's story, it is clear that some of the experiences related to her childhood disturbed her a great deal. When she grew up, she felt very unsure about what she wanted. For a long period in her life, she was very unhappy. At a certain point in her life, the opportunity came to her to receive therapeutic help, and she grabbed at it. She knew that she needed a great deal of help to sort out her inner confusions. After many years of inner work and searching to find peace, Jill still feels that there are places within her consciousness that she has not unravelled. But in the process of searching for her own personal salvation, Jill has gained much inner strength and compassion. In the process, she has become a very good counsellor with the ability to listen and help people with their problems.

In my life, I believe that I did not face conditions as harsh as that of Jill as a child. Nevertheless, by the time that I was a teenager, I could sense that much of what my family wanted and expected of me felt claustrophobic and I could not feel at ease with it. At that stage, I knew very little of what I wanted, but needed a space to find out. I felt a determination in myself not to compromise myself to either my family or society. Finally, in my early twenties, I left Australia and went to live on the other side of the world. I needed that physical space to build my own identity and discover what I wanted.

I do not want to suggest that we all should separate from our families and break our families apart. However, I believe that once we can be sure that we are living a life fairly true to ourselves, then it is much easier for us to love members of our family than if we are not. The family can be a melting pot for building up much hatred and antagonism if people within that family are not living lives where they are being true to themselves.

We all need spaces in our lives to be with people where we feel a sense that we belong. Without that, we may feel rootless and unable to find a focus for our activities. This can produce its own frustrations. The family can meet that need, but it may not.

Adoption

Children who are adopted are placed in situations removed from their 'blood' parents. This can produce its own wound and sense of rootlessness. Usually, children are adopted at a very young age and it is the breaking of the link with the mother that is most painful. Having worked with a number of clients who were adopted, I know that the memory of separation from the mother is something that adopted people carry even if they don't realise it. Often people who have been adopted coming to me as clients complain about vague feelings of loss and lack a sense of 'belonging' in their lives, however much their adopted parents may have tried to compensate for this.

When I have led these clients into regression, typically, they will feel a tremendous healing and release by enabling them to contact the memories of being with their mother, and perhaps their father. There may be much buried emotion and need to communicate within these experiences. For instance there may be a need to say goodbye, a need that was never met at the time. Losing parents through adoption can be like a death. Even though it may be a memory from when the person is very little, it seems that people still have awareness of what is happening for them. They know it instinctively.

Once I had a client who had been a twin. Her sister died when they were both very little. Her life has never felt complete since then, as if part of her was missing, and she has needed much help to try to come to terms with this.

My partner Eleyna was adopted. She has described in her story how she met her 'natural' mother and I have mentioned about her much more recent meeting with her 'natural' father. Eleyna feels that when meeting her mother, her mother wanted to treat her like a baby, wanting her baby back. She felt a barrier towards her mother, feeling that her mother never fully accepted her or knew her. Yet in relation to both her 'natural' mother and father, when they were not existing as part of her life, for Eleyna it felt like there was a huge hole inside of her. It has been important for her to know them.

I sense that Eleyna has suffered through being adopted. She has carried an enormous craving to be loved unconditionally, even though her inner beliefs have tended to support the notion that this was not possible for her. Concurrent with this, she has

224

wanted at times to cling onto members of her family desperately, wanting their love and acceptance, as if there was no one else in the world who could meet this need in her. Very often she has felt let down and disappointed by especially her 'two mothers' in this regard. I have wondered how much the pain of separation from her mother soon after birth has contributed to these feelings and urges. The counselling she has received in recent times has been very much orientated to help Eleyna loosen her ties to her 'mothers' and former husband, so that she could open herself to expect love from more reliable sources than these people.

I have a daughter who was born outside my marriage. She has been brought up by her mother who lives in Brazil. Her mother has asked me not print her name. For me, being separated from my daughter has been very painful. However, I have been fortunate enough to meet her on a few occasions when her mother has travelled to Britain.

When my daughter was three and a half years old, I met her in Scotland. I was aware that she did not speak my language and I had little hope that we would form very much of a bond. Her mother had similar expectations. As things turned out, when I met her, I got down to her level and played with her. Soon she wanted to sit on my lap and hold my hand. It felt amazing to me that she wanted to be close to me. Her mother was confounded too. She told me that my daughter was a very shy girl who tended to withdraw from people that she was meeting for the first time. The way that my daughter was relating to me was very unusual for her.

I sense that my daughter instinctively recognised me as her father even though we had had hardly any previous contact. The fact that we bonded delighted me. It made me appreciate that people do have an innate knowledge of their 'kin', something that is very precious.

Our Wider Family

For some of us, we may find that we feel a greater affinity and bond with people outside our family. From a soul perspective, those with whom we share the closest links may not be members of our 'blood' family on Earth at all. By making warm and strong bonds with people outside our family, we may be increasing our capacity to love and helping form links between people that does not depend upon blood ties. All people are worthy and deserving to receive love. If we restrict our loving attention to the members of our 'blood' family, then we may be blocking ourselves from loving others who need it. By opening ourselves to love others as if they were our 'family', we may begin to feel a sense that all of humanity is our family, and that our task is to go and be where we are needed most, without any preconditions or expectations.

By not including others outside our 'blood' family as people that we feel open to love, this means that we will tend to look upon these other people as strangers, and not be prepared to trust them. If we feel that we can only open ourselves to our family and if we have a difficult relationship with various members of this family, then we may not have very much emotional support in which to live our lives happily. When we do not trust people outside our family and regard them as strangers, then our hearts will remain closed and our lives will become smaller.

As we open ourselves to the potential of loving others beyond our family, then this may offer opportunities for us to learn about people and ourselves in a way that would not have been possible previously. It may help us to gain a wider view of our world and our place within it. If we do not feel part of our family, but at the same time, we cannot open ourselves to love and trust others, then we may feel very wretched and rejected indeed. This may be a very dark place for us in which to enter, and we may be only able to emerge from this, as we are able to reach out for help and question our previous expectations.

Chapter 26-
Facing Death and Illness

Models of Reality

As we live our lives, we like to feel that we have some degree of control, so that to some extent at least, life is progressing how we want it to go. When the elements of our lives seem to move out of our control, and we cannot manage them, then we may find it very difficult to cope. In situations where people feel that they are powerless and helpless, with no control over their lives, then this can precipitate anxiety or in more difficult cases, a nervous breakdown. Our 'Ego' self likes to know the boundaries of our existence so that it can feel safe. If these boundaries are breached or disturbed then, this can prompt a nervous reaction of fear.

Because of the influence of the Ego, people create their own sense of reality. They can place memories, thoughts and feelings that they do not want, out of the way so that they will not be disturbed by them. People can perceive events around them coloured by their own expectations and prejudices, experiencing life through a kind of filter system, so that only what is judged to be safe will be allowed to enter. Probably, we all do this to some degree.

The Ego does perform a useful function. If it is weakened, then a person may suffer from mental illness, not able to manage his or her thoughts and emotions.

What people create by their various belief systems to support the Ego, may not correspond very closely to what is true. People can become very fixed in their opinion about how they want their lives to be, and not be willing to perceive it in any other way. With this attitude, they will not learn very much.

People may decide that what they perceive and can control with their Ego, is the only possible reality, that this is life in total. Of course, life is not so predictable to allow this model and outlook towards life to be easily sustained. But when we are fixed in our attitudes about some aspect of our lives, we may feel very angry if some circumstance or event comes along to challenge our perception. We may want to close our minds so that we feel that things stay the same for us. With this outlook, change can appear to be quite threatening.

From my own perspective, I believe that our Ego is only one aspect of our being, that we have a sub-conscious and Spiritual aspect to our being as well. Altogether, these three aspects of our being make up our soul. When we allow the Spiritual aspect of our being to permeate our Ego, then we can come closer to the truth of our soul pathway. To do that though, we need to be open to learn, to acknowledge that what our Ego knows is very limited, and to trust that if we ask for help inwardly, then we will be supported through change.

Approaching Death

In my mind, I feel that every moment of life is new. Change is occurring with every breath, and there is nothing that I can really hold onto in my physical life. My physical body ages, my circumstances alter like the weather, the relationships I share with people go through cycles and transformations in spite of what I may wish. If I try to resist change, then I will suffer, because I will be exerting my Will against what wants to happen.

Sometimes it can feel very difficult to go through major change in our lives. From the Spiritual aspect of our being, we may have chosen to go through a particular experience, but when our Ego self becomes aware of that, we may want to refuse and back away from what has been presented to us. This may be a test for our soul. When our Spiritual self and our Ego self are in conflict with each other, we may feel very unhappy. The act of surrender is needed by our Ego self in order for such conflicts to be resolved, but if our Ego is afraid, it may be inclined to build a fortress around itself rather than to give way.
We can be very complex beings, with many inner conflicts and self- judgements affecting us at any given time. There may be an

inner task for us to be able to release our attachment to what is keeping us stuck in some pattern or situation that no longer serves us. When we surrender to the inner truth of what we need to do and how we need to be in our lives, then there can be an exhilarating release of energy that makes us very happy.

Probably the biggest soul test for each of us is about how we die. When we die, all the structures that we have built up in our lives collapse and are gone. Our personality and possessions, our physical comforts and sense of identity is no longer ours to keep. We have to let go, physically at least, of all the relationships that are dear to us. Death forces us to let go of control completely.

People may want to fight Death and not want to accept it. For some, it may feel very unfair. We may be afraid, feeling that it is a big step into the unknown. As we approach Death though, we will be confronted with the spectrum of the life that we have lived, what has really been important, and where we know that we have been deluding ourselves and others. When people near Death, they may feel an urgency to put things right, before it is too late.

An example of this from the life stories in this book is that of Jill's mother. Although she was not dying, she knew by her age that her time was coming. Bravely, she has dared to tell Jill how much she loved her, and was prepared to admit her mistakes from the past. She wanted to feel as complete with herself as she could before she died. The compassionate side of her nature wanted to assert itself and she could recognise that it was not as much present when Jill was little.

It is not always the case that people will feel good about dying. They may feel bitterness and resentment, and want to deny what is happening to them. Their anger may be directed at God, Spirit or whatever has made them so that they have to endure this.

Whatever our faith, we cannot be certain what we will experience when we die. For people who release themselves to Death with love when their time has come, there is generally great peace and tranquillity around that person when that moment arrives. However much pain that the person may have had to withstand in the time leading up to the death, then this will be so. On the other hand, people who fight Death may find that even their final moments are like torture. They may wrestle with unresolved feelings within them.

From my work with past life regression and channelling, I am inclined to believe that passing through Death is often a very peaceful and liberating experience, although not always. When people do not have any faith or hope for what they may experience after Death, then this can affect what they experience when they die. People are accountable for the life that they have lived and will become very much aware of both the quality of love in their interactions with others from their life span and any hurt that they have caused. But there are Spiritual beings to support them and acceptance. It would seem that it is usually the ones who have been left behind for whom it is harder.

Dealing with Death

Many years ago, I lived in a community with some other families. Among these families, there was one where the couple had five lively children, ranging in age from toddler to two teenage girls. This family expressed such a lot of vitality, adventure and fun that they were really at the heart of the community. When I first arrived to live at this community, I used to be in awe of the energy and creativity they expressed.

That summer, they went away together on a holiday to the seaside. Then one evening we had a phone call that the mother, Liz, had suffered a heart attack and drowned in the sea while they were all out swimming together. She was only 39 years old.

I remember when they all returned home and they could not be consoled. They were wailing. It was a most terrible sound. I can imagine that people could ask if we have a loving God, how such an awful thing would be allowed to happen.

I am sure that all of those children and Rob, the father, were scarred by that experience. Their hearts were made heavy by that loss and their lives more difficult. Within a year or two, the

230

community fell apart. I know that Rob needed to search deep within himself to find reason and meaning to go on living. He had his children of course, and their needs had to be considered as a priority.

Liz's death was so sudden that none of them had the chance to say goodbye to her while she was still alive. So many unresolved feelings came bursting forth in the months that followed. There was grief, sadness, anger, guilt and bitterness. They all needed a huge amount of help and support. It was an enormous challenge to all of them.

Yet, Liz as a soul may have chosen to die at that time. It may have been necessary for the others in her family to have to cope with her loss and learn to live without her. Life can be very mysterious and hard at times. I do not know how they have all managed but I hope that they have been able to meet their challenges and find peace.

When someone close to us dies or becomes very ill, this can bring strong and intense feelings to the surface that otherwise we may tend to ignore. Through love, we can become very bound up with other human beings so that if we discover that we are going to be separated from them, our inner world of thoughts and feelings can collapse. Much of our behaviour, belief systems and expectations can be linked to those that we love, so that without them we may feel lost. We can wrap the fabric of our existence around those people we love so much that other people and events beyond those loved ones will not seem to matter.

When we are aware that someone we love is dying, then our feelings connected to that person could be intensified. If there have been any deficiencies in the relationship, then we may compulsively feel that we have to remedy them. Any rivalries and jealousies associated with other people may also come into much sharper focus. If we have not been fully expressing the love and appreciation that we feel for the person who is dying, then we may feel that we have to do so. Communication becomes very important in these circumstances, if we can do it. Where love can be expressed, then this may be very healing.

Problems arise if we are not able to communicate what we feel to our loved one who may be dying. Perhaps, as with Liz, death may come before we can say goodbye. It will be difficult then for us to feel how we can complete with that person adequately. We may feel guilt and resentment about any inner conflict or unresolved issue relating to that person.

To fulfil these needs people may feel prompted to develop faith, and to contact their loved one in Spirit. Where people feel that they cannot do this, then they may feel despair and emptiness. I have witnessed many instances where people have felt, whether it is through dreams, meditations or spontaneous events, that they have sensed the presence of their loved one in Spirit. By doing this, they may come to believe that separation by death is not final, that Spirit does exist and can help us.

When we lose a loved one through Death it may be very hard for us to let them go. However, as we do that, it may free our love and compassion to embrace more people and situations than it may otherwise have done. If this is our path, to spread and share our love, then the Death of a loved one may actually serve us as a useful and significant stepping stone along our way. This depends upon our life purpose.

We may also choose not to let go of our loved one, but want to hang on to them internally. Perhaps we may fear that we cannot live without our loved one, or we may not want to live without holding that person close. The effect of this choice of not letting go will be for us to remain closed and limited in our outlook.

Emotionally, I feel that dealing with death can be one of the toughest challenges for us as human beings to face. If we have been blocked emotionally, then situations of death may prompt our emotions to flow, as they need to do. If we try to suppress our feelings when someone close to us dies, then the effort we need to make to sustain this will probably make us ill unless we find an outlet for our feelings. What we feel when someone close to us dies may not always be very nice, so we need to be with one or more people who can listen and accept us whatever we need to express, to support us. For the listener, this can be challenging as well. However, I know that in situations where people have felt safe and supported to express their deeply felt emotions, then this can be very healing, and those people have tended to feel much better afterwards.

Suffering With Illness

As well as witnessing ones who are close to us dying or being very ill, there will probably be times during the course of our own lives where we endure illness ourselves, and we have to cope with that.

To suffer from a debilitating illness can be one of the worst experiences to go through. The feeling that our body has let us down, that it will not function as we want, can be very frustrating and frightening. With our Will, we may want to do so many things and yet feel that we have no control to be able to accomplish our goals. The pain and discomfort of illness may be so much to bear that we can only think of survival from one moment to the next. We may feel ourselves drifting and not want to live anymore.

Illness is a great leveller. Whether we like it or not, it generally forces us to some extent or other, to surrender our personal wants so that we are in a more passive state of being. We may struggle or try to fight against this because we may not want to be ill. As we release this struggle though, we have to slow down, and the illness may force us to consider our lives in ways that we would not do otherwise.

People may ask themselves, 'What have I done to deserve this?' If we believe in past lives, then we may wonder if we have done something awful in a past life and now are being punished. But all these thoughts place us in a kind of victim consciousness, which supports the fear that we are totally powerless and without responsibility for what has befallen us.

From a Spiritual perspective, it is possible that we choose our illness as a soul from the period before we are born, as a kind of soul test to help our character to develop. Therefore, on a deeper level, we may have created or allowed the illness, because we may

233

feel that the experience from this would be useful to us and perhaps to those close to us. However, this does not imply that there may have been lives in the past where we have been hurtful to others and now, therefore, we have to experience the same conditions, ourselves. In our background, there may be experiences like that, but the soul choice for us to take on an illness may be for other reasons, most probably because we wish or need it for our development.

When we are rolling around in agony, it may be quite difficult for us to appreciate that we have chosen our illness. We may want to rebel. But, if in our heart we know that we have chosen an illness, and yet we resist this, then we will be in conflict with our essential Self. As with other experiences, our soul may want us to be ill, but if with our personality, we deny and refuse to accept this, then we will be cutting ourselves off from Spirit and our inner truth.

So what can be gained, and what needs to be learned when we suffer from an illness? Many of us just wish for some pills from our Doctor so that we will not suffer from any inconvenience and be able to get on with our lives. For many illnesses, this solution may apparently solve the problem without giving us any insight. It is possible, of course, that many illnesses may be largely physical in nature, without having deep Spiritual connections. Doctors in our modern world tend to treat illnesses purely as physical disorders, without exploring any deeper layers of meaning. But what if there is deeper meaning and significance to the illness?

In confronting any illness and the challenges that it offers, I feel that the most important step is to reach a stage of acceptance. To achieve this, it may be necessary to go through many emotional reactions and inner conflicts, and find the means to resolve those problems. However, once we accept an illness, we can ask inside what we need to learn and how we can move forward. We may then be open for inner guidance and help so that the illness may become a more positive experience in our lives. Whilst we continue to struggle and resist the illness, wishing that we didn't have it, then our energies will go into our struggles and we will not find peace.

From my own personal experience of illness, reaching that point of acceptance is not necessarily easy and a lot of pain can be felt before it is found.

When my marriage broke up, for several months, I suffered from severe sciatica. Physically, I was immobilised - for much of that time, I could hardly walk or sit and I was in great agony whenever I moved. On several occasions, I felt panic and the irrational fear that I was going to die. I needed help from others to a degree that I had never needed it before. Thankfully, my friends did help me.

During this time, I was most grateful for any help, which I could receive. This was a change because normally it felt as though I would be the one who would be giving. So this was a balancing exercise for me. However, I know that my main lesson was patience. Much as I wanted to rush on ahead, on many levels, I had to adjust to a new life and the pain of leaving an old life, which had seemed to serve me well. Over the months, I needed to let nature take its course and heal me. Gradually, this did happen, but only once I started to accept my illness did I feel happier. I noticed how this acceptance of my illness corresponded with a growing acceptance of my new situation too.

Chapter 27 -
The Illness of Eleyna's Mother

Earlier in this book, my partner, Eleyna, has related her life story. In her account, she related about the difficulties that she had felt in connection with the relationship she shared with her adopted mother.

Some months after completing her initial story, her mother collapsed and was rushed to hospital, remaining critically ill for a considerable time. This series of events has been a catalyst for Eleyna and her mother to go through some very intense exchanges in their relationship. In what follows, Eleyna relates her story of what took place.

Eleyna's Story continued -
My Mother's Illness
Following my separation from my husband and the formation of a new relationship with Paul, my mother played a somewhat difficult role. She felt my husband to be a good man, who worked hard and provided well for his family. He had also frequently been kind to them and helped them in many ways. She did not want to hear any of my reasons for leaving my husband, feeling that it would be too distressing for her, and she also wanted to maintain contact with my husband in a friendly way.

I felt these choices she made in a very hard way. Frequently, I felt that in the same way that I had lost my way of connecting with my children, I was also losing my relationship with my parents and my mother in particular. In addition, I felt that my mother was betraying me, even feeling that if she could have had her choice of who to adopt now, she would have chosen my former husband over me. Following my marriage separation, there were frequently conflicts between my former husband and myself, which spilt over and affected my mother. Whenever this occurred, Paul was at great pains to ensure that my mother understood as much as possible what was happening to cause these conflicts, so she could know my side of it as well. Frequently it would look as though I was reacting without provocation because of the way my former husband would be charming and pleasant to maintain his positive image.

While I had still been living with my former husband, I had rarely talked to my mother about my troubles, preferring to remain silent out of a sense of duty to him. Also, sadly, I did not have much confidence that my mother would be sympathetic to me.

Slowly, then, with Paul's help, the communication between us began to improve and this did begin to redress the balance a little. I felt that she was starting to see me and appreciate me more. It was still not really possible to communicate fully with my mother concerning all aspects of these crises because of her frail health. However, I did notice a change. My mother would regularly phone me for a chat, a thing that she never did in the past.

One Saturday my mother went to town as usual to do her shopping. She liked to be busy and had a very particular way of doing things. No matter how ill she felt, she would be determined to carry on with her routine. However, the night following this shopping trip, she could not sleep because of severe chest pains and was unable to breathe.

My father tried to call the doctor. He was used to my mother waiting on him and doing things for him. It was three in the morning and he was told by answer machine to ring the emergency number. My father, in his state of stress and confusion, dialled the number three times incorrectly before finally contacting the operator, who tried to calm him down and contacted the emergency services. When the paramedics arrived they worked for nearly an hour before taking her to hospital.

My former husband rang me and told me that my mum had been taken to hospital. I can only assume that my father was unable to find my number. Feeling shock and swirling emotions, I could not decide what to do. Knowing how my mother would be terrified, she hates hospitals, I wanted to be there to hold her hand, but I did not even know if I would be able to get onto the ward. As I was having these discussions with Paul, my former husband rang again and told Paul that he was going to the hospital. Immediately when Paul communicated this to me, I rang back to say I would go, for I did not want him to be there in my place. The phone kept ringing, and I realised with frustration that my former husband had already left.

I was furious. Here again was a situation where my former husband was going to take control and I was not going to be able to be true to my own wishes. What I wanted was to be there personally to comfort my mother. Quickly, I dressed and hoping that Grace, my six-month-old baby would sleep, left for the hospital.

When I arrived, I found my mother in some distress and very afraid. She was unable to breathe and felt as though she was drowning. Mustering as much self-restraint as I could, I said to my former husband that I wanted to be with her now and that he could leave. Thankfully, he left without argument.

Trying to help her to be calm and give her as much love as I could, I told my mother how much I loved her, and she responded that she could really feel my love. What we shared was a very warm and rich experience despite the difficulties my mother was having.

After staying with my mother for two hours, she seemed to be settling and, on her insistence and the advice of the nursing staff, even though I felt uneasy about it, I went home, intending to come and see her as soon as possible in visiting hours later that day. On returning home, I slept, and then we resumed our normal Sunday family activities. After we came back from one of our activities, there was a message on the answer machine to get to the hospital as soon as possible. Imagining the worst, I felt panic because I did not want my mother to be dead.

When I got to the ward, they told me that my mum had had two cardiac arrests and had been transferred to intensive care. Rushing over to the intensive care unit, I did not know what I would find.

I had always thought that my mother was more fragile than my father because of her inability to rest and take care of herself. Now as I faced her possible death, I was filled with a huge sense of loss. Having only just begun to heal some of the rift I had felt with my mother, my emotions longed to feel closer to her. Now, just as I was beginning to feel a more loving openness between us, I feared that I was about to lose her. As I thought about this, I also understood that I could not fight the Universe. Whatever was intended for my mother, I would need to accept. Inside myself, I began to feel a sense of peace as I placed my mother and myself in the hands of God and trusted that whatever the outcome, it would be for the very best.

When I finally saw my mother, she was unconscious, being connected to numerous tubes, and on life support systems. The next hours were going to be critical as to whether she survived or not. As the family gathered in the waiting room, the consultant explained about my mum's collapse and gave her a fifty - percent chance of survival. My father, in particular, was shocked, but I felt relieved, because I had fully expected my mother to be dead.

Every moment longer that my mother was alive seemed precious. The hours of waiting drained me emotionally, but I wanted to be there to comfort her.

During this time while she was unconscious, there was one occasion when I was alone on a corridor where I felt my mother's presence talking to me. This was a very powerful experience for me. When I looked at my mother's body, it felt as though she was not there and I felt certain that she had left her body and would not return. However, gradually this changed.

Over the next days I spent as much time with my mother as I could. The initial signs were not good. Her heart was failing, her lungs were filled with fluid and not functioning adequately, and her kidneys were also not working properly. Some days, even though I was at the hospital for many hours, I only saw my mother for a few minutes, as she frequently needed to be worked on and receive treatment.

During one of these precious moments, my former husband's girl friend turned up with one of my daughters. The nurse told me that there were visitors for my mum. Not knowing whom it could be, I was shocked when this woman entered with my daughter. Instead of leaving my daughter with me and going to the waiting room to wait for my former husband, she sat down on a chair and watched while I held my mother's hand and talked to her. I felt invaded. Having only spent a few moments with my mother that day, now during these intimate moments, I was being watched by a woman with whom I did not wish to have any contact. Even with the intense feelings of resentment rising up inside me, I felt unable to say anything without causing some kind of scene on the intensive care unit.

Later that evening I rang my former husband and, trying to use as much self-control as I could, I very calmly described how uncomfortable I had felt that afternoon. I made the request that if he and his girlfriend were to visit my mother in hospital, could they please wait in the waiting room until I had left. I tried to make the point to him that it was my mother and not his.

He became enraged, calling me every conceivable kind of insult. Using the strongest language, he finished his tirade of abuse by telling me that in the short time that his girl friend had known my mother, she had been a better daughter than I had ever been.

I was stunned. The cruelty of his words went deep inside and became engraved upon my heart. These were words and deeds not easily forgotten.
Later that week, the consultant gathered us together and said that my mother now only had a twenty-five percent chance of survival. At this stage she had still not regained consciousness and so it was important to find out whether her brain had been damaged whilst her heart was stopped. To do this whilst she needed so much support for her breathing, they would have to

perform a tracheotomy. I signed the consent forms and wondered what would happen as they reduced the sedation. This was a particularly anxious time.

However, slowly, as the sedation was removed, my mother began to show signs of regaining consciousness. From initially showing physical movements that indicated only a vegetative state, her movements became more coherent and she showed signs of responding to people around her. Amazingly, this progressed, until she opened her eyes and could recognise her surroundings. I felt enormously grateful. Talking to her, my poor mother was able to understand what had happened to her. It became clear that her brain was totally unaffected by the cardiac arrest.

Earlier a friend of mine had asked what he could do to help and I had replied that I needed a miracle, but that I wasn't necessarily going to get it. I had surrendered my mother to the will of God and was also able to find peace within myself to accept the outcome of events. So, with my mother able to regain consciousness and communicate, I felt I had been given this miracle.

The crisis was not over yet though. As the week went on, her chances of survival did not improve. She was still very frail and none of us could be sure if she might die at any time. But by her being awake and aware, each of the family, including my children, was able to speak to her and communicate as fully as possible their love for her. I know that however things turned out, this sharing of love would be very helpful and healing for all the members of the family.

During my time with her, I shared with my mother some of things my former husband had said and she made it very clear to me that I was number one in her life. It became clear to me through the next days that these were not just words. My visits were her most highly prized contact and to all other people she found it an effort, because she felt she had to be civil and put on a performance. With me she was more able to be herself and speak her mind.

While all of this had been going on, my own health had been failing. The stress had been too much for me and this, coupled with the cruel remarks from my former husband and the stress of my job, caused me to have a mental breakdown. I tried desperately to get help from counsellors, and doctors, but in vain. Becoming more and more depressed, I finally had to be placed upon medication to help keep me calm. However, I was determined to carry on at work, visiting my mother, caring for a baby, and helping my father as well.

The consultant had said when giving us the odds of my mother's survival that he did not treat statistics, he treated people. At all times I felt my mother was receiving the best of care. Slowly she began to improve. She wanted to live.

During one of our conversations I was very interested to ask her about what she had experienced whilst unconscious. She had said that she had seen figures walking up and down and that a woman wearing a cloak had come to speak to her. This woman had said that it was not time for her to come home and that she was very ill. When I suggested to my mother that this could have been a dream my mother responded that it could not because it had been too real.

My mother's condition continued to improve and, despite having a tracheotomy, was transferred to the ward. She was not very happy there. The speed of the transfer and the unfamiliar surroundings made her very anxious. For twenty-four hours she seemed OK but when I saw her the next day there had been a huge deterioration. I could feel death around her. For some reason, she had sent a message to me via my daughter, insisting on seeing me that day. As I said my good byes I felt within myself that this could be the last time I saw my mother alive.

Later that night, the phone went, and it was the hospital. They said that my mother had had another collapse. Once again not knowing what I would find, I went to the hospital. Collecting my father, we reported to the ward where my mother had been. There were still numerous doctors and nurses huddled around her bed and we were ushered into the sister's office.

When they came to speak to us, they told us that my mother had suffered another cardiac arrest because the tracheotomy tube had become blocked. Once again, she was rushed to the intensive care unit. We waited until she was stable, even though she was unconscious. Knowing that there was no more I could do, I reluctantly went home. Next day I returned to begin my vigil, and was greeted with the news that she had regained consciousness and was fine!

As I write this part of my story she is still in hospital and I am uncertain what the future may bring. It is possible that her heart could give up on her at any time. Whatever happens though, I am grateful for every minute I am able to spend with her and for the opportunity to tell her how much she is loved.

My own story too is moving at a pace. I have really felt the love from my mother and come to realise how important I am to her. Also, I have begun to realise more fully at a deeper level that I am not a failure, simply because I was unable to make a marriage work with a person with whom I am incompatible. There is much that I still need to resolve inside myself, and I know that at times I struggle to value myself sufficiently. However, there are many elements of my life that are very beautiful now and I am hopeful of a brighter future.

Chapter 28 -
Channelled Teachings

I have indicated at various stages of this book that I believe that we each have a Guardian Angel or Spiritual guide protecting us and supporting us from within, if we are open for that help. Once we begin to wish to live with integrity and search for the inner meaning of our lives, I feel from experience, that it may be possible that indications of the presence of our guides could come forward. Depending on our expectations and belief systems, we may interpret unusual experiences from within in numerous ways. From my work with Hypnotherapy, even when unprompted, people's consciousness can produce and reveal many very wise and healing experiences if the space is given for this.

People may become aware of a brilliant healing light, of Spiritual beings that they can see, of helpful thoughts coming into their minds that they had not had previously, and of peace and tranquillity. All of these phenomena, to my mind, may be indications of the presence of our Spiritual guides. For people to experience these things, I have found is not unusual, once people have begun a process of inner exploration.

Some people seem to have the capacity to access these experiences even if they are not particularly interested in inner exploration. It may, of course be the soul pathway of these people to make good use of these experiences. But whether they do or not is up to them.

As people develop their relationship to their Spiritual guides, they may become more aware of thoughts coming to them from their guide. Through practice, they may also be able to allow the presence of their guide to approach closer. This can be very comforting and people may feel this like having an inner friend available and close for when there is a need.

A further stage of advancing our relationship with our guide is to allow our guide to speak through us. This process is called channelling. As people get to know their guide, they may find that their guide has quite a different personality to themselves. This personality may be reflected in the manner of any channelling that takes place.

For people learning to channel for the first time, there is the challenge to discern how much of what is being imparted is our own thoughts and how much is actually coming from the guide. It is a worthwhile practice to learn to open to all thoughts that may be given to us, not to inwardly censor them before we can express them or digest them. In our consciousness, we may only be open to a certain framework of thoughts, so working with our guides may enable us to open our awareness. This can help us on a thought level to learn more about the positive potential in our lives and to overcome inner restrictions that we had placed upon ourselves.

Some people are able to learn to put their own consciousness fully to one side so that the guide can speak without interference. I believe that people allow themselves to do this because they trust their guide completely to support them and they recognise their guide as a living distinct entity working with them. People learn to trust their guides because of the love that they feel from them. To channel, for them, is an act of service.

However, because guides need to use the inner consciousness of the person channelling to speak, I feel that the thoughts of the guide will never be completely free of the inner attitudes of the channel. Therefore, I believe that channelled teachings do tend to be coloured by the thoughts, feelings and attitudes of the channel, even if that channel is able to move completely to one side.

I do feel though, that teachings, which come from Spirit in this form, do have authenticity and can be very inspiring. In that it appears to be becoming easier for people to learn to channel, the Spirit realm is perhaps drawing closer to ours and I believe that a co-operation is possible. Our Spiritual guides are naturally concerned with our welfare and much more easily familiar with that aspect of our souls that is in Spirit. Therefore, I feel that channelled teachings from Spirit can have relevance to our quest to learn about our soul pathways.

In the next chapters of this book, I am going to include the channelled teachings of two guides, one connected to my partner Eleyna, and one that has been associated with me. I hope that these may be helpful additions to the stories and commentaries that have gone before.

Chapter 29 -
The Thoughts of Echmael

Meeting Echmael

Echmael is the name of Eleyna's, Spiritual guide. She has described briefly how she met him and some aspects of her relationship with him in her life story. However, when she has channelled him, Echmael has indicated a wish not only to help Eleyna personally, but also to teach others and especially to help people to connect with their life purpose.

When Eleyna first became aware of Echmael, she felt his presence very strongly as energy like a tickling sensation coming down the right side of her head. She did not see him as such because she tends not to possess a strong inner visual faculty. But her inner sense for picking up both thoughts and feelings is very accurate. So, Eleyna could discern the presence of Echmael as someone separate from herself and quite distinct from her original guide Jonah.

When I first engaged with Eleyna in some experiments to discover how well she may be able to channel him, Eleyna had this strange sensation whereby she felt, as I invoked his presence, that there was his consciousness and hers trying to occupy a very limited space inside her. It felt squashed and like a pressure that was quite uncomfortable. But at first, Eleyna very much wanted to be present so she could witness and even censor what Echmael may wish to express and so she would not move completely aside.

In the beginning, they had an uneasy relationship. Echmael could be much more forthright and confrontational than Eleyna would ever dare to be. But there were occasions when Eleyna felt Echmael's love and compassion. She did not always want to listen to him, but when she did take notice, he often made suggestions that were ultimately very helpful to her. As a result, the trust that she felt for him gradually increased.

After a while then, Eleyna allowed herself to fully move to one side so that Echmael could express himself without interference. At the end of these sessions, Eleyna would not remember the contents of what had been spoken. She would typically feel numbness in her hands and nose that would need a little time to clear as she returned. Grudgingly, she admitted that she enjoyed the channelling experience because it would give her a deep feeling of peace that would linger for quite a while afterwards.

It has often puzzled me that Eleyna could be so reluctant to channel Echmael at times, but I know that she is a strong minded individual and it must be quite a strange feeling for her to let that Self go for someone else. When she was pregnant with Grace, Eleyna did not want to move completely to one side, as she wished to remain in contact with her baby.

When Echmael has channelled for our Healing group, members of our group have sometimes experienced anxiety at what Echmael would say. In responding to personal questions, he could be very honest and direct, and the answers he gave may not always be what people have wanted to hear. However, in my own case, my respect for Echmael has grown appreciably. He has frequently challenged my thinking about situations and made me consider my own motives for things more closely. I feel that his main concern has been for people to face their inner truth and live that truth as fully as they can.

We have often laughed when Echmael has suggested to one of us that some action we propose would be 'good'. He has not necessarily meant that following through with that action would be pleasant or easy, but more that we may learn something fundamental by doing what we propose, even if it causes us quite a bit of struggle along the way.

In this chapter, I wish to include a question and answer session that I recorded with Echmael, about the challenges we face in life. Following this, there is the text of a life purpose meditation transcribed from a session he led with a group of people.

248

Channelling Session with Echmael

Paul: Can you tell about yourself, the work you do, and what it is you wish to teach people?

Echmael: *I have been in Spirit now without coming to visit the Earth for incarnation for quite some time, for thousands of your years. And during the time I have been in Spirit, I have worked mainly with Souls that have come over after death, that have not been in connection with Spirit and have not really had any faith in their lives. These souls then find that in passing over, they are confused and often do not know what to do.*

It is not a very easy task to do this work, because it involves much patience and waiting on the part of Spirit - waiting for these souls to reach out and to ask for help. It can take a very long time for this to happen. Although we often speak of there being a different sense of time in Spirit - and this is so, it is often in your terms a very long time before people, when they have passed over, connect with Spirit just a little, and ask for help. We are talking thousands of years sometimes. And it is hard to watch and wait, to see a soul in torment, to see such confusion around a soul, and to have to wait for them to recognise and realise that they have to ask for help.

However, when the step has been made, and the soul has reached out and just said 'Can somebody help me?' - then a great sense of relief is felt by all. And we are very willing to very gently and kindly guide this soul and help them to see where they have been and what they have just experienced. However long ago it may have been, whatever their most recent experience, we help them to recover and rebuild and start to look forward as to what their next steps may be. But it is a very difficult and quite a sad task at times.

As well as there being souls who are lost in Spirit and not knowing what to do, there are similarly people on the Earth who live their whole life in the same kind of darkness and separation from Spirit. And the same is true for them. It is very much a parallel - that if they choose to live their lives in that way, then they will feel a great deal of trouble and isolation in their lives. If they can just turn and ask for help, then they will immediately find their lives transformed - not in such a way that their lives become easy, but more that they now have a sense of support. They will feel that there is love there for them, no matter how difficult the situation may be.

Paul: Can you say more in depth what happens for people when they live their lives on Earth 'in the darkness', without Spirit?

Echamel: *Well this can appear in a large number of ways. Some people can live their lives, they would say, quite happily without Spirit. They have to wish this to be part of their lives, and they very consciously choose to live their life without Spirit. And they may still work with people, care for people, and show concern for their fellow man. But, however much that they may feel that they have their lives in order and well-sorted out, deep in their hearts they will know and they will feel that there is something missing from their lives. Yes, they are doing all these things, caring for their fellow man, but somehow there does not seem to be any real purpose in what they are doing.*

There will be others that while they do not have any connection with Spirit, will live lives that are very dark. They will feel very empty and alone, and you may call it depression where they really feel that there is no purpose in their lives and that they cannot find any sense in what they are doing at all. Between these two extremes: where someone is very clear and level- headed and quite purposeful but somehow lacking the meaning; to the other extreme, where there is almost complete desolation - there will be people living their lives without Spirit occupying the full spectrum between these two ways of being. But, all of them have the same thing in common, that when they look deep into their hearts, in moments of reflection, they will question what they are doing and why, and wonder what is the purpose of it all.

Paul: How is it that people begin to make contact with Spirit and what difference does this make?

Echamel: *Well first of all, it needs to be made clear that some people are almost determined that they will not have this as part of their lives. And so, even though we in Spirit may show them various things and they may encounter things that they cannot explain, events unfolding not as they would expect, but rather in a better way, they would rather not notice that or put it down to good luck or something like that. There are many people living in that way even though Spirit is there for them and continually waiting and watching, very much as I was describing before.*

It only takes a very small change in people's hearts and minds though, for them to begin to allow Spirit to come into their lives. Then they will start to notice, if they can only open themselves a little, just how much Spirit is there trying to help and guide them in all sorts of ways as they go through their life. This is done because Spirit loves and cares for them, their guide understands them and tries to help them as best they can. It is not as if we are going to solve problems, or that we are going to answer every question that someone has. But it is just to have someone that loves and cares for you and just gives you that little helping hand when you reach times of trouble, so as I have said before, you know that you are loved and cared for and you are not alone.

Paul: What challenges are possible for people once they start living a Spiritual path?

Echmael: *Well, as I said before, it is not as though you will have any answers particularly, or that life will even be any easier. In fact, frequently, once you have recognised Spirit, and begin to live a life where serving Spirit and being aware of the part that Spirit plays in your life, this can often make life more challenging for people. Because now you are aware that you are not alone, that you are not just an island, and someone that is just responsible for themselves. Now you become aware that everything you do affects people and in turn will affect you. Therefore, you are not isolated from Spirit, and you are not isolated from other beings, other people. Everything you do is important, how you care for people, and how you treat people. Therefore, you have responsibilities that you perhaps ignored before or you could pretend that they did not exist. When you are aware of Spirit and the way in which Spirit* *works and the ways in which souls have to learn, then you begin to realise how important it is to live a life that is as good and caring, with as much love as you possibly can.*

I would also say there are many paths that people can follow as they go through their lives. The choices that you make are obviously very important. One of the most fundamental choices that a person makes in their life is to live a life with connections to Spirit being important to them, and to live a life that is as much aware of all the consequences of their actions as they possibly can be.

So once you have made that choice at that particular crossroad, it is not that you have then chosen the easy route, the easy path. It is probably more likely that by choosing that particular path, you will have chosen for yourself the more difficult route. Because, if you consider it, it is probably easier to live life if you have the attitude that thoughts and feelings are not important and that you do not have any real responsibilities. However, as soon as you consciously chose to live your life with Spirit, then you have also accepted responsibility for your life as well.

Paul: What incentives do you feel there are for people to follow a Spiritual path?

Echmael: *I do not think that I have ever looked upon it in that way. I think that you have to realise that if you start to live your life more consciously and with more awareness, then it will bring you great challenges.*

If you want to say to someone 'Do this because it would be easier for you', I think that would not be the truth. I think that what you have to realise is that the benefits are a form of great joy and great peace that can be achieved when you feel the love of Spirit around you and you feel that you are really loved and held. If then you can know and feel that you are truly loved and cared for, it follows that all beings are accepted in this way.
Any individual that may have gone through a great deal of their life feeling unloved and uncared for, or feeling that they are unworthy in some way, then to feel this love that is so deep and

does not require anything of the person, is a wonderful thing. It is something that they would never have experienced in their life before. Therefore, this is a great blessing.

But I do not think it is a good idea to say to someone that if you turn to Spirit, I guarantee that your life will be wonderful, and you feel this and you feel that. I rather feel that it is something that really only comes from the heart of the person themselves. When, through all their different thoughts and feeling in their life, they begin to realise that there is something more and there is something that they wish to connect with, then they will gain that insight and understanding and they will begin to accept and love themselves, and begin to accept and love others.

But I do not think that you can say to someone, who does not have Spirit in their lives, 'Look if you just allow Spirit into your life, life will be wonderful'. I do not think that will work. Therefore, I find it difficult to talk in terms of incentives or benefits or even reasons why you should turn to Spirit, because it is really down to the heart of the individual concerned.

Paul: How can people best deal with pain and fear, which they feel in themselves?

Echmael: *I think, as you know Paul, that it is very important that people do not hide from these things. I know that it is very tempting, and particularly, from spending a great deal of time with Eleyna, I am very aware of how people can react to these. But it is absolutely essential that people do not hide from these. No matter how uncomfortable or how difficult they may find a situation to be, or something that they have experienced in the past, they must deal with these particular fears or a particular source of pain. This needs to be done in such a way that is loving, and this really is where Spirit can help, because Spirit will help to bring light and love into a particular area of darkness within a person. This will help that person to feel more that they can be with that pain or that they can experience that fear and that they can survive from that experience and become stronger at the other side of it.*

I think that Spirit also has a part to play, in that when people have experienced and processed, in whatever way was necessary for them, fear and pain, then Spirit can also be very healing and very cleansing. By the influence of Spirit, people do not have to feel that they are forever weighed down by these various difficulties in their life. Rather, once they have seen what they need to learn from a particular situation, and they have really felt that light and love have moved in, in its place, then Spirit can help to cleanse them of these things. Then these difficulties can become just a part of their memory and their past rather than feeling that it is something that pulls them back and weighs them down in their life.

Echmael's relationship with Eleyna

Paul: Can you speak of your relationship with Eleyna and how you came to be associated with her?

Echmael: *First of all, it was always intended for me to be her guide, but only if she made certain steps in her life.*

As you are aware, the plan is made in Spirit as to the general purpose and path that a particular life will take. But as I have already mentioned, there are many various points upon the path where people can take different routes. I'd say that for most people, they can delay things and frequently they can go a little astray. The majority of people tend to return to the path that they were originally meant to travel, at some point in their lives. Obviously, there are some people who head off in the opposite direction and then somehow are determined not to return to the correct path, no matter how many opportunities are given. I would say that the majority of people feel themselves drawn back to their correct route.

So it was planned that should Eleyna make the relevant steps and open her heart to Spirit, then I would become her guide. And if she failed to do this, then Jonah, her earlier guide, would have stayed with her. But really, his purpose was to try and help her make that important choice and recognise that within herself. So, having done that, then I could step forward and become her guide.

There have been some important things in Eleyna's life - for instance, her long period of depression and her feeling of isolation, that have been really essential parts of building her character and disposition in this life, and also her understanding. In this way, she was prepared and attuned, if you like, for me, so that we could work together in harmony. Essentially, she has some very relevant experiences from living on the Earth this time that very much parallel the experiences that souls have when they come into Spirit when they have not lived a life connected to Spirit. And so, because of my interests, we have a very harmonious relationship in that way.

I would say that our relationship has not always been easy though, and that certainly to begin with, she was very nervous and frightened of allowing me to come through. She could feel that I was a much stronger character than Jonah, and her fear of what I may say to others was difficult for her to overcome. Even now, I know that she becomes nervous, though I am certain that over the time that I have been channelling through her, I have moderated the way in which I speak so that I am now a little more gentle, than I was in the beginning.

Paul: Why did you make yourself known to Eleyna at the time when you did?

Echmael: *It was only because she made her connection with Spirit in a deep and meaningful way, that this then meant I could come forward. But even when she was depressed and alone, she was open to Spirit, because she has a sensitive nature. She has been very much aware when events around her have been influenced and guided by an outside force. And so, even during the time when she was very much alone and in the darkness, she was not completely immune to the fact that there was Spirit and guides around her. It is more that she would tend, as a great many people do, to dismiss or say 'No, this is not really happening. I am not going to pay any attention to that', and try to push it away.*

And so, when the shift inside her took place, where she began to more and more accept this side of her life, and allow it to really become important to her, then it became possible for her to

255

experience the full love that can come from Spirit to her. She experienced, as she has told people, this feeling of love really filling her. At that moment, she knew that there was really Spirit and God, and that she could have faith in this. As soon as she recognised that, and allowed this experience to enter her heart, then it became possible for me to become her guide.

Paul: How do you feel that you need to support Eleyna nowadays?

Echmael: *Well, this is sometimes quite difficult, because although she is now much more open to Spirit and very much recognises it as part of her life, she is also very much used to operating as an individual. And so she uses her Will and only allows Spirit a very small part in her life. This is not always the best way forward. But there is very little that I can do about this because she is very stubborn.*

It is much better if the choices and decisions come from her, because then her heart will be open and she will allow our connection to be good and for my advice and for my love to flow freely to her. If she is at all pushed, or tried to be forced into connecting with Spirit or doing anything that is not in keeping with her own way of thought, at that particular time, then it won't work.

But I have to say that I do find it very frustrating at times. I know that if she would just rest and allow Spirit to come close, allowing herself to feel the love that is there for her, then she would be much more at peace within herself.

Paul: What is the work that you wish to do with Eleyna?

Echmael: *I think that once again, it is in parallel with the work that I do in Spirit - that work where people are moving from darkness into light. Because Eleyna has been through similar processes herself, she can offer a great deal of help and support to these people. She could help people who are perhaps in darkness but have reached that point where they are asking for help. They may be ready to move into light and be ready to open themselves to*

Spirit and understand what is there for them.

Also, I would say, that she can help people by giving them love and opening her heart to them, allowing love to flow through her, so that people who have not experienced love in their lives can feel loved and cared for. This is particularly important when she is giving healing, that she opens her heart and really concentrates, allowing not just the healing energy to flow through but also love to flow through from her heart.

Life Purpose

Paul: How do people come to have a life purpose? Does this change according to the choices people make in their lives?

Echmael: *Essentially, the purpose of any particular life does not change.*

All that really happens is that some people arrive with a particular purpose and never actually do anything in their whole life to help, learn or understand more about that purpose. They basically do not learn anything new in their life

Then there are others that, whilst they, as we've said before, move along a path and then will be drawn away this way and that way, they may also be drawn back to the correct path. As they do this, they will be learning, sometimes a little, and sometimes a lot, about that particular purpose. Basically though, the purpose of someone's life does not change.

All that really changes is how much a person connects with that purpose or how well they understand it. And that is how people may feel that their life changes and takes a new direction.

Paul: What is the importance for people to understand their purpose?

Echmael: *Well, it really links in with some of the things I was saying at the beginning. If you become aware of your purpose in life, so that you are very conscious of how it is there in the* *background for you, then your life has an additional dimension to it. If, as I said before, by opening to Spirit, you then become aware of how Spirit is guiding you, and you become aware of your life purpose, then you immediately become aware of how all the situations and all the people that you meet are actually helping you to learn more and to understand that particular purpose.*

So, rather than going through a particular life wondering and questioning why particular events are happening to you, and what it can all mean, it is as though you now have more insight. It is as though, instead of feeling that everything is happening to you randomly, that you have no understanding at all, now at least everything becomes a little clearer to you. Whilst you go through any particular difficulty or trouble, you can at least have this feeling of peace and understanding in yourself, that no matter how difficult a trial or test may be, it has a purpose and you are loved and cared for.

This understanding is not always very helpful to people at the time. In fact, it can also make people angry because they may feel aware of their particular purpose or lesson and here they are being challenged, having to learn something about that lesson again. They may feel quite angry that they need to do this. But that is just one passing emotion. Quite often, when they have had time to reflect and to think about all the different things that they have learnt and experienced, and they have reached a more tranquil and peaceful time in their lives, then they will often feel grateful and be able to say 'thank you'.

Paul: How can people find the courage to live their life purpose?

Echmael: *I believe that a great deal of courage is needed to help people to find the determination to take the step of living life with Spirit and live a life fully understanding their life purpose. But there is no one pushing them or expecting them to take huge leaps or huge steps into something that is unknown. If they can only manage to take a tiny step and then pause, then that is perfectly reasonable. The most important step they can take is to realise that Spirit is with them.*

If they know that they are not taking these steps alone, then they will be fine. It is also important for them to know that they are the ones making the decisions in this, that they are the ones making the steps. But as I say, no one is pushing them or making them do anything that they do not wish for in their heart.

They will only be expected to do things for which they are ready. And even though it may feel that they are attempting the impossible, or that it is too much for them at times, there will be friends around them and there will be Spirit supporting them. And the most important thing that they can learn is to trust that we will be there for them.

Paul: I know that you have a particular meditation that you like to lead to help people to connect with their life purpose. How can people prepare for that?

Echmael: *If people are wishing to do this, then they either need someone with them, or they need to record the meditation for themselves first, so that they can really give themselves fully to the meditation. It is not something that you can do in a light and superficial way. It is something that needs full concentration and devotion to it, and so it does need preparation.*

The other important thing is that the thoughts and impressions that come to people come in a variety of ways. Some people obviously see very clear pictures and it unfolds very much as a story. But for other people, it may be that they experience emotions, or they may see just symbols or still images. However the information comes to them though, it is important to allow it, and not to question it at that time. Whatever thoughts and impressions come, need to be accepted.

This process is quite a serious undertaking, and if you open yourself in this way to receive guidance, two things may happen. It may not be the time for you to receive such guidance. There may be other steps that are necessary in your life, before you are ready and able to be more aware of your own life purpose. People may then need to get some guidance about what steps are needed if they have done the meditation and not really received anything.

259

But the other thing is, that once you have opened yourself to Spirit like this, then you cannot necessarily expect all of the information to come during the time of the meditation. You may also receive guidance or further information through your dreams or impressions that come to you at any time of the day or night.

So you must be prepared that, once you have undertaken such a meditation, you have really opened yourself and asked for this information to be given to you.

Chapter 30 -

Echmael's Life Purpose Meditation

Echmael's Introduction

It is important for people to become aware of their life purpose because it will help them ultimately to live a better life. If you live a life where you are not really in harmony with your purpose, with the reason why you are here, then you will find yourself continually in conflict with yourself. You may not even understand why you are unhappy or unsettled, because often superficially, your life will be complete. It may have all the elements that many people would consider are needed to be happy. And yet, for many people, this still leaves them feeling unsettled and ill at ease. These feelings arise because they are not fulfilling their purpose in the way that they are supposed to do. This purpose is held within you, and if you can reach a very quiet place within yourself, then it is possible for you to start to become aware of what is really important to you, and what you can do to help move your life in a better direction.

I would like to point out though that it can be quite difficult to become aware of this purpose, because people are often quite good at using their will or imagination to create for themselves what they think would be a better situation. Often what they really need to do can be quite different from this. But also, what they really need to do may be more difficult. So, it is commonly a process whereby you get small glimpses and small insights into what you need to do. And people may sometimes step away from this or become afraid and will again try to avoid doing this.

But, it is a fact that whilst they avoid the inevitable, then there will continue to be this feeling of inner conflict inside them. I would say to you that although people may be at different stages, as you do this exercise more than once, then you may become aware in many aspects of your purpose. As you continue to repeat this process, then you can expect or be aware that more may be revealed to you.

For people doing this for the first time, it is important to realise that to begin with, you may not experience very much at all. It is very unlikely that you will do this meditation and everything will be revealed to you. But what you could perhaps expect, is that you start to get glimpses and impressions of things, and these might not even make sense to you at this time. It is important therefore, to record them and reflect on them. And once you begin to do this, you may also have begun to unleash a process where other impressions will come to you in the next few days. So you must maintain your openness to this. Be aware that no matter how strange or unexpected, you may receive information in all kinds of ways.

The Meditation

For this meditation, be in a room or place that is quiet where you can be reasonably certain that you will not be disturbed. You can either choose to lie down or sit, as you prefer. Have notepad and pen and possibly drawing materials by your side. Make yourself comfortable and close your eyes.

I would like you first of all to become aware of your breath. Notice the rhythm of how you breathe. Don't try to alter it. Just notice the rise and fall of your chest as you breathe. Perhaps you are breathing slowly because you have been sitting still or resting for some while. Perhaps you are breathing a little faster because you are uncertain of what may come, or you may have just moved. However it is for you, just allow yourself to drift with your breathing.

And I would like you to feel yourself moving deep within yourself, leaving behind thoughts and impressions of the day, leaving all of that behind, and moving very gently, very easily, within yourself, to a place of stillness, a place of quiet. This place is very warm, very secure and very safe.
And as you find yourself here, allow yourself to become aware that

you can become connected to Spirit or to your Higher Self or to your guide - connecting to some loving power and presence that is there for you to help you gain knowledge of your purpose in this life. And with this connection, as it forms, you can find impressions and thoughts coming to you. Try not to have any expectations, and do not question or judge what may come. Just simply notice it and remember. There may be pictures that you see or you may have feelings. However this comes for you, is right. And if you do not feel that you are receiving anything, that too may be all right. So then, as you rest in this place, just allow these feelings and thoughts and possibly images to come to you. So for some time now, allow yourself to stay with this and experience it fully.

(Long pause)
And then, very slowly, and only when you feel that you are complete with this, slowly return and write down what you have been given. If however, you feel that you have more that you wish to experience, then stay in this place, for as long as you need. And only when you are ready, come back to normal consciousness. But, whatever way you do this, it is important for you to write down all the impressions that you have received so that you can meditate upon these, and consider their importance to you.

263

Chapter 31 -

The Path of Service

Introduction

When I was twenty years old, I was invited to help at a camp for children suffering from Asthma. At that time of my life, as I have said previously, I was rather shy and withdrawn, but I welcomed this opportunity, even though I had never done anything like it before.

Once I started playing with the children, I was surprised about how energetic and creative I felt. Up until then in my life, I had only surrounded myself with a small circle of friends and I knew very little about anything to do with my life purpose. With it being holiday time, I tended to feel quite bored. However, in this environment, where there were thirty or forty children, my task was merely to play with them and care for them so that they could be content. Somehow, I felt extremely happy. I wanted to help these children, to love them and share love with them.

By the end of this camp, something had changed in me and I had gained an insight that I had not realised before. I wanted to help people. It gave me so much pleasure to help these children and it did not matter whether I received any reward for what I did or not. The more that I was able to help these children, then the more energy I seemed to have.

I do believe that the opportunity of this camp taught me quite a lot about my life purpose and the experience gave me a feeling of contentment inside that I had not had before.

Since then though, I have wondered what it means to really help people and to serve. When I consider a definition of the 'path of service', I think of 'servant', somebody who is not very important but does what he is told. With my own actions, there have been times when I have been very focussed upon helping another.

Typically, this may be in my therapy work, with my partner, friend or one of my children. When I have concentrated my attention upon the needs of this other person, I have done what I felt I had to do, with little thought for any advancement or reward for myself. If someone has praised me for my efforts, I have usually found this to be very uncomfortable because I was not doing what I did for myself.

In my therapy work, I often feel that I have been no more than a catalyst for change and inner transformation, so that if someone gains some benefit from their work with me, it comes from their own motivation and readiness to change and not from me. I can try and provide a loving and safe space for them so that they feel supported, but the rest is up to them.

When I was younger, I used to wish to want to change people and make the world a better place. I still have the idealism to want to do that, but nowadays I do not feel that my contribution is so vital. Often, I feel grateful if people feel more peace in their lives after being associated with me, but I don't know how much this is really due to me. I can only do what I can, and the consequences then go beyond me.

As I observe other people, I feel that there are those that seem to want to help and serve others and also many who do not. Some people appear to be very caught up in their own desires for themselves and little concerned about anyone else. The path of service seems to be about caring, and it is a choice that we have as to whether we do that or not.

When I have studied channelled teachings from Spirit, my own experiences and the experiences of others relating to the more Spiritual realm, I have felt that loving and caring is fundamental to that realm of existence, and happens quite naturally. Further, I believe that when we as souls decide upon our soul pathway for our lifetime on Earth, one of the most important tasks that we would generally set for ourselves would be to do with caring and loving, and perhaps learning to do that in some new way.
But it is not always easy to love, especially if we are provoked or challenged in some hurtful or unpleasant manner. Inside we may

feel that we don't want to love other people. However, that is not the truth of our soul. There may seem to be attractions in seeking power and position, but without love and caring, these achievements may feel very empty.

In this chapter, I would like to express some thoughts about the value relating to the path of service. It may not be something that everyone wants to choose. But because it links with Spirit and our essential Spiritual nature, I thought that I would include some channelled teachings from my guide Clemond. I enjoy the simplicity of his teachings and I would also like to share the story of how I came to open to my connection with him.

Meeting Clemond

In the Autumn, after my marriage break up, I was living in a flat with Eleyna. It was a difficult time and for both of us I believe that there was much turmoil and confusion in our minds, as we tried to sort out our lives. We were both trying to cope with guilt, loss and the shock of what we had been through. During all these months, I was experiencing continual physical pain and agony from the acute sciatica which was troubling me. Meanwhile, my client numbers dropped, and due to my physical immobility, I felt quite trapped for a lot of the time. Naturally I became introspective and it was a struggle for me not to become depressed. I am grateful to Eleyna and my friends for helping me.

Despite my struggles though, I did not lose faith that something important and necessary was happening to me through these changes. It was not all bleak either. With Eleyna, we shared much of ourselves with each other. We started to overcome barriers, learning about each other's habits and personal histories and becoming more intimate. Amidst all our individual difficulties, we both felt a depth of love towards each other that we had not felt with anyone else. From that place of love we conceived our child - Grace.

One of the activities, which we shared, was in having mutual channelling sessions with each other. I would guide Eleyna into trance so that she could channel her guide Echmael and similarly she would guide me into trance for me to access my personal guide Sebastian. Doing this helped me to gain a measure of calm and clarity about my situation, and the experience of accessing my guide gave me some peace. It was often late at night or even in the early hours of the morning when we would be having these sessions. Somehow, it was a time when we wanted to talk or share with each other in some way. There were occasions when we pondered how many other couples would spend their nights lying in bed together and channelling rather than sleeping.

Because of the pain I was experiencing, I did not channel very frequently at first. I found it very difficult to concentrate or to be physically comfortable. What was challenging for me was to cope with the fear I experienced around my pain. On many occasions I called privately for Sebastian's help over and over again so I would be able to settle. Eleyna and my friends tried to support me with healing and therapy to try to make it easier for me. I remember one evening when I awoke in the middle of the night and I was shaking and shivering with fear for well over an hour. This release though helped me to accept my condition so I could carry on.

Gradually, as the months crept by, the pain eased and I could feel more normal again. It was around this time when the worst of the pain had passed, but while I was still immersed in family problems, that I first came into contact with Clemond.

Eleyna was guiding me into trance for her to have a conversation with Sebastian. By now, I was quite used to channelling Sebastian. I still could not move completely to one side, as some of my friends could do. But I could gain an impression of him, and I could feel sensations on my forehead as he came near. Typically, I could feel a light energy spread across my inner vision. In the area where I remained, it was darker. Then, into this light area would come Sebastian's thoughts. As Eleyna would ask me questions, I would find myself speaking words in answer to those questions. When the connection was strong, I could feel Sebastian's love, like a very good comforting friend.

267

On this occasion though it was different. As I was entering the trance, the name Clemond kept coming into my mind repeatedly. I saw an image of a man with long dark hair and a beard. His manner was very kind and considered, like a friendly philosopher. His thoughts hammered onto my forehead in a fashion that was much more intense that I had experienced with Sebastian, but somehow I welcomed his presence.

When I spoke his words to Eleyna, he introduced himself as Clemond. He was a Spiritual teacher and his work was in helping people and Spiritual beings learn about the path of service. His intention was to help me personally and members of my group. Also, he wanted to provide teachings for this book. Clemond had a very different energy to Sebastian. He had a very slow and dignified pattern of speech. My voice altered considerably when I was channelling. I felt as if I was speaking with a French accent.

For me, I found it astonishing that a Spiritual being should come to me at such a time when I was so low and self-absorbed, to teach about the path of service. I felt so little able to reach out to others. However, Clemond was interested in the trials, learning and suffering people need to go through so that they can truly serve. He suggested that I was going through a trial in my life. This was quite helpful to my rather shaky faith, and did give me some encouragement to endure and try to move forward. Certainly, I felt that serving people was what I wanted to do. Therefore, it was most frustrating to feel emotionally in turmoil so I was not able to do that to my best ability. I kept on getting messages to be patient, but I did not find that to be very easy to do.

For two or three months I felt Clemond's presence strongly and I continued to have channelling sessions with him. After allowing myself to speak his words, I always felt very settled and at peace.

Below is the transcript of one of the channelling sessions from this period, which we recorded in the flat where we lived. I formulated a series of questions, which Eleyna then read.

Channelling Session with Clemond

Eleyna: What is the essential aim of your work?

Clemond: *As you are familiar, my main interest is to teach about love and service. I believe that at the core of what people need to learn is love. There are many facets of love and many ways in which learning about love can proceed, about trusting in love. The energy of love is the most essential truth of your universe, and once people in your world can feel love and express love in all aspects of their life, then they do not need to be in physical reality any more.*

With regards to service, this is about people on your plane reaching out to help others, not only people, but other life forms as well. You see, by people choosing to serve rather than being concerned only with their narrow self-interests, then this can lead to an evolution of the soul, and also assisting the quickening of the vibration of all life on your planet. We believe that the life on your planet at the moment is waiting to move to a higher level, so people may be more caring and sensitive to each other, and become more aware of the reality of Spirit. This is not only my aim but also a collective wish for many of us who are working in Spirit. Whether we are successful or not will depend very much upon how many people choose to orientate themselves in this way, and how well they may be able to link together.

Eleyna: What does it mean for people to offer themselves in Spiritual service?

Clemond: *It is first of all, an inner choice on the part of that soul. There may be an important point in a particular individual's life, a moment that the soul may have chosen before birth. This then could be the moment when the soul could be ready and equipped to be able to help others, to draw on what life experience has been gained, as well as the strength of character, of soul experience, from within. Then there needs to be a dedication, where the soul chooses to fulfil not only their individual needs, but to help with*

269

the fulfilment of other's needs as well.

It is not uncommon for human beings to give themselves the opportunity to serve. For instance, every time a mother gives birth to a baby, there will be an instinct to place the baby's needs before her own. However, for someone to consciously choose a life of service is a brave and courageous act, because it does involve to some extent, a measure of sacrifice. To care for others may mean that there is not the possibility for people to pursue their individual pleasures as much as before. This may feel like a restriction. Also, to serve willingly and truly is a responsibility that may not be very easy to fulfil.

One of the main challenges for a person engaging in Spiritual service is that people closest to that person may not necessarily be attuned to this outlook and orientation. Therefore, when people choose to do this, they may have to cope with the possible alienation of those closest to them. Once a person is engaged in Spiritual service, that person may be called upon by Spirit, to help with people and in places where help is really needed, and this may not always be with the people with whom they have been closest.

This dilemma can manifest in relationships, where one partner feels an urge to serve and the other does not. It could be that on the level of soul, the two individuals are choosing different paths from that moment, and if both people can allow it, this may lead to the break up of the relationship. There are many possible tests and it will be for people to find the truth for themselves.

Many trials and changes can occur once people have engaged on the path of service. It is a challenge, therefore, whether the soul is ready and willing to agree to this or not. There will be challenges. Any attachments, longings or desires, which keep those people connected to what they just want for themselves, for their smaller wants and needs, rather then the needs of the greater whole, may be presented to them as a course of action which is no longer appropriate. It may be quite difficult for people to let go of attachments, which are no longer needed as part of their life. People may be convinced that what they are doing is right even though this may not be true. When people go on the path of service, they may need to go right to the foundations of their belief systems and re-evaluate what is there. People may feel then that they do not know any more about the meaning of their life, but have to search for answers. So the path of service may be like a Spiritual quest, an opening to learn and perceive, and a listening from the heart.

A life in service may not be very grand, but may be very simple and humble. The needs of Spirit may not involve rising above the crowd, but for another soul this may indeed be the path that is needed.

Eleyna: What can people really do to help others?

Clemond: *Firstly, people need to learn to listen to Spirit and reach that very quiet place within them. This may not be easy and take discipline to learn to do this. But skills will increase with practice. For deep inside, everyone knows what they need to do, to be happy and fulfilled, to be acting faithfully according to their purpose. People need to learn to distinguish the various drives from within them. It is not what they feel they should do, or what others tell them they should do, or even what they want to do with their own will that is important - it is what they need to do, and how they need to be, not only for their own sake, but also for the sake of others. People can ask themselves where the love needs to flow from their hearts.*

Some people, when they become aware of their purpose, may find that their life does not involve much service at all - they may be mainly concerned with learning some new knowledge or mastering a particular relationship, which is mainly connected with them only. However, for those who do have a path of helping others, they have to learn to ask for help from within, and be willing to accept guidance.

When people feel an urge to act from a source within them, acting in a way that is caring and loving, with no intention for personal gain, then this impulse may be coming from their true self. It is not so difficult once a person gets used to doing it. People can learn to follow their intentions and urges, especially those coming in response to their inner asking for help, and by doing so, people will learn to be in harmony with their inner self.

The path of service is one where a person will give without necessarily knowing what they will receive in return. It is a kind of unconditional giving and it is not something that is very easy for any person to do in the beginning. Much learning and practice is needed, and very often, as I have hinted, there may be a strong need for emotional, mental and even physical purification. People need to give themselves freely and not be tied by things that would restrict them - that would prejudice really, how far and how well they can give.

Some souls who wish to serve may really only ultimately be able to do this in quite a limited way, due to the restrictions that they have within them, the various fears and attachments that hold them to a very small sphere of activity. For others, there may be the potential to operate in a much wider scope. For these souls, the challenges and growth that is needed may be more severe and testing. There may be childhood factors and events that prompt strong fears and attachments that need clearing. However, the drive to release those fears and attachments will be the same impulse to encourage compassion and the wish to help others undergoing similar suffering.

It is a test for souls because although they may be aware inside themselves of a feeling that they need to do something about their fears, there will be a challenge as to whether they are prepared to ask for help when the opportunity is given. Also they will be tested if they are willing to confront the fear or rather try to ignore it. When souls decline to face their fears and get the help they need to release them, then they may feel a vague sense of unease, and live lives that feel rather flat and uninteresting. Choosing a path of service may provide challenges that are quite daunting, but it will not prompt a life that is boring - rather one that is fell of intensity and vitality.

People may be afraid that if they follow a path of service, they may lose those they love. Indeed, there have been traditions from the

272

past where to take up a Spiritual path often meant that the person concerned was isolated from other human beings. But this does not need to be the case. As human beings, you have a natural inclination to be with other humans. And since the path of Spirit is essentially about learning to love, people can generally express that best in the company of other human beings. It is not necessary for any separation. When people agree to serve Spirit, they gain a much deeper sense of whom they love, and how they can help those they love, and because love is such a strong bond, it just means that this love will be enhanced and operating from a deeper place.

When someone serves another, it is giving for the love of giving, and giving because that other person needs help. Nothing happens by accident, and whoever comes into your sphere at a particular moment needing help, will be the one needing your attention. Sometimes you may also need to be active and either move into a new sphere where you are needed to be or alter the sphere of activity where you are living in such a way so that your service may be more effective.

Eleyna: What are the benefits for the one wanting to serve?

Clemond: *Well, there are benefits of course, for the soul growth of the person serving. As that person gives, and learns to give to others, learns to give unconditionally, learns to give from the heart with love, and without prejudice, and without being restricted in the scope or direction in which this is expressed, then this person - this soul is becoming more like 'God', more Spiritually-minded, and this essentially is what each soul desires.*

Usually, when people serve, there will be feelings of peace and contentment, feelings of joy that they are being true to themselves. There may also be growing feelings of being connected with many other people and with life forms around them. To give unconditionally can also help to dissipate any residues of emotions like jealousy, hatred, resentment or bitterness that may be clogging up a person's system. To serve others can be a very cleansing and healing process. Often people will gain awareness of themselves through doing this.

Eleyna: How is Spiritual service linked to love?

Clemond: *Spiritual service is basically love. It is a giving of energy, a giving from the heart, without condition and without expectation of any specific response, to what is being given. This in essence is love and how love can be manifested.*

Many people regard love as a kind of tie, where you give and expect something in return, and expect a kind of loyalty as a result of what is being given. But in the way that love is expressed in Spirit, it is really something that helps another soul to feel more free. It is basically a giving of energy that helps that soul to feel happier, helping their energy and helping that soul in whatever way the soul needs. It is a connecting, a giving and a letting go.

In the end, the person who wants to give Spiritually, in service, needs to fully release whatever thoughts they may have about what they need in return from the person to whom they are giving.

Sometimes the person to whom they give may not even respond positively. There may be rejection. The person receiving may not appreciate what is being given. This may be a test for the person giving. Yet it may still be appropriate to give to that person. One of the challenges of love is to give, not only to those people who respond and will be very happy with what is given to them, but also to those who may be more difficult. If you feel the inclination or urge to give to someone like this, then there may not be any obvious rewards. But it may be that this is the person who needs love most. So, without realising it, you may be actually giving more and serving more by giving to this person, rather than to someone who may give lots of hugs, and say how wonderful you are.

Eleyna: What are the main challenges needing to be faced by someone wanting to serve?

Clemond: *The primary challenge is for people to face their own fears. Every soul on the path is learning - with qualities that may have been developed over many lifetimes, and qualities that they may still be developing. So there is usually a mixture of strengths* and weaknesses within the soul.

Because souls are wanting to evolve, it is often the case that a life will be chosen that will produce tests in those weaker areas - the aspects of being that need to be refined and developed. The soul will wish to make progress in these areas, to become more whole.

Consequently, when a soul chooses to serve, there may be tests relating to the weaker aspects of that soul's being, so that soul can learn as well as help others. This co-operation may be planned in advance by the souls concerned before birth. For both the giver and receiver, there may be lessons to be learned and challenges. Sometimes the greatest service a soul can give to another is to allow himself to receive help from this other soul. There are many possibilities, and it depends on the need that is there. Hence, it is not always obvious who is serving whom in a given situation.

Life in the universe continues to function in a way to give opportunities to all beings. The main challenge then, for someone choosing the path of service, is to say 'yes' and to be willing to go forward and trust in 'God' and the underlying Spiritual reality, and not to refuse this.

Eleyna: How can people help someone who does not want help?

Clemond: *This is very difficult. There are times - even for souls who have chosen to serve - when people may find themselves at a particular point on their path of life, where they may not wish to go any further. They may come against some fear or attachment, which feels too fundamental within them for them to give this up or in any way to move forward. This may produce a particular crisis for that individual where they become very closed off at that time. Ultimately that soul needs to make their own choices about what to do. Nobody can do that for them.*

Even a soul on the path of service may turn away before they have completed all their tasks. They may make a wrong decision and feel guilt and shame about what they have done. People may feel very lost and isolated in their little worlds.

275

However, in the end, it is still possible to give love to these people. Through prayers it may be possible to ask for help that they may be true to themselves. Even though they may be stuck and not wanting to receive help, it is still possible to accept them. When people are having difficulties, it may be very comforting for them to feel loved and accepted.

When a soul is in this condition, then usually they will be feeling very uncomfortable inside and they will not be enjoying the slightest bit being in the position that they are in. They may also be finding it very hard to accept themselves for what they are going through, for they will know that they are not living the kind of life that they really want to live. But fear or negative emotions inside them that feel too difficult for them to let out may affect them - or they may feel that life is too much for them to bear - to make any difference, or to change where they are situated.

If they can feel that they are accepted and loved, even in this position of being stuck then that is the best that you can do for them. Sooner or later it may be possible that they will become open to listen once more from within themselves. And from that place, where they act upon guidance they are given, they will find a way forward, because there is a way forward for every soul. There is never really any stuck place except for what becomes stuck in the creation of that soul's mind. Once that souls opens their mind to Spirit, they will find their way forward, and if they listen to this, they can step forward to the next stage of their journey.

No one is given the situation of living on your Earth to be stuck. It is only something that you do yourselves.
Eleyna: What is your vision of how Spiritual service could help humanity?

Clemond: *I feel that humanity is in great need of help at the moment - a need to connect with Spirit. As I have spoken, Spirit is love. Love is needed in your world at this time. There are many that are treading very dark paths in your present age. There is much confusion in your world. The structures of living are very fast paced. There are so many distractions, taking people from what is essentially inside of them. For people to know that there* *are people and places where they can find peace is really very important.*

Your world could become much more peaceful than it is at this time. If people were able to learn that they have the possibility of connecting with Spirit within themselves, then they could also learn that they have an access to what is most true within themselves. And if more people could live like this, then it may affect your education systems and ultimately help everyone on your planet to feel more optimistic, with a sense of collective purpose of what you want to achieve and do together.

Not everyone of course wants to follow their own truth. But many people in your world today would follow more a path of Spirit and truth, if only they knew how they could do this. These are the people we want to reach and we want to help. I believe that if more souls engaged on a path of service that they have chosen, then this may be possible.

Chapter 32 -
Update

As 'Soul Pathways' nears publication, a year or more has passed since the life stories from this book were written. Lives have moved on. For all of us, the path of our life continues to unfold. Challenges and opportunities are presented to us. The dramas we face form shapes and contours for what we can create for ourselves in terms of experience.

I thought that it may be of interest to comment briefly about what I know concerning the contributors to this book and how their lives have fared since they finished their writing.

Eleyna
Eleyna has continued to endure many trials and difficulties in her life. Her mother slowly recovered from her illness and was able to leave hospital. However, shortly after she returned home, her father died. Eleyna felt no sense of loss at his passing. She felt that they could have become closer while her mother was ill but they didn't do so. In the meantime, her mother returned to her old habits, including smoking! Her strong allegiance to Eleyna's ex-husband has been retained and has resulted in strains and tensions between Eleyna and her mother. It is clear that Eleyna's mother has not really wanted to change, even after her husband died. There has been warmth though, in the relationship between Eleyna and her mother and this has been a blessing for both of them.

As the year went on, Eleyna suffered a lot of stress connected to her workplace at school. Coupled with this, there were still outbursts of aggravation between her and her ex- husband concerning matters relating to their divorce. These tensions came to a peak in November, and perhaps as a consequence, Eleyna suffered the tragedy of a still birth while seven months pregnant.

We called our baby Gabrielle and were able to bury her in the churchyard near to our home.

For a while, Eleyna was in a desperate state of grieving, but she received help from some unusual sources, including an Astrologer, who suggested that Gabrielle had come as a messenger. Anyway, from this event, Eleyna resolved firstly that she had to sort out her divorce with her ex-husband as quickly and as efficiently as possible. Secondly she decided that she needed to change her job.

In the time since then, she has been on sick leave from her job. She has begun taking counselling courses and is retraining in the field of psychology. Through making these steps and seeking alternative employment, Eleyna is learning more about herself. She knows that she needs to be living in situations where she receives respect and appreciation.

Her relationship with her former husband grows ever more distant and her relationship with all her children is good. I believe that my own relationship with Eleyna has strengthened and we enjoy the home that we share together.

Although I feel that there is still a long way to go, I feel that all the changes that Eleyna has faced are gradually helping her to build a better life for herself.

Michelle

I do not know Michelle's entire story over recent months. For a while after she had done her writing I tried to help her, but I did not have the tools to help her to release her dependency upon Heroin. During the autumn I had no contact with her, and I sense that during this time she went into a very dark place. I believe from what she has told me that she felt that her plight was hopeless and that she would never be free from heroin.

However, in the New Year, something must have shifted in her. She began to see some hope. Recently, she made contact with a local group of Narcotics Anonymous. This group follows much the same principles as Alcoholics Anonymous. From this initiative, she has begun to connect with other people who are former

279

addicts, people who know the kind of experiences that she has been through. I believe that this has helped her a great deal. She has not only found people with whom she could gain help and support, but she has been looking for that support as well.

In the last couple of months, she has started studying some short courses at the university and she has a part time job, one night per week. Her relationship with her mother and her boyfriend Tee has remained good.

For the last six weeks she has been off heroin and is reducing her methadone intake. During the last three weeks, as part of her programme with Narcotics Anonymous, she has stopped drinking alcohol completely.

When I saw Michelle some days ago, I felt that she looked brighter and healthier than at any time since I got to know her. There is certainly promise with the steps that she is now making in her life. It could herald a new dawn in her life. I am aware though, that there are still many pieces for her to pick up in her life. We will have to wait and see how she does.

Denise
After months of procrastinating and prevaricating, Denise finally did leave the hospital that has been her workplace for the past thirty plus years. For many of those years, Denise had hardly any life besides her work and therefore her identity was very wrapped up in the place. She felt a duty and responsibility to be there, struggling to know how her department would cope without her. However, underneath, I believe that she suffered from the fear of not knowing how she would be without her workplace, even though in her heart, she no longer wanted to be there.

As it happened, I feel that Denise handled the situation very well. Because of strains in her back, she has been able to retire on the grounds of ill health. In the process, she received the full backing of her management, and much appreciation from the staff for all her help and dedication over the years. To top it off, after all the money troubles that she had earlier in her life, she has been able to secure a good pension to make life easier in the times to come.

Now, Denise is moving ahead with her dream to be a crystal healer. A group of us have opened a Healing Centre, and so now the opportunity is there for Denise to carve out a practise for herself, where she can express her gifts and skills with this therapy to help people.

This new phase of her life represents a challenge for her to embrace a sense of her own worth. I believe that she is not yet as confident with that as she could be, but I also feel that she has much less fear now that she has made her important step. Inside, I feel that her heart is singing.

Helga

Within a few months of making her life story contribution for this book, Helga learnt that she had contracted cancer. In typical style, she told no one, fearing that if anyone knew, then they would reject her. With one friend, I believe that she did confide some details of the illness, and received a negative response. This seemed to confirm to her what would happen on a larger scale if more people knew.

The cancer was quite widespread and needed intensive treatment. To her family, she explained her illness as having to do with the diabetes that she was suffering. For Helga, this development marked a very dark chapter in her life. I believe that she often felt that she did not want to live any more.

After some months, she shared about her condition with me. I suppose that it felt safe to share with me because I lived a long way away and did not impinge upon her everyday life. Although Eleyna and I both urged her to share about the illness with her family, and especially her children, Helga refused to do so. However, she did appear to value me sharing my thoughts with her.

For a while, because Helga felt so weak and ill, there was a big doubt as to whether she would be able to continue her work or not. I feel that the thought of losing her independence was terrifying to her.

Gradually though, Helga tried to work things out in her own mind. The cancer was like all kinds of dark thoughts and emotions eating away at her. In the New Year, she formed a brief relationship with a man and felt much brighter and optimistic. She decided that she wanted to live. Immediately, this decision had a positive impact upon her health. She felt better and the cancer went into remission.

Helga realised that through her own attitudes, this could affect her health either positively or negatively. Consequently, even though the relationship she had entered ended, Helga made efforts to put things from the past behind her and get on with her life. With this attitude, she has been able to start a new job and her health has stabilised.

Her family still does not know about the cancer and I feel that the issues and problems of not being able to trust continue to be avoided. She feels that the only way that she can cope is by dealing with her problems on her own. Not surprisingly, she has felt a lack of contact with the Spiritual side of her nature since she learnt about the cancer. It is clear to her that she could open to this contact if she wished. However, she also recognises that if she were in contact with this, it would light up the pain that is there that she would prefer not to feel.

Jill
After an extended period of time on sick leave, Jill was understandably nervous about her return to work, but actually coped surprisingly well. My impression is that Jill enjoyed leading her new social work team and took an assertive attitude into meetings with her management. Rather than compromise as she may have done in the past, she was determined to remain true to her beliefs and principles. The staff appreciated her for both her dynamism and her caring, listening approach.

Concurrent with this, Jill felt passionately interested in learning about Sound Therapy and felt at last that she had found a tool that she could use to serve and help others. She enjoyed very much the training course in Sound Therapy that she was undertaking. This is where her heart lay. Consequently, she wanted to spend more time with this and less time with the Social Work.

Now she has made the first steps towards this goal. Shortly she will reduce her hours as a Social Worker by two days per week, and in that space she wants to develop her practise as a Sound Therapist. She is part of the group that has opened the Healing Centre and feels very happy about this. Jill feels confident that her life is improving and looks forward to the years in front of her.

Claire and David
I have not had any further contact with either Claire or David in recent months.

Chapter 33 -
Conclusions

The aim of this book has been to help people who are having difficulties facing the problems of their lives. What I have tried to show, through the different life stories and commentaries about various conditions with which many of us are confronted, is that life has common fundamental challenges for us all. Nobody is really above these challenges, whatever their position in life may be. We all have our own unique 'soul pathway', the experiences that we have chosen for ourselves to present our challenges, and these experiences give us opportunities to learn and test our character.

I feel that no one who is born on Earth is immune from suffering. Whenever we are given a challenge we suffer because we cannot have everything that we want. The choices that we are given in life usually involve some form of releasing. For all of us, it is hard to let go of things that we want, but we have to do this sometimes so that we can move forward.

I have likened suffering to a state of living in the darkness, because generally people feel very cut off and alone when they cannot decide what to do. It is typical for people to feel that no one would understand their suffering and they have to try and cope with it all by themselves. But this is not true. What I have suggested in this book is that the first and most important lesson for people to learn, especially when they are facing difficulties, is to reach out for help.

This is necessary in terms of making contact with other human beings and allowing help that way, where possible. However, help can also come from within, when people are prepared to ask for Spiritual support and to face the inner truth of how they need to live, even when people may doubt if they are capable of that.

People are often afraid of what their soul path may be demanding of them and this is one reason that people may not seek for Spiritual help as much as they would otherwise. Usually, people's soul path, once it is revealed to them, may involve considerable changes and taking up of responsibilities that can feel as if it could be beyond them. People may feel that it would be much more comfortable for them to refuse to know about these things. But if they do refuse to take up their soul challenges, they will never be quite satisfied in their lives either.

I have suggested that once people have decided that they want to know the inner truth of their being and what they have come here to do, then an inner process will be initiated to enable this truth and pathway to be revealed. It may take considerable time, while layers of understanding and life experience is built up. People may falter in their tracks. However, I have suggested that we each have a Spiritual guide or, as some people may regard it, a Guardian Angel, who is with us and can give us peace and clarity if we turn to that source for help. It may be quite easy for people to make this contact if they sincerely wish for it. The first step would be asking for help and seeking through prayers and meditation for guidance.

However, it is not only on a Spiritual level where people need to rely on help. As human beings we want so much to be loved, but we need to learn to give love as well and reach out when we need support or a shoulder to cry upon. As has been discussed in the chapter about the path of service, very often people's soul path may involve some form of service to others. But before we can serve anyone else, we need to know how we can seek and receive help for ourselves as well.

In many of the life stories in this book, people have shared of their stumbles in life and their despair. I have also shared of my own mistakes and moments where I have felt lost and confused. The main message that I want to convey to people is that there is hope and that we are not alone.

There is much that people share in terms of their fundamental inner experience. If we could break down our inner barriers so that we could acknowledge what is common to us and feel with our hearts how much linked we are with each other, then I believe that this could help many of us to overcome our problems.

If we feel that we have closed ourselves away in some very dark inner place, then this is something that we have manifested ourselves. We decide our own reactions to situations however nasty or hurtful another person may have been towards us. Therefore, although we may need help, it is only through our own intentions that we can overcome our difficulties once we are struggling with them.

I have found in my own life in recent years that I have been struggling with problems much more than I have had to do at other stages of my life. Although this has been hard for me, I have also felt myself more immersed in life than I have previously too. This has had its reward. Every so often when my head has come above water, I have felt a real joy to be alive, that somehow for me to confront my challenges and move on in the journey of life is a wonderful thing. I have felt stronger and more fully myself.

If I could express a wish for anyone reading this book, then it would be that some of the experiences shared in these pages could help you, reader, to lift your head above the water, to see a shaft of light showing you your pathway. Then, I would urge you to say 'yes' and go ahead along that way that you have seen and help others to do the same.

AUTHOR CONTACT

Paul Williamson offers workshops and individual sessions on themes such as Past Life Therapy, Healing the Inner Child, Meeting Spiritual Guides and other psychotherapy work.

For more information or to offer feedback on this book, Paul can be contacted at:

Paul Williamson. PO Box 121 Lancaster LA1 5GS

Please enclose an SAE or two International Reply Coupons

FREE DETAILED CATALOGUE

Capall Bann is owned and run by people actively involved in many of the areas in which we publish. A detailed illustrated catalogue is available on request, SAE or International Postal Coupon appreciated. **Titles can be ordered direct from Capall Bann, post free in the UK** (cheque or PO with order) or from good bookshops and specialist outlets.
Do contact us for details on the latest releases at: **Capall Bann Publishing, Auton Farm, Milverton, Somerset, TA4 1NE.** Titles include:

A Breath Behind Time, Terri Hector
Angels and Goddesses - Celtic Christianity & Paganism, M. Howard
Arthur - The Legend Unveiled, C Johnson & E Lung
Astrology The Inner Eye - A Guide in Everyday Language, E Smith
Auguries and Omens - The Magical Lore of Birds, Yvonne Aburrow
Asyniur - Womens Mysteries in the Northern Tradition, S McGrath
Beginnings - Geomancy, Builder's Rites & Electional Astrology in the
        European Tradition, Nigel Pennick
Between Earth and Sky, Julia Day
Book of the Veil , Peter Paddon
Caer Sidhe - Celtic Astrology and Astronomy, Vol 1, Michael Bayley
Caer Sidhe - Celtic Astrology and Astronomy, Vol 2 M Bayley
Call of the Horned Piper, Nigel Jackson
Cat's Company, Ann Walker
Celtic Faery Shamanism, Catrin James
Celtic Faery Shamanism - The Wisdom of the Otherworld, Catrin James
Celtic Lore & Druidic Ritual, Rhiannon Ryall
Celtic Sacrifice - Pre Christian Ritual & Religion, Marion Pearce
Celtic Saints and the Glastonbury Zodiac, Mary Caine
Circle and the Square, Jack Gale
Compleat Vampyre - The Vampyre Shaman, Nigel Jackson
Creating Form From the Mist - The Wisdom of Women in Celtic Myth and
        Culture, Lynne Sinclair-Wood
Crystal Clear - A Guide to Quartz Crystal, Jennifer Dent
Crystal Doorways, Simon & Sue Lilly
Crossing the Borderlines - Guising, Masking & Ritual Animal Disguise in the
        European Tradition, Nigel Pennick
Dragons of the West, Nigel Pennick
Earth Dance - A Year of Pagan Rituals, Jan Brodie
Earth Harmony - Places of Power, Holiness & Healing, Nigel Pennick
Earth Magic, Margaret McArthur

Eildon Tree (The) Romany Language & Lore, Michael Hoadley
Enchanted Forest - The Magical Lore of Trees, Yvonne Aburrow
Eternal Priestess, Sage Weston
Eternally Yours Faithfully, Roy Radford & Evelyn Gregory
Everything You Always Wanted To Know About Your Body, But So Far
    Nobody's Been Able To Tell You, Chris Thomas & D Baker
Face of the Deep - Healing Body & Soul, Penny Allen
Fairies in the Irish Tradition, Molly Gowen
Familiars - Animal Powers of Britain, Anna Franklin
Fool's First Steps, (The) Chris Thomas
Forest Paths - Tree Divination, Brian Harrison, Ill. S. Rouse
From Past to Future Life, Dr Roger Webber
Gardening For Wildlife Ron Wilson
God Year, The, Nigel Pennick & Helen Field
Goddess on the Cross, Dr George Young
Goddess Year, The, Nigel Pennick & Helen Field
Goddesses, Guardians & Groves, Jack Gale
Handbook For Pagan Healers, Liz Joan
Handbook of Fairies, Ronan Coghlan
Healing Book, The, Chris Thomas and Diane Baker
Healing Homes, Jennifer Dent
Healing Journeys, Paul Williamson
Healing Stones, Sue Philips
Herb Craft - Shamanic & Ritual Use of Herbs, Lavender & Franklin
Hidden Heritage - Exploring Ancient Essex, Terry Johnson
Hub of the Wheel, Skytoucher
In Search of Herne the Hunter, Eric Fitch
Inner Celtia, Alan Richardson & David Annwn
Inner Mysteries of the Goths, Nigel Pennick
Inner Space Workbook - Develop Thru Tarot, C Summers & J Vayne
Intuitive Journey, Ann Walker Isis - African Queen, Akkadia Ford
Journey Home, The, Chris Thomas
Kecks, Keddles & Kesh - Celtic Lang & The Cog Almanac, Bayley
Language of the Psycards, Berenice
Legend of Robin Hood, The, Richard Rutherford-Moore
Lid Off the Cauldron, Patricia Crowther
Light From the Shadows - Modern Traditional Witchcraft, Gwyn
Living Tarot, Ann Walker
Lore of the Sacred Horse, Marion Davies
Lost Lands & Sunken Cities (2nd ed.), Nigel Pennick
Magic of Herbs - A Complete Home Herbal, Rhiannon Ryall
Magical Guardians - Exploring the Spirit and Nature of Trees, Philip Heselton
Magical History of the Horse, Janet Farrar & Virginia Russell
Magical Lore of Animals, Yvonne Aburrow
Magical Lore of Cats, Marion Davies
Magical Lore of Herbs, Marion Davies
Magick Without Peers, Ariadne Rainbird & David Rankine

290

Masks of Misrule - Horned God & His Cult in Europe, Nigel Jackson
Medicine For The Coming Age, Lisa Sand MD
Medium Rare - Reminiscences of a Clairvoyant, Muriel Renard
Menopausal Woman on the Run, Jaki da Costa
Mind Massage - 60 Creative Visualisations, Marlene Maundrill
Mirrors of Magic - Evoking the Spirit of the Dewponds, P Heselton
Moon Mysteries, Jan Brodie
Mysteries of the Runes, Michael Howard
Mystic Life of Animals, Ann Walker
New Celtic Oracle The, Nigel Pennick & Nigel Jackson
Oracle of Geomancy, Nigel Pennick
Pagan Feasts - Seasonal Food for the 8 Festivals, Franklin & Phillips
Patchwork of Magic - Living in a Pagan World, Julia Day
Pathworking - A Practical Book of Guided Meditations, Pete Jennings
Personal Power, Anna Franklin
Pickingill Papers - The Origins of Gardnerian Wicca, Bill Liddell
Pillars of Tubal Cain, Nigel Jackson
Places of Pilgrimage and Healing, Adrian Cooper
Practical Divining, Richard Foord
Practical Meditation, Steve Hounsome
Practical Spirituality, Steve Hounsome
Psychic Self Defence - Real Solutions, Jan Brodie
Real Fairies, David Tame
Reality - How It Works & Why It Mostly Doesn't, Rik Dent
Romany Tapestry, Michael Houghton
Runic Astrology, Nigel Pennick
Sacred Animals, Gordon MacLellan
Sacred Celtic Animals, Marion Davies, Ill. Simon Rouse
Sacred Dorset - On the Path of the Dragon, Peter Knight
Sacred Grove - The Mysteries of the Forest, Yvonne Aburrow
Sacred Geometry, Nigel Pennick
Sacred Nature, Ancient Wisdom & Modern Meanings, A Cooper
Sacred Ring - Pagan Origins of British Folk Festivals, M. Howard
Season of Sorcery - On Becoming a Wisewoman, Poppy Palin
Seasonal Magic - Diary of a Village Witch, Paddy Slade
Secret Places of the Goddess, Philip Heselton
Secret Signs & Sigils, Nigel Pennick
Self Enlightenment, Mayan O'Brien
Spirits of the Air, Jaq D Hawkins
Spirits of the Earth, Jaq D Hawkins
Spirits of the Earth, Jaq D Hawkins
Stony Gaze, Investigating Celtic Heads John Billingsley
Stumbling Through the Undergrowth , Mark Kirwan-Heyhoe
Subterranean Kingdom, The, revised 2nd ed, Nigel Pennick
Symbols of Ancient Gods, Rhiannon Ryall
Talking to the Earth, Gordon MacLellan
Taming the Wolf - Full Moon Meditations, Steve Hounsome

Teachings of the Wisewomen, Rhiannon Ryall
The Other Kingdoms Speak, Helena Hawley
Tree: Essence of Healing, Simon & Sue Lilly
Tree: Essence, Spirit & Teacher, Simon & Sue Lilly
Through the Veil, Peter Paddon
Torch and the Spear, Patrick Regan
Understanding Chaos Magic, Jaq D Hawkins
Vortex - The End of History, Mary Russell
Warp and Weft - In Search of the I-Ching, William de Fancourt
Warriors at the Edge of Time, Jan Fry
Water Witches, Tony Steele
Way of the Magus, Michael Howard
Weaving a Web of Magic, Rhiannon Ryall
West Country Wicca, Rhiannon Ryall
Wildwitch - The Craft of the Natural Psychic, Poppy Palin
Wildwood King , Philip Kane
Witches of Oz, Matthew & Julia Philips
Wondrous Land - The Faery Faith of Ireland by Dr Kay Mullin
Working With the Merlin, Geoff Hughes
Your Talking Pet, Ann Walker

FREE detailed catalogue and
FREE 'Inspiration' magazine
Contact: Capall Bann Publishing, Auton Farm,
Milverton, Somerset, TA4 1NE